PRAISE FOR *APPETITES* BY CAROLINE KNAPP

"[P]rofoundly insightful, compassionately perceptive. . . [Knapp] was an exceptional analyst of the female zeitgeist, one whose astute cultural observations and ruthless personal revelations leave a legacy that will resonate with women for generations to come."

—BOOKLIST

"Explor[es] in passionate detail what it feels like to be female. . . . [Knapp] uses her own experience with anorexia to talk about how American culture suppresses and perverts feminine desire."

—ORGANIC STYLE

"Eloquent. . . a skillful blend of memoir and social commentary."

—BOOKPAGE

". . . More than one woman's tragic story; multitudinous interviews with women with eating disorders, excerpts from classic feminist texts and sociological statistics lend credence and categorize the book under cultural studies as much as self-help. . . . Though Knapp admits it's 'easier to worry about the body than the soul,' she hopes creating a dialogue about anorexia will enable all women to nourish both."

—PUBLISHERS WEEKLY

"Her beautiful prose is bolstered throughout with nice anecdotes from research material and the author's personal experiences. An eloquent voice that will be missed."

—KIRKUS REVIEWS

"In lucid, effortless prose, Knapp explores the personal and cultural influences around appetites such as food, shopping, and sex and a woman's drive for recognition and fulfillment."

—LIBRARY JOURNAL (STARRED REVIEW)

"*Appetites* is a wise, compassionate, and important book about a subject that touches all of our lives. Knapp synthesizes thirty years of important thought on food, body image, and female identity and gets even more deeply inside these issues. Her writing is frank, personal and true. *Appetites* is an invaluable contribution to the literature of women's inner lives."

—BETSY LERNER,
AUTHOR OF *FOOD AND LOATHING: A LAMENT*

"How very sad to have lost brave Caroline Knapp, and how glorious to see her evolve whole lifetimes in the few years she was given. Read this book if you want to know why it is that women dismantle their bodies in search of—and in flight from—their souls."

—KATHRYN HARRISON,
AUTHOR OF *SEAL WIFE*

"Caroline Knapp chose searingly difficult subjects, and wrote about them with such grace that the horrible became eerily beautiful. . . . Her generous honesty and gifted writing leave something that is a valuable legacy."

—*THE SEATTLE TIMES*

"In her earlier works of cultural criticism Knapp began to explore a style that wedded memoir and sociology, the personal with the political. Although those books were successful, *Appetites* takes her idiosyncratic method to a new level."

—*THE BOSTON PHOENIX*

APPETITES

[APPETITES]

WHY

WOMEN

WANT

CAROLINE KNAPP

COUNTERPOINT

BERKELEY

For Herzog
And for Roxanne, Zoë, and Hallie

Copyright © 2003 by Caroline Knapp

Foreword © Gail Caldwell 2011

Hardcover edition first published in 2003 by Counterpoint

First paperback edition published in 2004 by Counterpoint

Set in 11-point Goudy

The Library of Congress has catalogued the hardcover edition as follows:

Knapp, Caroline, d. 2002
    Appetites : why women want / Caroline Knapp.
        p.   cm.
ISBN-10 1-58243-225-2 (hc.)
ISBN-13 978-1-58243-225-0 (hc.)
    1. Knapp, Caroline, d. 2002—Health.   2. Anorexia nervosa—
Patients—United States—Biography.   3. Appetite.   I. Title.
RC552.A5 K636 2003
362.1'9685262'0092—dc21

2002152118

Paperback ISBN 978-1-58243-808-5

COUNTERPOINT
2560 Ninth Street, Suite 318
Berkeley, CA 94710
www.counterpointpress.com

10 9 8 7

ALSO BY CAROLINE KNAPP

DRINKING: A LOVE STORY

PACK OF TWO: THE INTRICATE
BOND BETWEEN PEOPLE AND DOGS

ALICE K'S GUIDE TO LIFE:
ONE WOMAN'S QUEST FOR SURVIVAL,
SANITY, AND THE PERFECT NEW SHOES

APPETITES

CONTENTS

FOREWORD

BY GAIL CALDWELL

CAROLINE KNAPP AND I became friends in late summer of 1996, at a precious, crucial time in both our lives. In retrospect the friendship seems custom-made. We were both writers who lived alone, and we each had year-old dogs we adored. Our first walk together—a foray through New England woods—wound up lasting four hours. By autumn we were planning everything around those walks: meandering afternoons of shared silences and revelations, an intimacy both propelled and protected by the dogs we loved. Reluctant to interrupt this portrait of serenity for the usual holiday obligations, we decided to spend Thanksgiving together—another long walk in the emptied-out forest, then a meal at the end of the day.

She insisted we cook at my house. In most social negotiations, Caroline was both shy and diplomatic, but she was intractable on this one point. I remember being slightly annoyed at the notion because I thought that meant the lion's share of work would fall to me (an assumption that suggests how much I had to learn). On Wednesday afternoon, Caroline arrived at my door, sprinting up the stairs to my second-floor kitchen with bags of strawberries and fresh bread and cut geraniums. She hadn't just shopped; she had delivered the makings of a banquet, and I realized then that some tacit contract had been established. She would gather the wood if I would tend the fire.

Images of that Thanksgiving still return to me with deep pleasure: the autumn light of the woods we savored while the rest of the world was on the move; the dinner we lingered over as dusk turned to night. Now I believe I had passed some unconscious test that day, been offered some position of anchor in the free-fall bounty of life. It was the year that *Drinking: A Love Story* had appeared, and so I knew the public version of Caroline's earlier anorexia: the years spent hostage to the single apple—Eve's bitter meal—and the small cube of cheese that she had once allowed herself each day. In the months that followed, I recognized, as well, the leftover traces of her anxieties—most of them about how to manage the wants and demands of intimacy, of what was enough and what was too much, and how to approach this equation without being paralyzed by it. The meal she envisioned and that we prepared together represented some dyad of safety, much like the woods where we found sanctuary. For a recovering anorectic, the day was simple and profound: the primary act of feeding and being fed by someone you trust.

There were other crucibles ahead, some of them passed or failed before we even realized what they were, but the leap of faith she had taken that day became clearer as our friendship unfolded. As with any relationship, trust became the central component of our story. I had to trust her when she taught me to row in a 12-inch-wide scull; she agreed to trust me, even though she was afraid of water, when I showed her how to float on her back in a mountain lake. Eventually we came to trust each other with our shadows and our 3 AM dreads and the care of our beloved dogs. By the end of her life in 2002—she was 42—I trusted her with everything that mattered.

The public version of Caroline whom readers knew was not all that different from the private, personal one: She was brave and funny and psychologically astute as well as eloquent, willing to go down roads of emotional honesty where others might have fled in terror. I was nine years older and had spent much of my youth in angry rebellion; she had been the good-girl A-student, eager—she might say desperate—for the approval of everyone except herself. We had different histories and similar sorrows, and this complementarity, revealed and endlessly analyzed over the years, gave us both an education in compassion, I think, as well as a close-focus insight into the other. The thickets of being human turned out to be the same: despair and yearning, fear and desire, how to love without going bankrupt. And Caroline and I were always able to be kinder to one another than to ourselves. One of the things I miss most about her is that acceptance—the softened mirror on the soul that may be the essence of love.

Caroline struggled mightily with this book, by which I mean she worked with a kind of heroic deliberation to get it right: to render and comprehend an atmosphere, in late twentieth-century America, of women's deepest wants and the crevasses that often awaited them. She began the book with the intent of concentrating on anorexia, and as she thought her way through the next couple of years, she began to reach toward some larger idea about female desire and its desultory tributaries. "Find it, buy it, marry it," she would write, eventually believing that these disparate longings came from a similarly untended source. Caroline had a piercing precision in plumbing the most personal of emotions; as usual, her first research subject was herself. She was fearless in this regard, and smart, and she chose to eschew privacy and rosy self-reflection in favor of the truth. She finished the manuscript in the winter of 2002, a few months before she was diagnosed with the cancer that killed her.

When I immerse myself again in the story within "Appetites," more than a decade after she began what would be her last book, I can see the long span of the emergence of this spirit: the wounded girl—at one point, an 83-pound "temple of angle and bone"—and the courageous, self-possessed woman and writer she would become. Years after its original publication, the book seems to me to have mined and synthesized ideas about women and society that are now an established piece of the cultural dialogue. So much of what she wrote resonates today: the cruelty of girls, the sorrows of mothers, the hungers, met and unmet, that shape who we become. But then Caroline was always an archaeologist of women's secrets: the "rage-laced fatigue" of giving and giving, the lonely effort of searching for and listening to your own voice. Part of what readers loved about Caroline Knapp was that voice, crystalline and generous, that articulated not just the pain of her experience but also the path out. She left behind a lot of hope in these pages. I can't think of a legacy that she would have wanted more.

PROLOGUE

APPETITE BY RENOIR

*T*HE WOMEN LINGER *at the water's edge, and they are stunning in the most unusual way: large women, voluptuous, abundant, delighted. They lounge along the river bank, they lift their arms toward the sun, their hair ripples down their backs, which are smooth and broad and strong. There is softness in the way they move, and also strength and sensuality, as though they revel in the feel of their own heft and substance.*

Step back from the canvas, and observe, think, feel. This is an image of bounty, a view of female physicality in which a woman's hungers are both celebrated and undifferentiated, as though all her appetites are of a piece, the physical and the emotional entwined and given equal weight. Food is love on this landscape, and love is sex, and sex is connection, and connection is food; appetites exist in a full circle, or in a sonata where eating and touching and making love and feeling close are all distinct chords that nonetheless meld with and complement one another.

Renoir, who created this image, once said that were it not for the female body, he never could have become a painter. This is clear: there is love for women in each detail of the canvas, and love for self, and there is joy, and there is a degree of sensual integration that makes you want to weep, so beautiful it seems, and so elusive.

INTRODUCTION

APPETITE IN
THE WORLD OF NO

ONCE UPON A TIME, in a land as different from Renoir's
world as Earth is from Jupiter, I weighed eighty-three pounds. I
was twenty-one years old, five-foot-four, and my knees were
wider than my thighs. My normal weight is about 120 pounds,
and the effort to pare off thirty-seven of those—more than one
third of my body—was Herculean, life-altering, and, I believe,
exquisitely female.

In Renoir's world, a woman's appetites are imagined as rich
and lusty and powerful, the core of the female being celebrated
as sensual, deeply attuned to pleasure. In my world—a place that
unquestionably still exists, that's inhabited with varying degrees
of intensity by all too many women—appetites had a nearly opposite meaning, the body experienced as dangerous and disturbing and wrong, its hungers split off from each other, each one
assigned multiple and contradictory meanings, each one loaded
and fraught. This disparity eluded me at the time; had I seen a
Renoir painting, I would have thought: *Feh, fat women*, and
turned away in fear or contempt, perhaps both. For three years, I
ate the same things every day: one plain sesame bagel for breakfast, one container of Dannon coffee-flavored yogurt for lunch,
one apple and a one-inch cube of cheese for dinner. I ran: miles
and miles, a stick-figure with a grimace. I was cold all the time,
even in summer, and I was desperately unhappy, and I had no
idea what any of this meant, where the compulsion to starve
came from, why it so drove me, what it said about me or about

women in general or about the larger matter of human hungers. I just acted, reacted.

Nearly two decades ago, at age twenty-four and hovering near ninety pounds, I started to see a therapist, a specialist in eating disorders, who began to broach the subject of appetite in ways that baffled me for a long time. The word disturbed me—my associations went straight from food to loss of control to fat—but when he used it, he struck a broader chord, hints of Renoir in the undertones, as though describing a more complicated, possibly even gratifying matter of passion and sensuality and psychic hunger instead of a strictly physical issue of food. He'd use the word in strange contexts; when he questioned me about joy, for instance, or worried aloud about whether I was having enough "fun" in my life. I don't recall many specifics from those early meetings, only that such references seemed to hold a key of sorts, a code that one day might decipher or at least reframe the various struggles and tangles that had brought me to his office in the first place. What gave me delight? What fully engaged me, turned on all the senses? These seemed to be appetite's pivotal questions in his framework—they had to do with what a person really hungers for, with what makes one feel truly fed—and like the stubborn and recalcitrant patient I was, I found them annoying for many years, as though he were missing the point instead of illuminating it.

This spring, the therapist and I began to finish our work together, not because I'm "done" or "cured" or conflict-free but because I've finally (or so we hope) gotten the point. Appetite is the hook on which all my ancillary struggles have hung, the ocean from which all internal rivers (my own, those of so many women) have sprung. Appetite is about eating, certainly, and that's a piece of it that defines life for many women, a piece I, too, know well, but it's also about a much broader constellation of hungers and longings and needs. It is about the deeper wish—often experienced with particular intensity and in particularly painful ways by women—to partake of the world, to feel a sense of abundance and possibility about life, to experience pleasure. At heart, it's about our

+ so fuckin' true!

distance from the women in that Renoir painting, and about our abiding, often poorly articulated hunger for what they appear to have joy, peace with body and soul, bounty. *✗*

I have probably grappled with the matter of appetite my whole life—a lot of women do; we're taught to do battle with our own desires from a tender age, and reinforcements are called in over time on virtually every front—but if I had to pinpoint a defining moment in my own history, I'd go back twenty-three years, to an otherwise unmemorable November evening when I made an otherwise unmemorable purchase: a container of cottage cheese.

Innocuous as it sounds, this would actually turn out to be a life-altering event, but the kind that's so seemingly ordinary you can't consider it as such for many years. Certainly, I didn't see anything remarkable happening at the time. I was nineteen years old, a junior at Brown University, in Providence, Rhode Island, vaguely anxious, vaguely depressed. I was also, less vaguely, hungry. This was 1979, Thanksgiving weekend. I'd gone home to see my family, then returned to campus the next day to write a paper. My roommates and most of my friends were still away, I didn't especially feel like slogging over to the campus cafeteria to eat by myself, and so I put on my coat and walked up the block to a corner grocery store, and that's what I bought: a small plastic tub of Hood's cottage cheese and a solitary package of rice cakes.

Cottage cheese, of course, is the food God developed specifically to torture women, to make them keen with yearning. Picture it on a plate, lumpy and bland atop a limp lettuce leaf and half a canned peach. Consider the taste and feel of it: wet, bitter little curds. Now compare it to the real thing: a thick, oozing slab of brie, or a dense and silky smear of cream cheese. Cottage cheese is one of our culture's most visible symbols of self-denial; marketed honestly, it would appear in dairy cases with warning labels: THIS SUBSTANCE IS SELF-PUNITIVE; INGEST WITH CAUTION.

I didn't know this back then, which is important to note. Naturally thin, I'd never given my weight much thought before, and although I knew plenty of women who obsessed about their thighs and fretted over calories, I'd always regarded them as a rather alien species, their battles against fat usually unnecessary and invariably tedious, barely a blip on my own radar. I, in turn, had very little personal experience with cottage cheese. I'd never bought cottage cheese before, I'm not sure I'd even *eaten* cottage cheese before, but on some semiconscious level, I knew the essential truth about cottage cheese—it was a *diet food*—and on some even less conscious level, I was drawn to it, compelled to buy it and to put it in the mini-refrigerator in my dorm room and then to eat it and nothing else—just cottage cheese and rice cakes—for three consecutive days.

And a seed, long present perhaps but dormant until then, began to blossom. A path was laid, one that ultimately had less to do with food than it did with emotion, less to do with hunger than it did with the mindset required to satisfy hunger: the sense of entitlement and agency and initiative that leads one to say, first, *I want*, and then, more critically, *I deserve*. So as inconsequential as that purchase may have seemed, it in fact represented a turning point, the passage of a woman at a crossroads, one road marked Empty, the other Full. Not believing at the core that fullness—satiety, gratification, pleasure—was within my grasp, I chose the other road.

I stayed on that road for a long time; three days of cottage cheese and rice cakes became three years of anorexia, then three more, and the attendant battles around nourishment and pleasure would linger long after my weight finally stabilized, making their presence felt, albeit less extremely, in arenas well beyond the realm of food: in relationships, in questions about exercise, in matters of material indulgence, in just about any area, really, where longing can bump up against constraint. How much is too much? How much is enough? How hungry am I and, more to the point, for what? For *what*? These questions have dogged me like gnats, flitting into view whenever hunger announces itself, whenever it begins to rap on the door and demand a response, which it invariably, insistently does.

The *why* here—why I chose to starve, why appetite itself became so colossally complicated—is a big question, much of the answer idiosyncratic and personal. There is always a family at the center of an eating disorder, and I had a characteristically complex one at the center of mine, dominated by a set of brilliant, inhibited, often unhappy parents whose marriage was riddled with ambivalence (on my father's part) and frustration (my mother's). They were loving and generous people, but also reserved to the point of opacity, and their expressions of affection were so coded and veiled I wouldn't learn to decipher them until I was well into my thirties. Before then, I often felt mystified and apart and anxiously insecure, a kid who'd get dropped off at summer camp and never feel quite certain that I'd actually be retrieved at the end of the six weeks. My siblings, an older brother and a twin sister, seemed to have had a more innately secure sense of familial belonging, the result of a style that meshed with the family style, perhaps, or a kind of internal wiring that left them more apt to feel understood than unmoored. I lacked that. I suspect I felt personally responsible for my parents' quiet unhappiness and reticence, the bad kid who'd somehow poisoned the air we all breathed, and I felt compelled from an early age to compensate, as though my right to stay needed to be earned: I was quiet, shy, clean, perfectionistic. I got A's. I scrubbed the kitchen without being asked. My earliest memories, no doubt born out of the most intricate combination of family dynamics and brain chemistry, have to do with a sense of thwarted connections and emptiness, of a yearning for something unnamed and perhaps unnamable.

That sensation actually may date back to the very first days and weeks of life. I weighed four pounds, eleven ounces at birth, more than a pound less than my sister (she weighed in at six), and was dispatched immediately to an incubator, where I spent my first two weeks, basic needs attended to but probably not a great deal more. During the next several weeks, at home, part of my care fell to a nurse my parents had hired to help out, and as family legend has it, she determined early on that my sister was the healthy, vital one while I was sick and weakly. Apparently driven by some kind of twisted Darwinian logic, the nurse acted on this conviction by diluting my formula and increasing the strength of my sister's. My mother, who subsequently would refer to her simply as "sadistic," discovered this after a few weeks and fired her on the spot, and while I'm not sure how much weight to give to these early experiences, the stories feel resonant to me, threads of hunger and uncertainty about the concept of satiety woven into my life's fabric from the very beginning.

It would be tempting, and quite convenient, to end the story there—early experience sets the stage; the kid who never quite felt fed at home ends up having difficulty with the concept of feeding later in life—but if all it took to become anorexic were complicated parents and an inadequate ancillary caretaker, the vast majority of humans would be on that road. Starving, like all disorders of appetite, is a solution to a wide variety of conflicts and fears, or at least it starts out resembling a solution: Something feels perversely good, or right, or gratifying about it, some key seems to slide into place, some distress is assuaged, and the benefits of this are strong enough to outweigh whatever negative or painful feelings are aroused, such as shame, confusion, or physical hunger. This is very seductive stuff, the beckoning of demons, and I think it's bigger than family, the allure at once more all-encompassing and more specific to time and place.

That cottage cheese foray took place in a context of enormous promise and enormous anxiety, for me and for women in general. A year shy of graduation from an Ivy League college, I was facing a landscape of unparalleled opportunity, doors nailed shut to women just a decade or two earlier having been flung wide open. That year, I was thinking about moving to Arizona to live with a boyfriend. I was thinking about applying to medical schools, or Ph.D. programs in literature, or the Peace Corps, who knew? I was contemplating questions my own mother hadn't dreamed of at my age—whom to sleep with, where to live and with whom, what kind of future to carve out for myself, what kind of person to be—and as blessed and wonderful as all that freedom may have been, I suspect I found it terrifying, oppressive, even (though I couldn't have articulated this at the time) slightly illicit, as though the very truth of it somehow contradicted a murky but deeply-held set of feelings about what it meant to be female.

Into this, cottage cheese and rice cakes, which felt strangely alluring from the very start. I didn't begin to starve in earnest for quite a while after that purchase, several years, but I did spend a long time dabbling, an amateur scientist conducting experiments on the side, and even these initial flirtations with restraint had a seductive effect; something about the deprivation felt good, purifying almost. I lost some weight that fall and winter, my junior year, but I was only vaguely aware I was doing this deliberately. Mostly, I recall a detached feeling of curiosity, a pull to know more. *What if I skipped dinner? What if I didn't eat anything during the day, drank only coffee? I wonder how that would feel.*

It felt . . . interesting, little tests of will that gave me glimmers of things I seemed to covet: a quiet sense of strength, a way to stand out, the outlines of a goal. At night, I'd often go with friends to a bar near campus where the waitresses served oversized baskets of buttered popcorn along with pitchers of beer. I'd determine not to eat the popcorn, not even a single kernel, and I found this oddly pleasing, this secret show of resolve. Others would reach into the basket, grab handfuls, ask the waitress for more. I'd sit back from the table and smoke a cigarette, a little surprised and a little proud to find I could exercise such restraint.

I ate less and I grew thinner. People noticed, as they invariably do. "Oooh, you're so skinny!" they'd say. Or, "Oooh, you've lost weight!" I'd raise my eyebrows and shrug, as though I hadn't really noticed. "I have? Huh." But inside, that little kernel of pride sprouted, watered by the attention and by what I understood to be envy; without even trying very hard, I could do what others tried and failed to do. So many women lived and died by the scale, self-worth dictated by it. To me, it was just a game.

Anorexics are masters of exaggeration; they take a certain satisfaction in going the average woman one better, internalizing her worst fears and then inflating them, flaunting them, throwing them back in her face. Food had never been one of my big preoccupations, but I'd certainly witnessed its centrality in other women's lives, and in some rudimentary way I understood that this excruciating focus on size and shape—the fleshy curve of a hip, the precise fit of a pair of jeans—communicated something more complicated about the larger matter of female appetite and its relationship to identity and value, a notion that a woman's hunger was somehow inappropriate, possibly even grotesque. I saw how quietly tyrannized women could be by food and weight, how edgy they'd get when confronted by choices. I heard the high, anxious voices, the weighing of longing against deprivation, the endless, repetitive mantra: "Oh, I shouldn't, I really shouldn't." Decoded, the imperatives here were clear; we all live with them. Size matters. Control of size (of portions, of body, of desire itself) matters. Suppressing appetite is a valued ambition, even if it eclipses other ambitions, even if it makes you crazy. I paid attention. I lost five pounds, then another five. Message absorbed, amplified, and then ("How do you stay so *thin?*") duly rewarded. Other women might struggle with hunger; I could transcend it.

Starving, in its inimitably perverse way, gave me a way to address the anxiety I felt as a young, scared, ill-defined woman who was poised to enter the world and assume a new array of rights and privileges; it gave me a tiny, specific, manageable focus (popcorn kernels) instead of a monumental, vague, overwhelming one (work, love). Starving also gave me a way to address some nascent discomfort about my place in this newly altered landscape, a kind of psychic bargaining over the larger matter of hunger; permitted, at least in theory, to be big (ambitious, powerful, competitive), I would compensate by making myself small, fragile, and non-threatening as a wren. Starving also capitulated, again in exaggerated form, to a plethora of feelings (some handed down from my family, almost all of them supported by culture) about women in general and women's bodies in particular, to the idea that there's something inherently shameful and flawed about the female form, something that requires constant monitoring and control. And, of course, starving answered whatever long-standing feelings of yearning and emptiness and sorrow I'd carted off to college in the first place; it deflected all that longing into one place, concentrated it like a diamond. Food, over time, became a terrible, powerful symbol—of how much I wanted on the one hand and how certain I was that I'd never get enough on the other—and my denial of food thus became the most masterful solution. *I'm so hungry, I'll never get fed.* If that is one's baseline understanding of the world (and I suspect it was mine at the time), starving makes sense, controlling food becomes a way of expressing that conflict and also denying it. Your needs are overwhelming? You can't depend on yourself or others to meet them? You don't even know what they are? Then need nothing. At a time when I felt adrift and confused and deeply unsure of myself, starving gave me a goal, a way to stand out and exert control, something I could be good at.

I was very, very good at it. I grew smaller and smaller and smaller over time. I stopped menstruating. I began wearing jeans inherited from a friend's twelve-year-old brother, who'd outgrown them. I literally ached with hunger: My stomach throbbed with it; my ribs dug into my sides when I tried to sleep at night. I took painstaking note of these changes—how visible and pronounced my bones became, even the tiny finger bones; how my abdomen curved inward, a taut, tight "C"—and I found each one of them both profoundly compelling and inexplicably satisfying. I could not express what I'd been feeling with words, but I could wear it. The inner life—hunger, confusion, longings unnamed and unmet, that whole overwhelming gamut—as a sculpture in bone.

Today, I eat. That in itself is a statement of triumph, but the road toward a more peaceful relationship with food—which, of course, means a more peaceful relationship with my body, myself, my own demons—has been long, circuitous, and (would that this weren't so) full of company. It's hard to think of a woman who hasn't grappled to one degree or another with precisely the same fears, feelings, and pressures that drove me to starve, even harder to think of a woman who experiences the full range of human hungers with Renoir's brand of unfettered delight. Satisfying hungers, taking things in, indulging in bodily pleasures—these are not easy matters for a lot of women, and I suspect my own troubled relationship with food merely reflects the extreme end of a long continuum, and one venue among many others.

Food, sex, shopping: Name your poison. Appetites, particularly as they're experienced by women, have an uncanny shape-shifting quality, and a remarkable talent for glomming onto externals. One battle segues into the next, one promise proves false and another emerges on the horizon, glimmers, and beckons like a star: *Follow me, this diet will do it, or this man, or this set of purchases for body and home; the holy grail as interpreted by Jenny Craig or Danielle Steele or Martha Stewart.* In my case, starving gave way to drinking, denial of appetite—which made me feel highly controlled and rather superior and very safe—gradually mutating into a more all-encompassing denial of self, alcohol displacing food as the substance of choice. For others, the substances may be somewhat less tangible, but they're often no less gripping, and no less linked to the broader theme of appetite: Obsessive relationships with men; compulsive shopping and debt; life-defining preoccupation with appearances; "isms" of all kinds—all of these are about emptiness, about misdirected attempts to fill internal voids, and all of them tend to spring from the same dark pool of feeling: a suspicion among many women that hungers themselves are somehow invalid or wrong, that indulgences must be earned and paid for, that the satisfaction of appetites often comes with a bill. Eat too much, want too much, act too sexual or too ambitious or too hungry, and the invoice will arrive, often delivered with an angry hiss of self-recrimination: *You're a pig, a sloth, you suck.* Desire versus deprivation, indulgence versus constraint, nurturance versus self-abnegation; these are the constants on this stage, the lead players in a particularly female drama.

This, of course, is a profoundly human stage—the clash between the desire to satisfy appetites and the fear that they may overwhelm us, control us, lead us astray is as old as the story of Adam and Eve—but the female journey across it can be experienced and expressed in particularly painful and confounding ways, women being the gender born and raised on the notion that the female appetite is limited and curtailed to begin with, that female hungers should be reined in, permitted satisfaction in only the most circumscribed, socially sanctioned ways. "Eat to survive." A thirty-six-year-old television producer who's wrestled with weight for most of her adult life was raised on that mandate, spoon-fed the admonishment by her mother, who believed that anything beyond subsistence-level consumption was greedy, dangerous, unfeminine, wrong. "Don't be such a smarty pants; it's not becoming." A fifty-two-year-old scientist still has bad dreams about that one, which came from both parents and carried a similar warning: Good girls (interchangeable with desirable, deserving girls) have limited appetites for knowledge, limited brain power, limited aspirations. "So you really *do* wear high heels." A forty-two-year-old architect, just out of graduate school at the time and quite pleased with her new professional identity, recalls being met by those words nearly twenty years ago, when she picked her mother up at the airport for a visit; the statement was contemptuous, laced with disappointment, and still stings two decades later: "The implication wasn't that I was trying to be sexy by wearing high-heels and failing. It was that I *was* sexy, and therefore I was disgusting." These are tales from the World of No. The messages may be delivered far less directly, or they may be mixed and contradictory, but if you're a woman who came of age in the latter half of the twentieth century, you've no doubt heard them in one form or another: Don't eat too much, don't get too big, don't reach too far, don't climb too high, *don't want too much*. No, no, no.

That these mandates exist is hardly news, but their cumulative effect on women's lives tends to be examined through a fragmented lens, one-pathology-at-a-time, the eating disorder lit on the self-help shelves separated from the books on women's troubled relationships with men, the books on compulsive shopping separated from the books on female sexuality, the books on culture and media separated from the books on female psychology. Take your pick, choose your demon: Women Who Love Too Much in one camp, Women Who Eat Too Much in another, Women Who Shop Too Much in a third. In fact, the camps are not so disparate, and the question of appetite—specifically the question of what happens to the female appetite when it's submerged and rerouted—is the thread that binds them together. One woman's tub of cottage cheese is another's maxed-out MasterCard; one woman's soul-murdering love affair is another's frenzied eating binge. The methods may differ, but boil any of these behaviors down to their essential ingredients and you are likely find a particularly female blend of anxiety, guilt, shame, and sorrow, the psychic roux of profound—and often profoundly misunderstood—hungers.

With anorexia, I merely elevated to an art form what so many women do with their appetites all of the time, whether or not the behavior blossoms into a full-blown disorder. Weighing, measuring, calculating, monitoring. Withholding and then overcompensating. Reining in hunger in one area, letting go in another. The female appetite moves in guilty, circuitous ways, and although my own relationship with food is probably as normal today as it ever will be, I still carry around a flickering awareness of hunger's pushes and pulls all the time, a chronic tug between the voice of longing and the voice of constraint that feels like a form of heightened alert, something that can make its presence felt in any arena where taking something in is at issue. A woman I know determines exactly how much she will eat from day to day based on the amount of exercise she gets: If she runs two miles, she gets second helpings at dinner; three miles, she gets dessert; no workout, no extras, no goodies. She understands that this is irrational ("It's crazy," she says, "Who's keeping score?"), and she can't say when or why she developed the system, which she recognizes as completely arbitrary, but she adheres to the rules every day, and has for so long she can't fathom living any other way. Another woman, an economist who's been craving recognition in her field for years, found herself glaring at her reflection in the mirror the day after she was nominated for a major award. She was at the gym, pumping away on the StairMaster, her face tightened into a scowl, and she was thinking: *You fucking fraud; who the hell do you think you are?* "Where does *that* come from?" she wonders, unable to answer. "Why is it so hard to just take the good stuff in?" Appetites for sex, for beautiful things, for physical pleasure—all of these can feel baffling, and all of them can leave a woman confused about the most ordinary daily decisions. Are you eating that second helping because you're hungry or because you're sad? If you work out for an extra thirty minutes, are you heeding the call to health and well-being or engaging in a bout of self-punishment? If you spend $600 on a fabulous jacket you don't really need, are you permitting yourself a little well-earned luxury or are you spiraling out of control? Where are the lines between satisfaction and excess, between restraint and indulgence, between pleasure and self-destruction? And why are they so difficult to find, particularly for women?

Despite its common association with food, the word "appetite" has a fairly broad meaning. Webster's Third New International dictionary defines it as: (1) a natural desire; (2) an inherent or habitual desire or propensity for gratification or satisfaction; (3) an object of desire. I take a similarly wide view, using the word to refer to the things we take in and to the activities we engage in when we feel empty or restless or wanting, to the substances and behaviors that we imagine will make us feel full, satisfied, complete. In this sense, appetites differ from "needs" or "instincts" in that they're not necessarily matters of life-and-death (an unsatisfied need for food or drink will, in due time, kill you; an unsatisfied appetite for chocolate probably won't; a flight instinct that malfunctions in the face of a predator can be lethal; in the face of a destructive relationship, it will merely make you miserable). Instead, appetites inhabit the murky middle ground between survival needs, which are concrete and unambiguous, and desires, a more general and all-inclusive term. Appetite is desire in the "drive" gear, more revved up and goal-oriented than generalized wanting, a destination always on its agenda. Appetites give specificity to the inchoate and shape to the formless; they're the feelings that bubble up from within and attach themselves to the tangible and external, turning elusive sensations (longing, yearning, emptiness) into actions, behaviors, substances, things. This meal, those shoes, that lover. The most obvious appetites, of course, are the physical ones, for food and sex, but I also consider material goods, ambition, and (perhaps above all) recognition by and connection with significant others to be among our most central and life-defining strivings. Along with food and sex, these are the things that propel us forward, that ignite craving, that guide and often dictate our behavior and choices.

Today, at the turn of the most accelerated century in history, a woman's appetites are (theoretically at least) under her sole control, hers to indulge or satisfy at will, for we live at a time when our most compelling hungers are almost wholly divorced from their essential purposes. Thanks to the sexual revolution, to widely available forms of contraception, and (for the time being) to access to abortion, a woman's decisions about sex may have little, if anything, to do with reproduction; separated from procreation, sexual appetite becomes both less rule-bound and more personal, less socially and physically threatening and also more confusing. So do her appetites in other life-defining realms. Liberated, at least to an extent, from her economic dependence on men, a woman today exercises an unprecedented degree of control over such matters as what and how much to eat, what to do with her time, how to look, where to live, and what objects to acquire. More important, thanks to the period of abundance that has characterized national life almost without interruption for the last eighty years, those decisions are rarely matters of sheer survival. For the bulk of middle- and upper-middle-class American women today, even in our current economic downturn, questions about diet, material life, livelihood, and relationships have far more to do with individual striving and self-definition than they do with basic subsistence. In short, the things we once needed in order to survive—food, shelter, intimate partnerships—have become the things we want in order to feel sated.

But satiety is itself a tricky subject, in large part because our culture—visual, commercially rapacious, oriented toward quick fixes and immediate gratification—both fuels and defines the wish for it at almost every turn, on almost every front. To the internal voice that whispers, *I want, I want,* consumer culture offers the reassuring, seductive words, *You can, you can; it's right here, within your grasp.* And it does so relentlessly, so much so we may barely be aware of its persistence and power. In 1915, the average American could go weeks without observing an ad; today, some twelve billion display ads, three million radio commercials, and 200,000 TV commercials flood the nation on a daily basis—most of us see and hear about 3,000 of them a day, all of them lapping at appetite, promising satisfaction, pulling and tugging and yipping at desire like a terrier at a woman's hemline. This is true for both genders, of course, but women in modern consumer culture are in the odd position of being both subjects of desire—people who are encouraged to desire things for themselves—and desire's primary object, mass imagery's main selling tool, sultry and thin and physically flawless. Thus, women are told not just *to* want but *what* to want. And the unstated promise here—that to want properly will make you *be* wanted—can create a powerful feeling of discord: Although in theory we may have the freedom and resources to satisfy our own appetites any way we choose, we have comparatively little freedom in determining, for ourselves, what those appetites should be, what true satisfaction might look or feel like. In one of the largest surveys of its kind to date, nearly

30,000 women told researchers at the University of Cincinnati College of Medicine that they'd rather lose weight than attain any other goal, a figure that alone suggests just how complicated the issue of appetite can be for women. This is the primary female striving? The appetite to lose appetite?

In fact, I suspect the opposite is true: that the primary, under-lying striving among many women at the start of the millennium is the appetite *for* appetite: a longing to feel safe and secure enough to name one's true appetites and worthy and powerful enough to get them satisfied. That a lot of women lack both sen-sations in sufficient measure is evident not just in the numbers on dieting and preoccupation with weight (which are stunning) but also in the kinds of gnawing sensations that can keep a woman up at night, worrying over questions of balance and per-spective and priorities: There's the awareness, sporadic perhaps but familiar to many, that we spend entirely too much time try-ing to suppress appetite instead of indulging it; there's the sense that a lot of us waste precious energy worshipping false gods, try-ing to get fed in ways that never quite seem to satisfy (if losing ten pounds won't do it, maybe that job will, or that house or that lover); there's an ill-defined but persistent feeling that on the whole this is a painful way to live, that it leaves us more anxious than we ought to be, or more depressed, or somehow cheated, as though somewhere along the way our very entitlement to hunger—to want things that feed us and fill us and give us joy—has been stolen.

It could be argued, of course, that women (and men) *should* lie awake nights worrying about appetite: More than half of all Americans between the ages of twenty and seventy-four are overweight, and one fifth are obese, meaning they have body-mass indexes of more than thirty; obesity, which has been called a "national epidemic," is linked to diabetes, high blood pressure, and neurological disorders; the cost of obesity-related illness is expected to reach into the hundreds of billions within the next twenty years.

But obesity's relationship to appetite (specifically, to the inability to curb it) is hardly clear. Morbid obesity in many cases may be genetic in origin, and the expanding American girth has at least as much to do with contemporary lifestyles as it does with restraint (or lack of it). Innovations in food processing and agriculture have made food cheaper, more abundant, and much higher in calories than it was fifty years ago, while technological changes (labor-saving devices that have left us more sedentary) have decreased the collective caloric expenditure: We live, in other words, in a fat-fueled and fat-fueling age. Obesity also appears to be a class issue: Cheap (and fat- and carbohydrate-rich) fast food is much more plentiful and accessible in poor urban areas than free-range chicken and fresh vegetables; health care, fitness facilities, and preventive education are far less accessible; not surprisingly, the poorer you are, the higher your risk for obesity and obesity-related disease.

But appetite is not just about eating and weight gain, and in a sense the national hand-wringing over obesity distracts from a more nuanced emotional consideration of indulgence and restraint, particularly as they're experienced in women's lives. Our culture's specific preoccupation with weight—particularly women's weight—has a lot to do with our more general preoccupation with women's bodies, not all of which is benign or caring, and a woman's individual preoccupation with weight often serves as a mask for other, more intricate sources of discomfort, the state of one's waistline being easier to contemplate than the state of one's soul. More to the point, when appetite is framed narrowly— as a matter of proportion and calories and fat—the larger constellation of feeling aroused by a woman's hunger is eclipsed. How a women reacts to cultural mandates about beauty and sexuality, how much self-acceptance she does or does not possess, how much pleasure she feels permitted to have, how much anxiety or guilt or shame her hungers arouse—these are the kinds of issues a woman may bring to the scale (or to the bedroom or the shopping mall or the workplace), and as the female preoccupation with dieting and body image alone suggests, they can generate an ex-quisite amount of pain and confusion.

Granted, these are not (or not always) life-and-death issues; to an extent, the brands of unease I'm interested in can be seen as colossal luxury problems, the edgy blatherings of women who have the time, energy, and resources to actually worry about their thighs or their wardrobes or their relative levels of personal ful-fillment. And to an extent, that view is entirely correct. The women I describe and address in these pages are primarily white, affluent, and highly educated; they belong to one of the most privileged populations in modern history. While I won't speculate here about how race affects a woman's feelings about appetite (an African American or a Latina woman's experience of the body, her conceptions of beauty, power, and entitlement may be subject to forces beyond my scope), I do recognize the defining power of class and social context. My own battle with hunger is wholly dif-ferent from that of a single mother living below the poverty line in my own city, or an Afghani woman living under the Taliban, or a Kurdish woman trudging across a mountain, child on her back, in flight from her war-torn home. Worrying about losing a few pounds is not at all the same as worrying about survival.

But the struggle with appetite, even in its "luxury" form, is im-portant, at least in part because it gets at complicated questions about female entitlement and freedom, the psychic qualities that one might have expected to spring up alongside the legal entitle-ments and freedoms that this population of women now enjoys. Divorced from issues of basic sustenance and freed from legal re-straint, appetite becomes a largely internal phenomenon, its ca-pacity for satisfaction wrapped up in an emotional framework rather than a physical or political one, and so a woman's rela-tionship with hunger and satisfaction acts like a mirror, reflect-ing her sense of self and place in the wider world. How hungry, in all senses of the word, does a woman allow herself to be? How filled? How free does she really feel, or how held back? Feeding, experiencing pleasure, taking in, deserving—for many women, these may not be matters of life and death, but they are certainly markers of joy and anguish, and they may have much to reveal about where the last four decades of social change have left us, and where they're leading us still.

By all accounts, I should feel as free and entitled on the appetite front as anyone. I came of age in the 1970s, in the progressive city of Cambridge, Massachusetts, and like many women of my generation and the generation behind me, I had the luxury of believing, in a not-very-politicized and no doubt naive way, that the battle on behalf of women had been fought and won, the munitions stashed away in the great cupboard marked Feminist Change. Women my age were the heiresses of the women's movement, of the sexual revolution, of relaxed gender roles, of access to everything from abortion to education, and to a large extent, that legacy blasted open female desire: We had more opportunities and freedoms at our disposal than any other group of women at any other time in modern history; we could do anything, be anything, define our lives any way we saw fit. And yet by the age of twenty-one, I'd found myself whittled down to skeletal form, my whole being oriented toward the denial of appetite. And at forty-two, my current age, I can still find myself lingering at the periphery of desire, peering through those doors from what often feels like a great distance, not always certain whether it's okay to march on in.

That story, with its implicit conflict between the internal and external worlds, is in essence the story of appetite. It's about the anxiety that crops up alongside new, untested freedoms, and the guilt that's aroused when a woman tests old and deeply entrenched rules about gender and femininity. It's about the collision between self and culture, female desire unleashed in a world that's still deeply ambivalent about female power and that manages to whet appetite and shame it in equal measure. It's about the difficulty a woman may have feeling connected to her own body and her own desires in an increasingly visual and commercial world, a place where the female form is so mercilessly externalized and where conceptions of female desire are so narrowly framed. And it's about the durability of traditional psychic and social structures, about how the seeds of self-denial are still planted and encouraged in girls, about how forty years of legal and social change have not yet nurtured a truly alternative hybrid, one that would flower into feelings of agency and initiative, into the conviction that one's appetites are good and valid and deserve to be satisfied in healthy and reasonable ways.

Evidence of the female struggle with appetite is everywhere. Five million women in the United States suffer from eating disorders; eighty percent of women report that the experience of being female means "feeling too fat." More than forty percent of women between the ages of eighteen and fifty-nine report some kind of sexual dysfunction, from lack of interest or pleasure in sex to an inability to achieve orgasm. Estimates on compulsive shopping range from two to eight percent of the general female population, fifteen to sixteen percent of a college-age sample. Something is wrong here, and it's not anything as simple as Low Self-Esteem, that great pathologizing scrap heap onto which so many female behaviors (our obsessions with weight and appearance, our apparent proclivity for self-destruction) tend to get tossed. That's always felt like very thin gruel to me as a rationale, about fifteen ingredients missing from the soup. A woman who is actively hurting her body or beating it into submission, a woman who is clinging to a relationship that hurts her or who's shopping her way into stupor and debt is suffering from a good deal more than a poor self-image: The phrase captures none of the sorrow and emptiness that leaches up alongside a thwarted appetite, and little of the agony that accompanies a displaced need, the anguish of truly not knowing why desires get channeled in so many wrong directions, of not knowing how to live—and feel—a different way.

Today, nearly two decades into my own battle to live differently, I can't quite say I resemble a woman out of Renoir; whether individual or collective, change is glacial in nature, progress charted not in victories but in inches and slight degrees, and I imagine that for me, as for many women, the challenges surrounding appetite will be both lifelong and life-defining. But I can say, in a grudging nod to victory, that I've redefined both the holy grail and the effort to reach it, a process that's internal and deeply personal and bound up with the extraordinarily slippery concept of well-being.

Once upon a time, a "good day" for me meant eating fewer than 800 calories in a twenty-four-hour period: case closed, well-being measured by its absolute inaccessibility. Today, a good day might mean several different things. It might mean that I start the day sculling along the river near my home, an activity that makes me feel competent and strong and alive. It might mean that I put in a solid day's work, that I spend some time laughing on the phone with a friend, that I eat a good meal, that I curl up at night with the two beings I love most in the world, one human and one canine. A good day usually means successfully resisting my worst impulses, which involve isolation and perfectionism and self-punishment; it means striking some balance, instead, between fun and productivity and connection. Finding my way toward good days, and toward a more sustaining definition of well-being, has meant creeping, gradually and often painfully, in Renoir's direction, a sixteen-year crawl toward a kind of freedom to be filled.

What liberates a person enough to indulge appetite, to take pleasure in the world, to enjoy being alive? Within that question lies the true holy grail, the heart of a woman's hunger.

1

ADD CAKE,
SUBTRACT SELF-ESTEEM
ANXIETY AND THE
MATHEMATICS OF DESIRE

THE LURE OF STARVING—the baffling, seductive hook—
was that it soothed, a balm of safety and containment that
seemed to remove me from the ordinary, fraught world of human
hunger and place me high above it, in a private kingdom of
calm.

This didn't happen immediately, this sense of transcendent
solace, and there certainly wasn't anything blissful or even long-
lived about the state; starving is a painful, relentless experience,
and also a throbbingly dull one, an entire life boiled down to a
singular sensation (physical hunger) and a singular obsession
(food). But when I think back on those years, which lasted
through my mid-twenties, and when I try to get underneath the
myriad meanings and purposes of such a bizarre fixation, that's
what I remember most pointedly—the calm, the relief from an
anxiety that felt both oceanic and nameless. For years, I ate the
same foods every day, in exactly the same manner, at exactly the
same times. I devoted a monumental amount of energy to this
endeavor—thinking about food, resisting food, observing other
people's relationships with food, anticipating my own paltry indulgences in food—and this narrowed, specific, driven rigidity

made me feel supremely safe: one concern, one feeling, everything else just background noise.

Disorders of appetite—food addictions, compulsive shopping,
promiscuous sex—have a kind of semiotic brilliance, expressing
in symbol and metaphor what women themselves may not be
able to express in words, and I can deconstruct anorexia with the
best of them. Anorexia is a response to cultural images of the female body—waiflike, angular—that both capitulates to the ideal
and also mocks it, strips away all the ancillary signs of sexuality,
strips away breasts and hips and butt and leaves in their place a
garish caricature, a cruel cartoon of flesh and bone. It is a form of
silent protest, a hunger strike that expresses some deep discomfort with the experience of inhabiting an adult female body. It is
a way of co-opting the traditional female preoccupation with
food and weight by turning the obsession upside down, directing
the energy not toward the preparation and provision and inges-
tion of food but toward the shunning of it, and all that it represents: abundance, plenitude, caretaking. Anorexia is this,
anorexia is that. Volumes have been written about such symbolic expressions, and there's truth to all of them, and they are
oddly comforting truths: They help to decipher this puzzle; they
help to explain why eating disorders are the third most common
chronic illness among females in the United States, and why fifteen percent of young women have substantially disordered attitudes and behaviors toward food and eating, and why the
incidence of eating disorders has increased by thirty-six percent
every five years since the 1950s. They offer some hope—if we
can understand this particularly devastating form of self-inflicted
cruelty, maybe we can find a way to stop it.

I, too, am tempted to comfort and explain, to look back with
the cool detachment of twenty years and offer a crisp critique:
a little cultural commentary here, a little metaphorical analysis
there. But what recedes into the background amid such expla-
nations—and what's harder to talk about because it's intangible and stubborn and vast—is the core, the underlying drive,

the sensation that not only made anorexia feel so seductively viable for me some two decades ago but that also informs the central experience of appetite for so many women, the first feeling we bring to the table of hunger: anxiety, a sense of being overwhelmed.

There is a particular whir of agitation about female hunger, a low-level thrumming of shoulds and shouldn'ts and can'ts and wants that can be so chronic and familiar it becomes a kind of feminine Muzak, easy to dismiss, or to tune out altogether, even if you're actively participating in it. Last spring, a group of women gathered in my living room to talk about appetite, all of them teachers and administrators at a local school and all of them adamant that this whole business—weight, food, managing hunger—troubles them not at all. "Weight," said one, "is not really an issue for me." "No," said another, "not for me, either." And a third: "I don't really think about what I'm going to eat from day to day. Basically, I just eat what I want."

This was a cheerful and attractive group, ages twenty-two to forty-one, and they were all so insistent about their normalcy around food that, were it not for the subtle strain of caveat that ran beneath their descriptions, I might have believed them.

The caveats had to do with rules, with attitudes as ingrained as reflexes, and with a particularly female sense of justified reward: They are at the center of this whir, an anxious jingle of mandate and restraint. The woman who insisted that weight is "not really an issue," for instance, also noted that she only allows herself to eat dessert, or second helpings at dinner, if she's gone to the gym that day. No workout, no dessert. The woman who agreed with her (no, not an issue for her, either) echoed that sentiment. "Yeah," she nodded, "if I don't work out, I start to feel really gross about food and I'll try to cut back." A third said she eats "normally" but noted that she always makes a point of leaving at least one bite of food on her plate, every meal, no exceptions. And the woman who said she "basically just eats what she wants" added, "I mean, if someone brings a cake into the office,

I'll have a tiny slice, and I might not eat the frosting, but it's not like a big deal or anything. I just scrape the frosting off."

Tiny slices, no frosting, forty-five minutes on the StairMaster: These are the conditions, variations on a theme of vigilance and self-restraint that I've watched women dance to all my life, that I've danced to myself instinctively and still have to work to resist. I walk into a health club locker room and feel an immediate impulse toward scrutiny, the kneejerk measuring of self against other: *That one has great thighs, this one's gained weight, who's thin, who's fat, how do I compare?* I overhear snippets of conversation, constraints unwittingly articulated and upheld in a dollop of lavish praise here (*You look fabulous, have you lost weight?*), a whisper of recriminating judgment there (*She looks awful, has she gained weight?*), and I automatically turn to look: Who looks fabulous, who looks awful? I go to a restaurant with a group of women and pray that we can order lunch without falling into the semi-covert business of collective monitoring, in which levels of intake and restraint are aired, compared, noticed: *What are you getting? Is that all you're having? A salad? Oh, please.* There's a persistent awareness of self in relation to other behind this kind of behavior, and also a tacit nod to the idea that there are codes to adhere to, and self-effacing apologies to be made if those codes are broken. *I'm such a hog,* says the woman who breaks rank, ordering a cheeseburger when everyone else has salad.

Can't, shouldn't, I'm a moose. So much of this is waved away as female vanity—this tedious nattering about calories and fat, this whining, shallow preoccupation with surfaces—but I find it poignant, and painful in a low-level but chronic way, and also quite revealing. One of the lingering cultural myths about gender is that women are bad at math—they lack confidence for it, they have poor visual-spatial skills, they simply don't excel at numbers the way boys do. This theory has been widely challenged over the years, and there's scant evidence to suggest that girls are in any way neurologically ill-equipped to deal with algebra or calculus. But I'd challenge the myth on different grounds:

Women are actually superb at math; they just happen to engage in their own variety of it, an intricate personal math in which desires are split off from one another, weighed, balance, traded, assessed. These are the mathematics of desire, a system of self-limitation and monitoring based on the fundamental premise that appetites are at best risky, at worst impermissible, that indulgence must be bought and paid for. Hence the rules and caveats: Before you open the lunch menu or order that cheeseburger or consider eating the cake with the frosting intact, haul out the psychic calculator and start tinkering with the budget.

Why shouldn't you? I asked a woman that question not long ago while she was demurring about whether to order dessert at a restaurant.

Immediate answer: "Because I'll feel gross."

Why gross?

"Because I'll feel fat."

And what would happen if you felt fat?

"I hate myself when I feel fat. I feel ugly and out of control. I feel really un-sexy. I feel unlovable."

And if you deny yourself the dessert?

"I may feel a little deprived, but I'll also feel pious," she said.

So it's worth the cost?

"Yes."

These are big trade-offs for a simple piece of cake—add five hundred calories, subtract well-being, allure, and self-esteem—and the feelings behind them are anything but vain or shallow. Hidden within that thirty-second exchange is an entire set of mathematical principles, equations that can dictate a woman's most fundamental approach to hunger. Mastery over the body—its impulses, its needs, its size—is paramount; to lose control is to risk beauty, and to risk beauty is to risk desirability, and to risk desirability is to risk entitlement to sexuality and love and self-esteem. Desires collide, the wish to eat bumping up against the wish to be thin, the desire to indulge conflicting with the injunction to restrain. Small wonder food makes a woman nervous.

The experience of appetite in this equation *is* an experience of anxiety, a burden and a risk; yielding to hunger may be permissible under certain conditions, but mostly it's something to be Earned or Monitored and Controlled. $e = mc^2$.

During the acute phases of my starving years, I took a perverse kind of pleasure in these exhibitions of personal calculus, the anxious little jigs that women would do around food. Every day at lunchtime, I'd stand in line at a café in downtown Providence clutching my 200-calorie yogurt, and while I waited, I'd watch the other women deliberate. I'd see a woman mince edgily around the glass case that held muffins and cookies, and I'd recognize the look in her eye, the longing for something sweet or gooey, the sudden flicker of *No*. I'd overhear fragments of conversation: debates between women (*I can't eat that, I'll feel huge*), and cajolings (*Oh, c'mon, have the fries*), and collaborations in surrender (*I will if you will*). I listened for these, I paid attention, and I always felt a little stab of superiority when someone yielded (*Okay, fuck it, fries, onion rings, PIE*). I would not yield—to do so, I understood, would imply lack of restraint, an unseemly, indulgent female greed—and in my stern resistance I got to feel coolly superior while they felt, or so it seemed to me, anxious.

But I knew that anxiety. I know it still, and I know how stubbornly pressing it can feel, the niggling worry about food and calories and size and heft cutting to the quick somehow, as though to fully surrender to hunger might lead to mayhem, the appetite proven unstoppable. If you plotted my food intake on a graph from that initial cottage cheese purchase onward, you wouldn't see anything very dramatic at first: a slight decline in consumption over my junior and senior years, and an increasing though not yet excessive pattern of rigidity, that edgy whir about food and weight at only the edges of consciousness at first. I lived off campus my senior year with a boyfriend, studied enormously hard, ate normal dinners at home with him, but permitted myself only a single plain donut in the morning, coffee all day, not a calorie more. The concept of "permission" was new to me—it heralded the introduction of rules and by-laws, a nascent internal tyrant issuing commands—but I didn't question it. I just ate the donut, drank the coffee, obeyed the rules, aware on some level that the rigidity and restraint served a purpose, reinforced those first heady feelings of will and determination, a proud sensation that I was somehow beyond ordinary need. I wrote a prize-winning honors thesis on two hundred calories a day.

The following year, my first out of college, the line on the graph would begin to waver, slowly at first, then peaking and dipping more erratically: five pounds up, five pounds down, six hundred calories here, six thousand there, the dieting female's private NASDAQ, a personal index of self-torture.

This was not a happy time. I'd taken a job in a university news bureau, an ostensible entree into writing and a fairly hefty disappointment (I was an editorial assistant in title, a glorified secretary in fact, bored nearly senseless from day one). The boyfriend had left for graduate school in California, and I was living alone for the first time, missing him with the particularly consuming brand of desperation afforded by long-distance love. I was restless and lonely and full of self-doubt, and the low-level tampering I'd been doing with my appetite began to intensify, my relationship with food thrown increasingly out of whack. This is familiar territory to anyone with a long history of dieting: a fundamental severing between need and want begins to take place, eating gradually loses its basic associations with nourishment and physical satisfaction and veers onto a more complex emotional plane in which the whole notion of hunger grows loaded and confusing. Sometimes I was very rigid with my diet during this period, resolving to consume nothing but coffee all day, only cheese and crackers at night. Other times I ate for comfort, or because I was bored, or because I felt empty, all reasons that frightened and confused me. I'd make huge salads at night, filled with nuts and cubes of cheese and slathered in creamy dressings; I'd eat big bowls of salty soups, enormous tuna melts, hideously sweet oversized chocolate chip cookies, purchased in little frenzies of preservation (should I?

shouldn't I?) from a local bakery. I started drinking heavily during this period, too, which weakened my restraint; I'd wake up feeling bloated and hungover and I'd try to compensate by eating nothing, or next to nothing, during the day.

For a year, I gained weight, lost weight, gained the weight back, and I found this deeply unnerving, as though some critical sense of bodily integrity were at risk, my sense of limits and proportion eroding. I'd feel my belly protrude against the waistband of my skirt, or one thigh chafing against another, and I'd be aware of a potent stab of alarm: *Shit*, the vigilance has been insufficiently upheld, the body is growing soft and doughy, something central and dark about me—a lazy, gluttonous, insatiable second self—is poised to emerge. Women often brought pastries into the office where I worked. Sometimes I'd steadfastly avoid them, resolve not even to look; other times I'd eye the pastry box warily from across the room, get up periodically and circle the table, conscious of a new sensation of self-mistrust, questions beginning to flitter and nag. *Could I eat one pastry, or would one lead to three, or four or six? Was I actually hungry for a Danish or a croissant, or was I trying to satisfy some other appetite? How hungry—how rapacious, greedy, selfish, needy—was I?* The dance of the hungry woman—two steps toward the refrigerator, one step back, that endless loop of hunger and indulgence and guilt—had ceased to be a game; some key middle ground between gluttony and restraint, a place that used to be easily accessible to me, had grown elusive and I didn't know how to get back there.

This, of course, is one of appetite's insidious golden rules: The more you meddle with a hunger, the more taboo and confusing it will become. Feed the body too little and then too much, feed it erratically, launch that maddening cycle of deprivation and overcompensation, and the sensation of physical hunger itself becomes divorced from the body, food loaded with alternative meanings: symbol of longing, symbol of constraint, form of torture, form of reward, source of anxiety, source of succor, measure of self-worth. And thus the simple experience of hunger—of wanting something to eat—becomes frightening and fraught. What does it mean this time? Where will it lead? Will you eat *everything* if you let yourself go? Will you prove unstoppable, a famished dog at a garbage bin? Young and unsure of myself and groping for direction, I was scared of many things that year— leaving the structure of college was scary, entering the work world was scary, living on my own was scary, the future loomed like a monumental question mark—but I suspect I was scared above all of hunger itself, which felt increasingly boundless and insatiable, its limits and possible ravages unknown.

I suspect, too, that this feeling went well beyond the specific issue of food, that anxiety about caloric intake and body size were merely threads in a much larger tapestry of feeling that had to do with female self-worth and power and identity—for me and for legions of other women. This time period—late 1970s, early 1980s—coincided with the early stages of the well-documented shift in the culture's collective definition of beauty, its sudden and dramatically unambiguous pairing with slenderness. There is nothing new about this today; the pressure (internal and external) to be thin is so familiar and so widespread by now that most of us take it for granted, breathe it in like air, can't remember a time when we weren't aware of it, can't remember how different the average model or actress or beauty pageant contestant looked before her weight began to plummet (in the last twenty-five years, it's dropped to twenty-five percent below that of the average woman), can't remember a world in which grocery store shelves didn't brim with low-cal and "lite" products, in which mannequins wore size eight clothes instead of size two, in which images of beauty were less wildly out of reach.

But it's worth recalling that all of this—the ratcheted-up emphasis on thinness, the aesthetic shift from Marilyn Monroe to Kate Moss, the concomitant rise in eating disorders—is relatively recent, that the emphasis on diminishing one's size, on miniaturizing the very self, didn't really heat up until women began making gains in other areas of their lives. By the time I started to flirt

with anorexia, in the late 1970s, women had gained access to education, birth control, and abortion, as well as widespread protection from discrimination in most areas of their lives. At the
same time, doctors were handing out some ten billion appetite-
suppressing amphetamines per year, Weight Watchers had spread
to forty-nine states, its membership three million strong, and the
diet-food business was about to eclipse all other categories as
the fastest-growing segment of the food industry.

This parallel has been widely, and sensibly, described as the
aesthetic expression of the backlash against feminist strength
that Susan Faludi would document in 1992. At a time when increasing numbers of women were demanding the right to take up
more space in the world, it is no surprise that they'd be hit with
the opposite message from a culture that was (and still is) both
male-dominated and deeply committed to its traditional power
structures. Women get psychically larger, and they're told to grow
physically smaller. Women begin to play active roles in realms
once dominated by men (schools, universities, athletic fields, the
workplace, the bedroom), and they're countered with images of
femininity that infantilize them, render them passive and frail
and non-threatening. "The female body is the place where this
society writes its messages," writes Rosalind Coward in *Female
Desires*, and its response to feminism was etched with increasing
clarity on the whittled-down silhouette of the average American
model: Don't get too hungry, don't overstep your bounds.

The whispers of this mandate, audible in the 1970s and 1980s,
have grown far louder today; they are roars, howls, screams. The
average American, bombarded with advertisements on a daily
basis, will spend approximately three years of his or her lifetime
watching television commercials, and you don't have to look too
closely to see what that deluge of imagery has to say about the female body and its hungers. A controlled appetite, prerequisite for
slenderness, connotes beauty, desirability, worthiness. An uncontrolled appetite—a fat woman—connotes the opposite, she is
ugly, repulsive, and so fundamentally unworthy that, according

to a *New York Times* report on cultural attitudes toward fat, six-teen percent of adults would choose to abort a child if they knew he or she would be untreatably obese.

Hatred of fat, inextricably linked to fear of fat, is so deeply em-bedded in the collective consciousness it can arouse a surprising depth of discomfort and mean-spiritedness, even among people who consider themselves to be otherwise tolerant and sensitive to women. Gail Dines, director of women's studies and professor of sociology at Wheelock College in Boston and one of the nation's foremost advocates of media literacy, travels around the country giving a slide show/lecture called "Sexy or Sexist: Images of Women in the Media." The first half of the presentation consists of images, one after the other, of svelte perfection: a sultry Brooke Shields clad in a blue bikini on a *Cosmo* cover, an achingly slender leg in an ad for Givenchy pantyhose, a whisper-thin Kate Moss. Then, about halfway into the presentation, a slide of a postcard flashes onto the screen, a picture of a woman on a beach in Hawaii. The woman is clad in a bright blue two-piece bathing suit, and she is very fat; she's shown from the rear, her buttocks enormous, her thighs pocked with fleshy folds, and the words on the postcard read: HAVING A WHALE OF A TIME IN HAWAII. The first time I saw this, I felt a jolt of something critical and mean—part pity, part judgment, an impulse to recoil—and I felt immedi-ately embarrassed by this, which is precisely the sensation Dines intends to flush out. At another showing before a crowd at North-eastern University, the image appears on the screen and several people begin to guffaw, nervous titters echo across the room. Dines stops and turns to the audience. "Now why is this consid-ered funny?" she demands. "Explain that to me. Does she not have the right to the dignity that you and I have a right to? Does having extra pounds on your body deny you that right?" The crowd falls silent, and Dines sighs. There it is: This obese woman, this object of hoots and jeers, is a tangible focus of female anxiety, a 350-pound picture of the shame and humiliation that will be visited upon a woman if her hunger is allowed to go unchecked.

Dines, among many others, might identify culture as the primary protagonist in this narrative, a sneering villain cleverly disguised as Beauty who skulks around injecting women with a irrational but morbid fear of fat. There is certainly some truth to that—a woman who isn't affected to some degree by the images and injunctions of fat-and-thin is about as rare as a black orchid. But I also think the intensity of the struggle around appetite that began to plague me twenty years ago, that continues to plague so many women today, speaks not just to cultural anxiety about female hunger, profound though it may be, but also to deep reservoirs of personal anxiety. Fear of fat merely exists on the rippled surface of that reservoir; mass-market images are mere reflections upon it. Underneath, the real story—each woman in her own sea of experience—is more individual and private; it's about what happens when hunger is not quite paired with power, when the license to hunger is new and unfamiliar, when a woman is teased with freedom—to define herself as she sees fit, to attend to her own needs and wishes, to fully explore her own desires—but may not quite feel that freedom in her bones or believe that it will last.

Once, several months into that first year of weight gain and weight loss, I met some friends for Sunday brunch, an all-you-can-eat buffet at a local hotel restaurant. All-you-can-eat buffets terrify me to this day—I find them sadistic and grotesque in particularly American way, the emphasis on quantity and excess reflecting something insatiably greedy and short-sighted about the culture's ethos—and I date the onset of my terror to that very morning. Such horrifying abundance! Such potential for unleashed gluttony! The buffet table seemed to stretch out for a mile: at one station, made-to-order omelets, and bacon and sausage; at another, waffles and pancakes and crêpes; at another, bagels and muffins and croissants and pastries; at yet another, an entire array of desserts, cakes and pies and individual soufflés. If you're confused about hunger, if the internal mechanisms that signal physical satiety have gone haywire, if food has become symbolically loaded, or a stand-in for other longings, this kind of array can topple you. I couldn't choose. More to the point, I couldn't trust myself to choose moderately or responsibly, or to stop when I was full, or even to know what I wanted to begin with, what would satisfy and how much. And so I ate everything. The suppressed appetite always rages just beneath the surface of will, and as often happened during that period, it simmered, then bubbled up, then boiled over. I ate. I ate eggs and bacon and waffles and slabs of cake, I ate knowing full well that I'd feel bloated and flooded with disgust later on and that I'd have to make restitution—I'd starve the next day, or go for a six-mile run, or both. I ate without pleasure, I ate until I hurt.

Years later, I'd see that brunch in metaphorical terms, a high-calorie, high-carbohydrate testament to the ambiguous blessings of abundance, its promise and its agonizing terror. As a rule, women of my generation were brought up without knowing a great deal about how to understand hunger, with very little discussion about how to assess and respond adequately to our own appetites, and with precious few examples of how to negotiate a buffet of possibility, much less embrace one. Eating too much— then as now—was a standard taboo, a mother's concern with her own body and weight handed down to her daughter in a mantle of admonishments: *Always take the smallest portion; always eat a meal before you go on a date lest you eat too much in front of him; don't eat that, it'll go straight to your hips.* Sexual hunger was at best undiscussed, at worst presented as a bubbling cauldron of danger and sin, potentially ruinous; the memory banks of women my age are riddled with images of scowling mothers, echoes of recriminating hisses (*Take that off, you look like a slut!*), fragments of threat-laden lectures about the predatory hunger of boys. And the world of ambition was in many ways uncharted territory, one that required qualities and skills—ego strength, competitiveness, intellectual confidence—that were sometimes actively discouraged in girls (*Don't brag, don't get a swelled head, don't be so smart*), rarely modeled.

This is a complicated legacy to bring to a world of blasted-open options, each *yes* in potential collision with an old *no*, and it makes for a great deal of confusion. The underlying questions of appetite, after all, are formidable—What *would* satisfy? How much *do* you need, and of what? What *are* the true passions, the real hungers behind the ostensible goals of beauty or slenderness?—and until relatively recently, a lot of women haven't been encouraged to explore them, at least not in a deep, concerted, uniform, socially supported way. We have what might be called post-feminist appetites, whetted and encouraged by a generation of opened doors and collapsed social structures, but not always granted unequivocal support or license, not always stripped of their traditional alarm bells and warnings, and not yet bolstered by a deeper sense of entitlement.

Freedom, it is important to note, is not the same as power; the ability to make choices can feel unsettling and impermanent and thin if it's not girded somehow with the heft of real economic and political strength. Women certainly have more of that heft than they did a generation ago; we are far less formally constrained, far more autonomous, and far more politically powerful, at least potentially so. Forty-three million women—forty percent of all adult women—live independently today, without traditional supports. Women make the vast majority of consumer purchases in this country—eighty-three percent—and buy one fifth of all homes. We have an unprecedented amount of legal protection, with equality on the basis of sex required by law in virtually every area of American life. We are better educated than the women of any preceding generation, with women representing more than half of full-time college enrollments. By all accounts, we ought to feel powerful, competent, and strong—and many women no doubt do, at least in some areas and at some times.

But it's also true that an overwhelming majority of women—estimates range from eighty to eighty-nine percent—wake up every morning aware of an anxious stirring of self-disgust, fixated on the feel of our thighs as we pull on our stockings, the feel of our bellies and hips as we zip up our pants and skirts. Women are three times as likely as men to feel negatively about their bodies. Eighty percent of women have been on a diet, half are actively dieting at any given time, and half report feeling dissatisfied with their bodies all the time. There is no doubt that this negativity is a culturally mediated phenomenon, that culture gives the female preoccupation with appearance (which in itself is nothing new) its particular cast, its particularly relentless focus on slenderness. But the sheer numbers, which indicate an unprecedented depth and breadth of anxiety about appearance in general and weight in particular, suggest that something more complex than imagery is at work, that our collective sense of power and competence and strength hasn't quite made it to a visceral level.

To be felt at that level, as visceral and permanent and real, entitlement must exist beyond the self; it must be known and acknowledged on a wider plane. And this is where women still get the short end of the stick; for all the gains of the last forty years, we are hardly ruling the world out there. Congress is still ninety percent male, as are ninety-eight percent of America's top corporate officers. Ninety-five percent of all venture capital today flows into men's bank accounts. The two hundred highest-paid CEOs in America are all men. Only three women head Fortune 500 companies, a number that hasn't budged in twenty years. We also have less visibility than men; women—our lives, issues, concerns—are still featured in only fifteen percent of page-one stories, and when we do make front-page news, it is usually only as victims or perpetrators of crime. And we still have less earning power: Women continue to make eighty-four cents for every dollar a man makes; women who take time off from work to have children make seventeen percent less than those who don't even six years after they return; men with children earn the most money while women with children earn the least.

This gap, I think—this persistent imbalance between personal freedom on the one hand and political power on the other—

amps up the anxiety factor behind desire; it can leave a woman with a sense that something does not quite compute; it can give choices a partial, qualified feel. A woman, today, can be a neurosurgeon, or an astrophysicist; she can marry or not marry, leave her spouse, pack up, and move across the country at will. But can she take such choices a step further, or two or ten? Can a woman be not just an astrophysicist, but a big, powerful, lusty astrophysicist who feels unequivocally entitled to food and sex and pleasure and acclaim? Can she move across the country and also leave behind all her deeply ingrained feelings about what women are really supposed to look and act and be like? External freedoms may still bump up against a lot of ancient and durable internal taboos; they may still collide with the awareness, however vague, that women still represent the least empowered portion of the population, and these collisions help explain why appetites are so particularly problematic today; they exist in a very murky context, and an inherently unstable one, consistently pulled between the opposing poles of possibility and constraint, power and powerlessness.

The world mobilizes in the service of male appetite; it did during my upbringing and it does still. Whether or not this represents the actual experience of contemporary boys and men, our cultural stereotypes of male desire (and stereotypes exist precisely because they contain grains of truth) are all about facilitation and support: Mothers feed (Eat! Eat!), fathers model assertion and unabashed competitiveness, teachers encourage outspoken bravado. At home and at work, men have helpers, usually female, who clean and cook and shop and type and file and assist. And at every turn—on billboards, magazine covers, in ads—men are surrounded by images of offering, of breasts and parted lips and the sultry gazes of constant availability: Take me, you are entitled, I exist to please you. For all the expansion of opportunity in women's lives, there is no such effort on behalf of female appetite, there are no comparable images of service and availability, there is no baseline expectation that a legion of others will rush forward to meet our needs or satisfy our hungers. The striving, self-oriented man is adapted to, cut slack, his transgressions and inadequacies explained and forgiven. *Oh, well, you wouldn't expect him to cook or take care of his kids, who cares if he's put on a few pounds, so what if he's controlling or narcissistic, he's busy, he gets things done, he's running the show, he's running the company, he's running the COUNTRY.* That litany of understanding does not apply to women; it sounds discordant and artificial if you switch the genders, and if you need a single example of the double standard at work here, think about Bill and Hillary Clinton. Bill's pudginess and fondness for McDonald's was seen as endearing, his sexual appetite criticized but ultimately forgiven by most Americans, or at least considered irrelevant to his abilities on the job; Hillary got no such latitude, the focus on her appearance (hairstyle, wardrobe, legs) was relentless, the hostility released toward her ambition venomous.

The one exception to this rule, the one area where a legion of others might, in fact, rush forward in service to a woman's needs, is shopping, particularly high-end retail shopping, but in itself, that merely underscores how lacking the phenomenon is in other areas, and how constricted the realm of appetite is for women in general: We can want, and even expect, the world to mobilize on our behalf when we're equipped with an American Express gold card and an appetite for Armani. But beyond the world of appearances and consumer goods, expressions of physical hunger and selfish strivings rarely meet with such consistent support. Instead, the possibility of risk can hang in the air like a mildly poisonous mist; for every appetite, there may be a possible backlash, or a slap or a reprimand or a door that opens but has caveats stamped all over the welcome mat. A novelist tells me in a whisper about a glowing review she's received; she can barely get the words out, so strong are the chastising echoes of her family: *Now, don't you let it go to your head,* her mother used to say, and it took her decades to realize how truly defeating that phrase was. ("Where's it supposed to go," she asks today, "someone else's head?") A scientist, brilliant and respected, secures a major grant for a project she's dreamed of taking on for years and later describes what an emotional hurdle it was to fully take pride in the accomplishment, to really revel in it: "I couldn't say it aloud, I just couldn't get the words out," she says. "I don't think a man would *get* that." An educator, who's taught high school for thirteen years and is now pursuing a PhD in education, tells me, "For years, I've carried around the feeling that if I really allow myself to follow my passions, something bad will happen." She can't follow that line of thought to any logical conclusion; rather, it expresses an amalgam of worries, some specific (she's apprehensive about being consumed by work, and about making sacrifices in her personal life), but more of them generic, as though the admission of hunger and ambition is in itself a dangerous thing, quite likely a punishable offense.

This quiet, dogged anxiety, this internalized mosquito whine of caveat, may explain why the memory of that hotel brunch would stick with me for so long; the experience seemed to capture something about the times, about the onset of a complicated set of conflicts between an expansive array of options on the one hand and a sense of deep uncertainty on the other, a feeling that this freedom was both incomplete and highly qualified, full of risks. Certainly that's how I felt in those early unformed twentysomething years, as though I were standing before an enormous table of possibilities with no utensils, no serving spoons, no real sense that I was truly entitled to sample the goods, to experiment or indulge or design my own menu.

In fact, I brought the opposite sensation to the table: a simmering conviction that appetites were perilous, hunger and indulgence a gateway to disappointment and shame. This, I think, was part of a silent family code in my household, a place I recall from the earliest ages as muted and hushed, the air infused by a quality of imperative restraint that sometimes felt like gentility and sometimes like depression, I could never quite tell which. My parents never actively discouraged expressions of hunger—

growing up, there were no overt taboos against lust or gluttony or covetousness, no religious prohibitions, no moralizing. But there wasn't any clear embrace of appetite, either, and there was certainly no sense of indulgence as an admirable or even desirable part of ordinary life. My father (a psychiatrist) and my mother (a painter) were deeply private and undemonstrative people. They did not fight or hug. They weren't particularly interested in material luxuries; they didn't get excited by food (I can't remember either parent ever eating too much); and while they clearly valued intellectual appetites—it was good to hunger for knowledge, good to harbor professional ambitions, very good to do well in school—the world of pleasure felt off-limits somehow, a country we didn't visit.

Instead, we seemed to inhabit a realm of essential sparseness, sensuality and strong emotion not completely absent but muzzled and kept leashed in the yard. Anger or despair or yearning might leak out periodically—a sudden bellow of displaced rage when my father lost his car keys, a muffled hiss emanating from behind my mother's bedroom door when she shut herself in there to talk on the phone—but these expressions were too sporadic and nonspecific to add up to anything serious or telling, and they left me with only the most ill-defined impression of parental dissatisfaction, faint etchings of hunger, a cloudy sense that underneath all that privacy and reserve was an ocean of unmet need too stormy and vast to contemplate. At dinner, my parents and brother and sister and I sat huddled around the table in separate orbits, linked only by an aura of the most obscure shared sadness, and the food always felt a bit incidental, a footnote to the meal. My father served. He'd stand at the head of the table and dole out portions so small they wouldn't cover half the plate, not because he was deliberately withholding but because he was absent-minded and preoccupied, food a lesser concern. The message here wasn't that bodily appetites were base or sinful, but that they were (at best) beside the point and (at worst) a Pandora's box, best to keep the lid tightly sealed.

My own hungers, by contrast, felt powerful and striking and out of place. I think I was a hungrier kid than my siblings, in several senses of the word: I was needy even as an infant, a baby who wanted to be picked up and held more than my twin sister did; later, I'd turn into a grabby pre-adolescent whose tastes didn't quite square with the restrained family style. I can't remember a time when I didn't want *things*: patent leather dress shoes to wear to birthday parties when I was a girl; a pair of bright red corduroy pants; fancy bedroom furniture. My parents took us on annual winter vacations to the most remote spots— rented beach houses way off the beaten path in Puerto Rico or on the gulf coast of Florida—and while everyone else fell easily into a mute and solitary pattern of relaxation (reading, bird-watching, ambling along the beach), I'd fume and squirm with boredom, longing for plush hotels, places with TVs and heated swimming pools and room service and elegant restaurants. Want, want, want. I wanted laughter in those quiet houses and I wanted all of us to pull our noses out of books and *speak* to each other, even to yell, and I wanted affection. As a child, running around barefoot in the summer, I'd occasionally get a splinter in my foot, something I came to relish because it meant my mother would soak my foot in hot water, then pat it dry with a towel and hold it in her hands while she worked at the sliver with a tweezers. She was not a toucher, and so I came to love that feeling: the pressure of her hand around my foot, the softness of the towel as she dabbed it against my skin.

But wanting is a frightening thing, especially if you lack models for it, or permission to act on wants, or a sense that your own desires are valid and good and satiable. Not wanting, by contrast, can be far easier, at least in the short term. Long before I began to flirt with starving, long before I bit into my first cottage-cheese-covered rice cake, I suspect I'd learned a good deal about curbing appetites, disguising them, molding them into acceptable shapes and forms. I learned over time not to whine and storm on family vacations, withdrew instead into a stony adolescent silence. I learned to tolerate my father's unnerving remoteness and preoccupation, to anticipate the leaden silences that descended when we found ourselves alone together in a room. I learned not to expect my mother's touch. I learned that the most reliable way to feel valued and loved was to excel at school, to stamp my hunger on report cards: A-minus, A-plus.

I also learned to be furtive about the world of pleasure. Once, around age fourteen, I snuck into the master bathroom at a friend's house and spent several long moments poking through the shelves of cosmetics and lotions and potions. The friend's mother was a beautiful, elegantly dressed woman who maintained a luxurious home—thick Oriental carpets, exquisite antiques—and her bathroom brimmed with stuff, glamorous and sweet-smelling, all of it prettily packaged in small glass bottles and slim tubes and perfect little compacts. I explored: unscrewed a cap here and a lipstick there, examined delicate vials of perfume, sifted through tiny pots of eyeshadow. And then, for reasons that utterly eluded me at the time, I reached toward the back of a shelf, picked up a small translucent bottle of Clinique moisturizer—a pale yellow liquid, obviously expensive and equipped with some vaguely scientific but lovely-sounding soothing property—and I stuffed it into the pocket of my jeans and took it home. This tiny bottle probably represented a whole world to me—access to femininity, a capacity for indulgence that I saw in other mothers but not always in my own, a longing on my part to be soothed, inside as well as out; I'm quite certain it also represented a sensation—nascent but strong—that there was something covert and unacceptable about pleasure, that it needed to be stolen.

This feeling would grow, an inchoate wariness about indulgence that gathered momentum in adolescence, gradually coalesced into an understanding that hunger itself was a sign of weakness and greed, or an invitation to disappointment, something best satisfied only in secret. So I took to snatching pleasure on the sly: cigarettes here, dollar bills there, squares of Hershey's chocolate from the supply my mother kept hidden in her dresser drawer, a small cache from which she herself would retrieve one tiny piece each day. I discovered masturbation at age thirteen or so, a thrilling and guilt-ridden pleasure I discussed with no one, not even my closest friends. I discovered alcohol around that time, too, a transformative indulgence that washed away inhibition and unleashed social curiosity and required the utmost secrecy, not just from the watchful eyes of parents but also from my peers; privately I may have acknowledged the urgency I felt around drinking, the anticipation of its great golden relief, but I never said a word about that feeling to anyone.

Unnamed hungers become frightening hungers, sources of self-mistrust. This is another one of appetite's golden rules; we learn to fear what we cannot discuss or explore, we are both drawn toward and terrified of the forbidden, and over time I suspect I reacted to that understanding not just with furtiveness but with an increasingly sophisticated form of sublimation, appetites driven underground and channeled into safer places, less fearful routes. It was painful to differ from the family style, estranging and scary to hunger for things they seemed not to value, and so I learned what legions of good, approval-hungry girls learn, which was to want what others wanted for me. Blend into the environment. Scope it out. Determine what others expect and respond accordingly.

This strategy was hardly unique. Whole bodies of work on teenage girls (most notably Carol Gilligan's) have suggested that girls lose themselves in adolescence, that confidence and spirit and voice begin to go up in smoke, and that this is essentially a culturally supported phenomenon, the result of a girl's growing awareness that the things she most fundamentally values (close relationships and connection) are demeaned and trivialized in the wider world. In order to stay connected, Gilligan theorizes, girls surrender their own perspectives, steer clear of conflict, and focus on what others need and want, learning as they grow to accept traditional feminine mandates about being attractive and "nice." Simone de Beauvoir described the same dynamic in somewhat starker terms. Noting that adolescence is the time in a girl's life when she realizes that men have all the power and that hers can come only from consenting to become a submissive, adored object, she wrote: "Girls stop being and stop seeing."

I think there's truth to that idea, but I also believe that culture merely fanned the fire, kindling an already smoldering sense of mistrust in my own beliefs, judgments, wants. Appetites, which are selfish and self-serving and aggressive, are scary for many girls, particularly those who've been brought up to believe that such qualities are unfeminine and inappropriate; they're scarier still when they're shrouded in mystery and tinged with danger, when they make you feel like an alien at the table, orbiting a planet too frightening and solitary to inhabit for very long.

And so I landed, parked my hungers on smoother terrain. In high school, I wore what my friends wore, listened to the music they listened to, lusted after boys they identified as attractive. In college, I "chose" my major—nineteenth-century British history and literature—not because I had any abiding fascination with the subject but because a few of the professors in the program took an interest in me and thus gave me a familiar focus: approval to covet, people to please. I was an excellent student, always—that hunger, so wrapped up in parental love and approval, was clearly labeled, unequivocally rewarded, easily acted upon—and I was very adept at fitting in, and by the time I hit my early twenties, by the time I reached that expansive array of real choices (career, relationships, lifestyle), I was lost.

In a sense, then, that hotel buffet was a perfect metaphor, the specific question—what to eat—a stand-in for much larger and more daunting questions: Who to be? What to strive for, whom to sleep with, how to live? What to *want*? At the time, I didn't really have a clue.

Such questions not only persist for women; they've multiplied, the potential answers wildly varied, sometimes overwhelmingly so. Sexual tolerance is higher than it was even a decade ago; a woman can be straight or live openly as a lesbian or explore bi-sexuality. Gender barriers are diminished in more professions; a woman can be an engineer, a paramedic, a cop. The traditional adult trajectories (marriage, child-raising) are less clearly de-fined. Even the boundaries of biology are more flexible; at least theoretically, a woman can delay childbirth until she's well into her forties.

Barry Schwartz, a professor of psychology at Swarthmore Col-lege, has written about what he calls "the tyranny of freedom," ar-guing that the sheer volume of choices in American life has come to feel oppressive and overwhelming; the proliferation ratchets up expectations and anxieties (there's always something better around the corner) and overloads the psyche. Studies from the business world bear this out, indicating that when consumers are faced with too many choices, they feel overwhelmed, frustrated, and paralyzed with indecision. But this brand of stress also has a less generic, more privately felt counterpart, which has to do with the burden of knowing—or, more aptly, trying to know or not quite knowing—your own heart, who you are, where you belong in the world, what you're feeling, wanting, driven by.

This is daunting all by itself, more daunting still when the vol-ume of choices is relatively new, the sense of entitlement behind it not deeply ingrained. "Women have infinite choices," says Louise Kaplan, a New York psychoanalyst and author, "and this is very frightening. It means you're stuck with who you are. No one is going to tell you who to marry, or what career to pursue, or how to cut your hair, and so you're thrown back onto yourself." The freedom to choose, in other words, means the freedom to make mistakes, to falter and fail, to come face-to-face with your own flaws and limitations and fears and secrets, to live with the terri-ble uncertainty that necessarily attends the construction of a self.

This, I think, is the steady pulse of agitation behind an unset-tled appetite, this wobbling, reaching anxiety, which craves re-lief, stalks it, hunts it down in tangible forms: Eat that cake, which will assuage some internal emptiness; buy that jacket, which will cloak you in an identity; call that man, who will define and give shape to your life. In its most explosive forms, the steady pulse becomes a high and driving whine. *I was overwhelmed. I felt like a blank slate. I didn't know who I was, what I needed, how to take care of myself.* These are the whispers of half-formed selves groping in the dark, and you hear them voiced with particular clarity by people who've actively grappled with the conflicts and consequences surrounding hunger, who know that dark and shapeless territory.

A former compulsive shopper tells me about tearing into Saks Fifth Avenue in New York in the fifteen minutes before a blind date, pawing through the racks, spending $400 she didn't have on some sleek black outfit, then stuffing her old clothes in a bag and racing out, clad—she hoped—"in a uniform that would tell me who I was." An impossible task, literally shopping for an identity, but one that took her years to understand and tackle differently.

A long-time member of Overeaters Anonymous talks about the panic-laced insatiability that once drove the need to eat, about what it was like to consume an entire carton of Dunkin' Munchkins on the way home from work and to gain 120 pounds in a single year, about the way in which the endlessly daunting business of defining a self—naming one's needs, speaking up for oneself, tolerating pain and frustration and disappointment—simply ground to a halt in the narcotizing stupor of a binge, all anxiety focused on the procuring of food, then eased, briefly but powerfully, in its consumption. This, too, took years to undo, painful and painstaking lessons in teasing out physical hunger from the emotional brand, in identifying the yearnings so easily obscured by sugar and lard, in self-acceptance.

And a woman with a long history of promiscuity describes the deeply disorienting, utterly ungrounded sense of urgency behind sexual obsession, the life-shaping need for definition that can drive a woman to call a man's answering machine for four consecutive hours on a bad night, or to get in her car and spend an entire evening parked outside his house; she describes what it feels like to tie every molecule of your value and loveability to another person's sexual interest, to feel "as though you have to attach yourself to someone else in order to feel that you're even allowed to exist." Now married, monogamous, and far more familiar with the real hungers (for validation, acceptance, love) that propelled such frenzy, she recalls that period of her life as "eight years of blind terror."

This is what I mean about the strange solace of starving, the cocoon of safety it seemed to offer; in my own blind terror, anorexia beckoned, the memory of those early sensations of mastery and control seemed to promise the most exquisite relief. One morning, about eight months into my year of weight gain and weight loss, I sat at my desk reading a profile of an anorexic girl in the *New York Times Sunday Magazine*. I'd never heard the term "anorexia" before or the phrase "eating disorder," and I pored over the piece, read it straight through to the end then read it again. The woman in the profile was young, in her teens. Her weight had dropped to below eighty. She did thousands of sit-ups, late into the night, and she'd become so skeletal that her arms and belly had grown a soft dark downy fur called lunago, a sign of the body's attempt to compensate for the lack of insulating body fat. I don't remember any other details, but I do remember my response, which was so peculiar I wouldn't quite identify it for many years: I envied her. I envied her drive and her focus and the power of her will, and I suspect I saw in this poor girl's sheer determination the outlines of a strategy: one anxiety (weight) as the repository for many anxieties (men, family, work, hunger itself); emaciated thinness as a shortcut of sorts, a detour around painful and confusing feelings, a way to take all hungers—so varied and vast—and boil them down to their essence, one appetite to manage, just one.

Which is precisely what starving accomplished, precisely what any singular obsession accomplishes. Several months after I read that piece, my West Coast boyfriend returned from California to spend the summer with me. At the last minute, he decided to spend six weeks of that time traveling in Europe with a friend, then two weeks with me before heading back to school in the fall. I felt devastated by this change of plans, and I suspect his departure stirred up an old set of fears about the relationship between hunger and disappointment, about how painful it was to be deprived of something you felt you needed; I suspect it touched the hungry kid in me, too, scraped at some of the scar tissue that had formed around forgotten childhood wounds. But I said nothing about this at the time, and probably couldn't have articulated the feelings if I'd tried. Instead, I remember taking him to the train station in Providence, then walking back to my office by myself, and thinking: *Okay, I'll just stop eating.* The sentence just popped into my head, fully formed and nonnegotiable. A solution: I am overwhelmed (by need, by disappointment, by uncertainty) and this is how I'm going to react. By the time the boyfriend returned from Europe, I'd cut off all my hair and lost seventeen pounds.

From there, the line on the graph would dip and dip and dip: 110 pounds, 102 pounds, ninety-six pounds, eighty-three pounds. In the mathematics of desire, I chose the simplest equation: Just subtract.

To an extent, the strategy worked. When you're starving, or wrapped up in a cycle of bingeing-and-purging, or sexually obsessed with a man, it is very hard to think about anything else, very hard to see the larger picture of options that is your life, very hard to consider what else you might need or want or fear were you not so intently focused on one crushing passion. I sat in my room every night, with rare exceptions, for three-and-a-half years. In secret, and with painstaking deliberation, I carved an apple and a one-inch square of cheddar cheese into tiny bits, sixteen individual slivers, each one so translucently thin you could see the light shine through it if you held it up to a lamp. Then I lined up the apple slices on a tiny china saucer and placed a square of cheese on each. And then I ate them one by one, nibbled at them like a rabbit, edge by tiny edge, so slowly and with

such concentrated precision the meal took two hours to consume. I planned for this ritual all day, yearned for it, carried it
out with the utmost focus and care. And I did not think, during
those years, about how scared I was of the world, or how lost and
shapeless I felt, or how needy I might have been if I hadn't
slammed the door on need altogether. I did not think about,
much less participate in, the redoubtable realms of men and sexuality. I didn't hunger for anything but that apple and that cube
of cheese, I snuffed out all other desires, and with them all other
anxieties. I felt nothing but the taut pull of my stomach, throb-
bing with a hunger so tangible and distinct I could practically
hold it in my hand.

To say that I "lost" my appetite during those years would be a
joke. On the contrary, I ate, slept, and breathed appetite. I
thought about food constantly, pored over food magazines and
restaurant reviews like a teenage boy with a pile of porn, copied
down recipes on index cards: breads, cakes, chocolate desserts,
pies with the richest fillings, things I longed for and wouldn't let
myself have. In truth, I had appetites the size of Mack trucks—
driving and insistent longings for food and connection and bodily
pleasure—but I found their very power too daunting and fearsome to contend with, and so I split the world into the most rigid
place of black and white, yes and no. I'd eat nothing or I'd eat
everything, I'd clamp down on appetite or I'd yield to it utterly.

Obsessions—even mild ones, even the run-of-the-mill, mun-
dane daily obsessions that can pepper a woman's thoughts (Do
these jeans make my butt look too big? Should I go to the
gym?)—have such extraordinary deflective power. They stop desire in its tracks, drive it underground, twist and disguise its form,
then send it back out into the world in a wholly altered form,
one that's particularly insidious because it feels so very real; even
the murkiest desire can re-emerge with a face and a name and
the specificity of a goal. I want to be thin, says the woman on a
diet, who may actually want any number of other attributes, who
may want the sense of value and belonging and loveability that

thinness represents but cannot guarantee. I want that wardrobe, I need that relationship, I just need to lose ten pounds. These become the felt and articulated wishes, the tangible hungers, appetite's pressing focus, and they can take over landscape, override all other desires, coax into the background the real hunger and the anxiety behind it, a woman's sense of ravenous need, or her lust and fear of lust, or the anguished empty spaces she carries inside; these simply evaporate in the active daily thrum of worry, they coil out of sight like smoke.

This is what I want. I remember saying that to a therapist at the time: *this*, I meant, this angular body, this steely cocoon, this proof of transcendence over ordinary human need, this is my wish, my desire, nothing else.

And yet this is precisely the point, this is why the mathematics of desire can be so compelling. Few people will *tell* a woman what to want these days, at least not formally. Women are not marched off to Jenny Craig or Weight Watchers at gunpoint, we are not ticketed or fined if we choose to eat chocolate cake every night instead fat-free sorbet, there are no rules, no externally imposed sanctions against having an active sex life or a hearty appetite for food or a headful of ambitions and dreams. But the erosion of rules has created a vacuum, one that certainly frightens a lot of men and may well frighten a lot of women, as well, particularly today, when our general sense of safety in the world—our belief in American inviolability and endless economic stability—has grown so fragile. The mathematics of desire mitigates precisely that anxiety. A woman—particularly a woman who feels fundamentally disempowered and uncertain—makes up new rules, replaces external constraints with internal ones, installs systems of mastery that operate from the inside out, the tyranny of freedom reconfigured as the tyranny of self.

In a sense, this is a form of cooking the psychic books. Whether its form is extreme, as in anorexia, or more low-level and reflexive, the business of taking stock, of monitoring and calculating and tinkering with the budget serves a purpose; it gives the illusion of control, and logic and order, as though some independent second party—a meticulous inner accountant—is holding the reins on hunger, literally counting the beans. And although all that calculating may generate a fair amount of conscious anxiety—it can keep you actively worried about specific things, about what you ate last night, and how your clothes are fitting, and whether or not you should go to the gym—it does a masterful job of keeping less tangible, more daunting matters at bay. The flood of options is reduced to a manageable trickle. Unnamed anxieties are replaced with tangible ones. The formidable social and personal questions that might plague a woman (how to be in the world, how much space to occupy, where to direct her energy, how much to demand for herself) are reframed, minimized, broken down into small, individual questions, palatable bites: how the jeans look, what to order for lunch. You can't worry about Appetite (joy, passion, lust, hunger) when you're worrying about appetite (frosting, fat grams).

What the math cannot do, of course, is eradicate anxiety altogether. On the contrary, that needling voice of cans and can'ts keeps you scared—not in a large, existential, potentially radicalizing way, but in a mild and chronic daily way, which is ultimately corrosive and undermining. It feeds that reservoir of self-mistrust, where authentic hungers are unknown and unexplored. And it supports a larger system of discord, in which a woman's socially sanctioned appetites (for beauty, for slenderness, for shopping) are clearly defined and encouraged while her more complex internal ones are left on the back burner, fuzzy and indistinct.

A friend, who recently lost about ten pounds, says she's astonished at the number of people who compliment her. This is a proud, ambitious woman, someone who's worked very hard to figure out what she wants in her life, who's raised a healthy, well-adjusted child, and who's made great strides in her professional life, recently securing a book contract for a project she finds deeply engaging. But, she says, "You cannot believe how many people comment about the weight. Forget the book contract. Forget the achievements of motherhood. It's all, 'Wow! You've lost weight!' As though this is the supreme achievement of my life."

If a woman herself believes that weight loss is, or would be, a supreme achievement, the internal picture gets murkier still. Beverly, a thirty-seven-year-old physical therapist, hints at this when she starts musing aloud about what her life might be like were she genuinely liberated from concerns about diet and weight. Renoir would love Beverly; he would see in her a portrait of plenitude with smooth rosy skin and a wild mane of auburn hair pulled into a loose braid and ample breasts and hips, but she sees only fat. A veteran in the diet wars, she has wrestled with food for most of her life, gained and lost the same twenty pounds more times than she can count, tried everything from Atkins to the Zone. "Sometimes I think about how much of my time and energy has gone into this, and I'm truly appalled," she says. "It's like what people say about workaholics: Not many people lie on their deathbeds and say, 'Gee, I really wish I'd worked more hours.' It's the same thing. Am I really going to reach the end of my life and think, 'Gee, I wish I'd spent more time dieting'? It's scary. Because probably I'll end up lying there and berating myself for putting all this energy into my goddamn weight when I could have—you know, *had a life*."

Asked what that means, what "having a life" might look and feel like were concerns about food and weight simply deleted from consciousness, Beverly falls silent. "I don't know," she says, finally. "It's hard to imagine what it would be like to wake up in the morning and just be oblivious to all that. To not know and not care how much I weighed or how my butt looked or what clothes I could or couldn't fit into. It's sort of overwhelming to even think about that. It's like . . . what would I think about?"

Precisely. The great anxious focus on the minutiae of appetite—on calories and portion size and what's going into the body versus what's being expended, on shoes and hair and abs of steel—keeps the larger, more fearsome questions of desire blurred and out of focus. American women spend approximately $1 million *every hour* on cosmetics. This may or may not say something about female vanity, but it certainly says something about female energy, about where it is and is not focused. Easier to worry about the body than the soul, easier to fit the self into the narrow slots of identity our culture offers to women than to create one from scratch, easier to worship at socially sanctioned altars of desire than to construct your own, one that allows for the expression of all passions, the satisfaction of all appetites. The great preoccupation with things like food and shopping and appearance, in turn, is less of a genuine focus on hunger—indulging it, understanding it, making decisions about it—than it is a monumental distraction from hunger.

What is this drive to be thinner, prettier, better dressed, *other*? Who exactly is this other and what does she look like beyond the jacket she's wearing or the food she's not eating? What might we be doing, thinking, feeling about if we didn't think about body image, ever? These are the questions that pain me when I think of myself at twenty-one and twenty-two and twenty-three, a set of bones hunkered over a tiny saucer, nibbling at those miniature squares of apple and cheese. What was I feeling? What was I trying, so desperately, not to feel?

2

THE MOTHER CONNECTION

HUNGER AND
THE COSTS OF FREEDOM

NOT LONG AGO, I HEARD a story about a woman who went to visit her mother for the weekend. Their relationship was, and still is, stormy and complicated, but she got through it with relative serenity—counted to ten under her breath a lot, recounted like mantras lessons learned in decades of therapy, kept her cool. But then, on her way to the airport, this grown, self-aware woman—a paragon of reason and maturity—was overcome with the compulsion to pull her rental car into the parking lot of a 7-Eleven, walk in, and steal a bottle of water. She could not resist; she snagged eight ounces of Evian and fled, embarrassed and confused.

I love that story, it captures so perfectly the mysterious, changeable quality of appetite, the way it bumps up against a feeling and then molds itself into a new impulse, attaches itself to something so seemingly random. But I'd love the story even more if the woman in question had stolen a bottle of milk, perhaps even a jar of strained peaches. For if you peel back another layer from the onion, dig a little deeper toward the core of appetite and the complexity of feeling it can evoke, that's where you begin to go: to the realm of mothers and daughters, to the ancient places

where our sense of desire was first molded and shaped and observed. There can be love in this territory, and deep identification
and attachment, but there may also be a great deal of confusion,
and anguish, and a steady, pressing throb of guilt.

My mother did not know how to respond to anorexia, or how
to make sense of it; she'd never heard of it before, she couldn't
imagine what it meant or what purposes it might have served,
and although she noticed me grow thinner and thinner, she said
nothing about it for a long time. I think she didn't know
whether to worry, or how much, and I think I was deeply ambivalent about broaching the subject, desperate for her to notice,
but also unwilling to admit how seriously the compulsion had
taken hold, and mostly afraid; aware on some level that at least a
piece of it had to do with us: mother and daughter.

The desperate part broke through a few years in, my weight
below ninety pounds by then. I'd come home from Providence
one weekend early in the spring, and on the pretense of changing into warmer clothes, I pulled off my sweatshirt in front of my
mother and reached into my bag for a wool sweater. The two of
us were in the kitchen, where she took her afternoon tea. Underneath the sweatshirt, I was wearing a camisole and I stood
there for an extra moment, rummaging in the bag. I wanted her
to see how the bones in my chest and shoulders stuck out, and
how skeletal my arms were, and I wanted the sight of this to tell
her something I couldn't have begun to communicate myself:
something about pain certainly, but something about less accessible feelings, too, an amalgam of buried wishes and unspoken
fears, some exquisitely tangled blend of love and rage. I was
vaguely aware of the complexity of this feeling at the time: I remember standing there, bones exposed, hoping in the most inarticulable way that the sight of my body might wound her and
also cry out to her, and plead and sob and cling, that it might deliver both a slap and an apology.

I don't know what my mother felt at that moment; she said
nothing, she didn't know what to say.

My parents were not cold or unfeeling people; in many respects, they were two of the most psychically sophisticated people I've ever known, and they were also deeply devoted to their kids. I always could, and often did, call my mother at two A.M. on a bad night, sobbing over a boyfriend; neither my mother nor father were strangers to pain or depression or turmoil, but they did not make contact easily outside of a crisis and their sense of privacy was so pronounced it could make you feel invisible. Both of them came from households dominated by opinionated, strong-willed mothers, and both of them bent over backwards to avoid meddling, smothering, interfering. But sometimes a kid needs smothering. At dinner that night, I drank a lot of wine and finally started to cry at the table. I told my parents I was having "a problem," that I didn't know what to do about it. I said I thought I was anorexic. All I remember is the look in their eyes: concerned, a little scared, very helpless. They asked a lot of questions I couldn't answer: Why? But aren't you hungry? What can we do? It was a relief to talk to them, but only in the most general sense of generating their worry. Whatever I'd hoped to articulate in the kitchen that afternoon remained unexpressed; I don't think any of us, least of all my mother and me, knew where to begin.

About a week later, my mother sent me a note in the mail. On a small square of white paper, she'd written one word in large block letters: "EAT." I just stared at it, thinking: But I can't. You have no idea, I just can't.

EAT. Eat, *eat!* Those are the words of an Italian mamma, words of abundance and plenitude. They mean, Take what I have to offer, take this food, take this love, relish it, take it in.

This language was not familiar to my mother, at least not in an unequivocally nurturant way, and so it was not familiar to me; written down, the word looked strange and oddly threatening, and in a fundamental sense it was, not simply because starving had become a deeply-ingrained strategy and way of being by then but also because to truly eat—to take in, to relish, to partake in all senses of the word—would have involved a significant departure on my part, perhaps even a betrayal or a loss; it would have required adopting a new language, one I must have feared I could not share with my mother, might not ever share.

Like so many women of her generation, my mother had been introduced early on to a very clear language of desire, its grammar based on femininity and accommodation to specific ideals. Her parents, descendants of Russian Jews who emigrated to the United States in the 1890s and early 1900s, lived in Brookline, Massachusetts, outside of Boston. Her father was a self-made businessman, kind, gentle, cerebral, ultimately quite wealthy, and somewhat passive in family matters. That territory was ruled by my grandmother, an intelligent, extroverted, and opinionated woman equipped with a great deal of charm, a deep appreciation for the luxuries of new wealth, and an abiding interest in appearances. She maintained an impeccable, elegant home, filled with the finest furnishings; she loved shopping, fine dining, lavish parties. When we visited my grandparents' home for Sunday dinners, a weekly event when I was a child, my grandmother would sit at the head of the table in the chandeliered dining room, reveling in her role as matriarch. At the first sign of an imperfection—the basket of popovers was empty, the platter of roast beef required refilling, the china needed to be cleared—she'd press down on a button hidden beneath the plush carpet by her chair and summon the cook, who'd arrive as if by magic and silently carry out the task. If I inherited a taste for luxury and fine things, I'm quite certain the gene came from her.

My mother inherited no such gene. Much to my grandmother's chagrin, she never took much interest in womanly things, particularly appearances; she was whipsmart, painfully shy, bookish, and solitary as a girl, and if she found her mother's materialistic bent oppressive, she also knew it was a difficult force to resist. Maternal love, in her experience, was deeply entwined with judgment, and her own interests—books, art, the natural world—lay in realms her mother seemed either to disdain or to judge harshly. This made for a lot of powerful conflicts, literal and psychic. Some of these my mother won; she went to college at age seventeen, then took off to Paris to study art, then spent her twenties living on her own and cultivating a career as a painter, an occupation her mother never quite knew what to make of and almost never praised. Other conflicts she lost; in her mid-twenties, she fell in love with and nearly married a young man named Jerry, who'd received an injury during the war that had left him with a rather pronounced limp. Her mother could not get past the "deformity," could not accept it, and my mother could not get past the criticism and lack of approval: She obeyed her mother and ended the relationship.

In 1955, still unmarried at the then-advanced age of twenty-seven, she met my father, a handsome, intellectual, intensely introspective psychiatrist whose personal résumé raised all kinds of eyebrows; eleven years her senior, he was from upstate New York WASP stock, a non-Jew, separated, and father of three children, one of them blind and severely retarded. That summer, he spent six weeks in Nevada securing a divorce, and he wrote my mother the most beautiful letters, passionate and wooing, full of intellectual exchange (she introduced him to Melville, he introduced her to Joseph Conrad), and brimming with curiosity about her: how her mind worked, what drove her, what fueled her painting. He found her beautiful and deep, and he seemed both to see and to appreciate the sides of her that had been waved away at home for so long, the creativity and sensitivity and passion for ideas. They married the following June; her mother was suspicious and huffy about the decision but did not fight it, and the wedding, held in the garden of her Brookline home, was exquisite.

This was a radical move on my mother's part, this choice of a rogue psychiatrist, and it suggests how far she'd come in her efforts to free herself from her mother's grip, to create a language of desire that reflected her own intellect and aesthetic. But to say that my mother had unleashed herself from a world of stricture and constraint would be inaccurate. I think her own history of incurred disapproval, amassed from childhood in a small sea of petty criticisms and withheld praise, would dog her all her life, leaving her deeply unsure of herself and wary of her own hungers, as though she'd crossed into unfamiliar territory and wasn't quite sure what the rules were, or how safe she'd be.

I also suspect this sensation received its share of reinforcement over time, bolstered by both personal and cultural circumstance. By the early 1960s, my mother had three children: my brother, born in 1957, and my sister and me, born two years later. Her life had receded into a sea of diapers, bottles, blankets, small shrill voices shrieking in the night. Her canvases languished, untouched. Her marriage had proven to be difficult, less of a partnership than she might have hoped, and my father had come with a bit more baggage than she'd anticipated. Shortly after the wedding, no doubt livid about this new union, his ex-wife had claimed that she could no longer care for their blind son, then ten years old, and she'd dispatched him to live with my parents, where he would stay for nearly three years, an explosive, impossible child whose care fell almost entirely to my mother. My father, who buried himself in his work and never once cooked a meal or pushed a vacuum across a carpet, kept promising he'd help and never did. What must have been my mother's early sense of optimism—a feeling that she'd entered a world in sync with her own hungers—began a long slow evaporation. She was exhausted, frustrated, and quietly enraged, and when I try to picture her back then, I imagine a young woman feeling deeply agitated without always knowing why, conflicted about her own desires and wants, which she wasn't quite sure she was entitled to in the first place, and ashamed of her own needs, which she herself could barely acknowledge. It took all the courage she could muster to tell my father she could no longer take care of his child.

This could—perhaps should—have been a promising, hopeful time. It was, after all, the early sixties; my parents had begun their marriage in Cambridge, a place where the early whispers of feminism were not only audible but embraced, particularly in the left-leaning, liberal circles my mother and father inhabited.

But the mandates that defined femininity for her generation—the mandates that her own mother so fervidly adhered to and upheld—were still very much alive, and I suspect that like many women of her time, my mother found herself torn, some central part of her aware that certain rules were unequivocal: Women (wives and mothers in particular) were to defer, to meet and anticipate the needs of others, to seek self-definition through family, and—perhaps above all—to convert their own strivings (for love, work, sexual expression) into caring for and responding to others.

Culture certainly supported those rules, feminist stirrings notwithstanding. My mother married at a time when the institution of motherhood had been elevated to near saintliness, when female ambition was expected to find its expression in the cultivation and maintenance of domestic life, no more, no less. These ideals were by no means new—female desire has been tied up in apron strings and cloaked in domesticity for generations, centuries in some societies—but they were amped up in the years following World War II, during my mother's adolescence and young adulthood, given a distinct look and feel that I can't imagine she was immune to. The middle-class flight to the suburbs set the stage, ensconcing huge numbers of young women behind picket fences, fostering isolation in the process. The explosion of consumer culture set the tone; traditional assumptions about female desire were mass-marketed for the first time and writ large, given a particular June Cleaver twist on TV and in women's magazines, movie scripts, and ads: See the perfect table, see the smiling children, the contented husband, the sparkling kitchen. The specificity of such images—the ideal of flawlessness—gave their messages a new quality of seductiveness and urgency; it also made them insidious in a new way; they are images that obliterate all the drudgery of domestic labor—the exhausting, dull, unpaid work of scouring and dusting and cooking and caregiving —and show only the fruits. Nowhere, in magazines like *House Beautiful* or in shows like *Father Knows Best*, do you see the actual grunt work women do to create a gourmet meal or to keep the bathroom tile gleaming or to pacify the husband and children; nowhere do you see any evidence of conflict about that work, either, or any despair about the pencil-thin conception of desire behind it.

My father appeared to support this picture, in fact if not in theory. The domestic sphere was my mother's territory, always. He admired and respected her work, but made little effort to give her the time or space to pursue it. More insidiously, despite his early infatuated passion, he appeared to love her in what turned out to be a rather fantastical way, as an icon of idealized womanhood that didn't exactly resemble Harriet Nelson or June Cleaver but that didn't seem to give her much room to exist as a full human being, either, with a full range of human needs and passions and hungers. They had what he would describe to me years later, vaguely and with great discomfort, as "sexual problems," the result of what they would both refer to—equally vaguely—as some kind of "split" on his part, an inability to disentangle his feelings about my mother from his feelings about his own mother, a woman he'd worshipped as a child but also felt consumed by. Sexual and familial love appeared to exist on different planes for him; his first wife, a brassy, hard-drinking, extroverted woman, had represented the former plane, as well as an escape from his mother's upper-crust overbearance. My mother represented a return of sorts; she was the graceful, reserved, cerebral center of family, an asexual and untouchable figure. From fairly early on in their marriage, he began to have affairs.

Years later, all of this would make sense to me; it explained the Pandora's box sensation at home, the feeling that dark and dangerous feelings existed just inches beneath the hushed surfaces, the suspicion that my parents' reserve, with its faint edges of preoccupation and sharp frustration, masked some immense disappointment and rage. But as a child, I knew nothing of such turmoil, only that my mother seemed boxed up in an indefinable way, that her passions seemed somehow squeezed into the margins, as though in constant competition with the needs and expectations of others.

Which, no doubt, they were. My mother was hardly June Cleaver—she hated housework, loathed entertaining, didn't care a whit about the trappings of femininity or fashion—but in many ways she looked the part of a good, late-fifties wife and mother, nurturant and homebound. As far back as I can remember, she had breakfast on the table every morning, soup and sandwiches ready for my siblings and me every day when we came home for lunch, dinner on the table every night at six. With occasional help from a series of au pairs and none at all from my father, she did all the grocery shopping, all the laundry, all the cleaning and cooking. Dad boiled water for instant coffee; that's about as far as his ambitions on the home front went. Mom did everything else—organized birthday parties, baked cakes, cared for the dogs, sewed Halloween costumes, bought and wrapped all the Christmas presents, helped us with our homework, attended every last school play.

At the same time, she was one of the most intelligent and well-informed women I've ever known, an avid reader, a woman who could breeze through the *Sunday New York Times* crossword puzzle, in ink, in less than twenty minutes, who could wield a wrench as deftly as a knitting needle, who had strong political opinions and an even stronger commitment to her work. The conflicting strains emerge in odd, contrary juxtapositions: an image of my mother's studio, a small room crammed with canvases and frames and oil paints, located right next to the kitchen and steps from the washer-dryer; a picture of her bed, strewn with copies of both *Woman's Day* magazine and the *New York Review of Books*; the memory of her front hall, a place you'd walk into and find the acrid scent of turpentine competing with smell of spaghetti sauce. Not insignificantly, the maternal, other-directed strain left more of an impression on me than the autonomous, creative one: I grew up with the idea that my father had a job, while my mother had a hobby.

In *The Feminine Mystique,* first published in 1963, Betty Friedan began to articulate what women of my mother's generation were feeling, the "problem with no name." Friedan's descriptions are well-known by now—she wrote about fury seething beneath the placid suburban surfaces, about truncated lives and thwarted ambitions, about the extraordinary personal costs incurred by attending to everybody's needs but one's own—and although my mother's world was more progressive and politicized than the one Friedan described, I don't have to reach too far to place her in it, to recall the sense of strain and discord. I remember her as a woman who never actively raged or stormed but who sighed a lot, and slammed things around in the kitchen when she got "cross," as she'd rather delicately put it, who'd shut herself in her bedroom with a headache and stay there for hours, a weary, off-limits, don't-ask sensation emanating from behind the door. I remember the way she'd play hostess at periodic cocktail parties for my father's colleagues, a role she abhorred but executed gracefully: a woman smiling demurely, passing homemade pâté and crackers on a tray, her attendant efforts (a back-breaking day of dusting and vacuuming, of making the pâté, of scrubbing the bathroom and stocking it with little soaps and hand towels) both implicitly mandatory and invisible. And I remember how tired she'd be the next morning, exhausted in the bone-deep way I now recognize as almost entirely emotional: It's the rage-laced fatigue you feel after you've given and given and taken next to nothing for yourself.

Friedan and her feminist contemporaries described that feeling quite clearly; less clear are the ways in which that generation's struggle with muted desire got transmitted (and may still be transmitted) to children, particularly to daughters. How does a woman who's been raised to table her own needs, to sublimate her own desires and strivings into the care and feeding of others, to swallow her own disappointments, communicate to her daughter the very feelings of authority and entitlement that she herself lacks?

Perhaps she doesn't. One school of thought—one you might read about in a textbook on gender identity or socialization—argues that a certain degree of constraint goes with the female territory, that girls are piloted from the first months and years of life toward a style based on identification with the "feminine" qualities represented by mothers (accommodation, nurturance, orientation toward others) and disidentification with the qualities embodied by fathers (autonomy, self-seeking, an orientation toward the outside world). We learn about hunger at home, this view suggests, and in the cruel rigidity of gender differentiation, men eat, women feed.

There are certainly grains of truth to this idea: Even in this time of more relaxed gender roles, where mothers work and fathers change diapers, the gospel of femininity lives on, echoing in memory for some, preached in daily life for others, its commandments about appetite passed on in accumulated lacks: lack of comfort with it, lack of reinforcement for it, lack of embrace. A mother who is tormented by diet and weight, who appears preoccupied with her appearance and disgusted by her own body, cannot easily teach her daughter to take delight in food, to feel carefree about weight or joyful about the female form. A mother who finds her own sexuality frightening or dangerous or dirty can't easily revel in her daughter's. And a mother whose experience of desire is based on taboo and self-denial, on feeding others and concealing her own pangs of unsatisfied hunger, can't easily steer her daughter toward a wider landscape.

At the very least, the gospel of femininity, which is essentially self-negating, may explain why a quality of guilt and murkiness can so easily leak into a woman's experience of appetite, a profound uncertainty about entitlement, even a sense that desire itself is indefinable or inappropriate. A woman in her mid-thirties, whose mother was a "paragon of self-sacrifice," a woman who lived for her kids, who always took the smallest piece of meat on the platter and the most bruised piece of fruit, tells me she has struggled her whole life to believe that her own desires have any weight at all: Even something as simple as choosing a movie or a restaurant can tie her into a knot, evoking a bone-deep sensation that "it is just plain wrong to let my needs come first." Another, thirty-eight, talks about inheriting from the females in her family a certain "blankness about desire," as though that entire territory were simply off limits, shrouded in a fog. "The needs of men were always blaringly loud and clear," she says. "My father needed dinner at seven o'clock and got dinner at seven o'clock, my brothers needed the car for football practice and got the car for football practice. But my mother and my aunts—there was this feeling that it would be unbelievably selfish to let your own needs eclipse someone else's, so you didn't even think about it."

I've watched women do battle with that notion my whole life: agonizing about asserting themselves at work, or debating about whether they "deserve" a raise, or struggling to subdue the chronic press of worry about other people's feelings, or fighting the urge to apologize for things most men would never think to apologize for (bumping into a chair, overcooking a meal, the *weather*). This is learned behavior. There is not a shred of compelling evidence to suggest that such impulses are biologically based, that females are genetically more caretaking and less self-seeking than males, that we're hard-wired to be accommodating, that we have less natural hunger or aggression. You observe, you follow, live and learn.

But this muddy business of identification is more than a matter of role modeling. Beyond the simple dos and don'ts of femininity, there may also be a more complex communication of constraint, a daughter's hunger shadowed by a mother's vulnerability or frustration or despair. Psychiatrist Jessica Benjamin writes, "It is too often assumed that a mother will be able to give her child faith in tackling the world even if she can no longer muster it for herself. And although mothers ordinarily aspire to more for their children than for themselves, there are limits to this trick: A mother who is too depressed by her own isolation cannot get excited about her child learning to walk or talk; a mother who is afraid of people cannot feel relaxed about her child's association with other children; a mother who stifles her own longings, ambitions, and frustrations cannot tune in empathically to her child's joys and failures." That feels closer to the heart of appetite's puzzle, to the more subtle imprints of feeling that may be may be etched onto girls along with mandates about being good and pretty and sweet.

Like so many women I know, I grew up understanding that self-worth and likeability were inextricably linked, that a sizeable portion of my value would come from nourishing others: pleasing, avoiding conflict, concealing my own needs and disappointments. Granted, some of this had to do with what I observed and absorbed about women as a child, the standard messages about gender and female accommodation. Some of it, too, had to do with my own drive to fit in, the creeping uncertainty I felt in adolescence about my own likes and dislikes and desires. But a pivotal piece, I think, was rooted in a more visceral feeling of alliance with my mother, a sense of fated and necessary sameness, as though I'd been swaddled as a child with some of her own struggle with entitlement and voice, absorbed bits and pieces of her being the way a patch of earth absorbs a raindrop. This is the stuff of identity and attachment, the thick essence of a mother—strengths, weaknesses, hopes, disappointments, love, rage—taken in by a daughter, and known to her in a way that's so deeply internal and wordless it becomes part of her own marrow, as present and unquestioned as the air she breathes. Today, nine years after my mother's death, I still feel these impressions; they live on in an almost corporeal way, as though genetically embedded. My mother's manner was unfailingly polite, restrained, other-directed. Particularly with people she didn't know well, she had the most beautiful, deferential smile—gaze slightly averted, head slightly lowered, a faint blush—and when I find myself in an awkward or insecure situation, I feel the exact same smile come over me, as well as what I imagine to be the exact same self-diminishing instinct, boundaries slightly blurred, my own needs

instinctively tied to the needs of others, my own voice and perspective dialed down while someone else's grows louder.

What I did not learn, what was not seared on a cellular level,
was an alternative way of being. Not once, growing up, did I see
my mother refuse to make dinner, or fail to get the laundry done,
or boycott the grocery shopping, or shut herself in her studio for
a whole day because that's what *she wanted* to do, the rest of us be
damned. This is a picture of responsibility and unselfishness and
eternally delayed gratification and I find it very nearly tragic. For
lost in that picture—for her, for me—was any sense of what a
woman might look like if she had large and vigorous appetites of
her own: a woman with real passions and independent desires; a
woman who fed, in all senses of the word, herself as dutifully and
consistently as she fed her family. I certainly didn't know any
women like that as a child; I probably couldn't have imagined
one if I'd tried.

Neither could Lisa, a dark, pretty, soft-spoken woman of
thirty-six who spent several hours in my living room one summer talking about mothers and daughters and indulgence and
restraint. Lisa, a comedy writer, struck me immediately as a rep-
resentative soldier on the battlefield of appetite, partly because
she has veteran status (long history of struggle with weight in
her twenties, including a period of bulimia) and partly because
she seemed to have an appreciation for the subject's dark mystery: Her heart started racing as soon as I turned on the tape
recorder, and she couldn't quite explain why except to say that
the very word "appetite" seemed "so big and so close to the
bone, so tied up with old family stuff—mother stuff."

At the time of our meeting, Lisa's primary site of combat had
to do with professional strivings, ambition, a hunger for achievement and recognition. Comedy writing is a very male-dominated
field, and she has fought—with no small degree of success—
against many of the standard obstacles: sexist attitudes at work; a
sense of being isolated from the boys' club; a need (real and perceived) to be extraordinary in order to get the same degree of

recognition as her often less extraordinary male colleagues. Now firmly established and respected as a producer at a Boston-area television production company, she finds herself fighting a new set of obstacles, confusing and stubborn ones that she's tentative about even mentioning: "One of the things that's up for me now is the question of how big can I think? How much can I take on, or take in? I tend to be very belittling, getting in my own way. And now I think, Why *shouldn't* I think big?"

Thinking big, in her definition, would mean "kicking it up a notch or two. Or five or ten. Being a very successful producer, having more than just a tiny little success. Having more of an impact. I feel like I want to be contributing on a mass level."

And why is that so hard to say?

Lisa grapples with that question for a while, an exercise that covers many of the standard themes about gender and constraint. She talks about the lifelong absorption of messages about femininity: "Somewhere along the line I got the idea that it's not okay to stand out, that it's better to serve others—that sort of selfless, help-others-achieve-their-dreams thing." She talks about familial expectations, and about the number of rules her choices have already broken (appearances in her household were considered paramount for girls, sex ruinous, female ambition ideally limited to such "noble" spheres as teaching). And she talks about her father, an intellectual, charismatic, commanding presence whom she adored but who never quite gave her the kind of encouragement she needed.

This could be read as a fairly classic gender tale, a case study in the way in which female desire can be cauterized by mandates about femininity. Lisa's description of her father is particularly resonant, a poignant testimony to the kind of distance that so often characterized father-daughter relationships during her childhood and to the consequences of that distance. Lisa's father admired her curiosity, found her bright and sweet, but, as she puts it, he always left her with the feeling that "women were just not all that visible." He talked at her rather than to her; her identification with him always felt thwarted, a tad incomplete, as though she couldn't quite absorb the attributes she saw in him and coveted. The case-study reading would reach precisely this conclusion: a girl whose identification with her father is frustrated or compromised will fall back on her mother, identifying and absorbing the qualities associated with her, and in the process losing the sense that "male" qualities—strength, entitlement, power—are truly available to her. Active versus passive, self-seeking versus self-sacrificing, hungry versus not hungry, man versus woman: These were the rules when Lisa was a girl, distinctions still widely reinforced by culture and family; end of story.

And yet the story is not so simple, in part because humans are not quite so malleable nor appetites so yielding, and in part because so many of the traditional mandates about femininity have been challenged and thrown open for debate. Women can—and do—test those mandates all the time. Grown up, educated, inhabiting an altered world, we hold them up in the clear light, we decry them as sexist and self-limiting, we toss them aside. Lisa is one such woman: she believes, unequivocally, that women are entitled to every bit as much as men are, and like a lot of women, she's come to that belief the hard way, which is to say the angry way: By feeling the rage a woman feels when she's judged by appearances, or patronized by a man, or paid less for the same work, or considered "bitchy" when she dares to voice an opinion; by working extraordinarily hard to prove herself as competent and intellectually able; and by learning—step by angry step—to be less accommodating, less caretaking, more entitled, more deeply committed to her own heart and hungers.

This is appetite's grunt work, a daily battle against stubborn inhibitions and abiding taboos and lingering strains of sexism, and there's no question that it's tough going. It can take decades for a woman to feel comfortable with her own power and competence, to stop apologizing for her achievements, to resist explaining them away (it was a fluke, a product of luck or timing or circumstance), to fend off feelings of fraudulence, to truly internalize her achievements. It can take decades, too, for a woman to feel a sense of ownership and agency about her sexual appetite, to feel that she has a right not just to be desirable but to desire, that she's entitled to sexual pleasure, with all its implicit threats of selfishness and uncontrollability.

What may take even longer to work through—what nags and gnaws in more intricate and puzzling ways—is a deeper sense of unease, a vague disquiet that sometimes feels like abandonment, sometimes like betrayal, and that springs, I think, from the territory of mothers, that plane of merging and attachment where knowledge of the mother is enlaced with knowledge of the self. That "other" we long to be—the one who'd emerge if we lost the right amount of weight or found just the right clothes, the one who so often gets lost under the relentless focus on size and shape and appearance—is not a figure many women can conjure up from childhood; she is not deeply familiar or intimately known or felt at the core; a woman may have to invent her by herself. And in order to do so, she may have to leave something—or someone—behind.

Lisa hints at this when she talks about her mother, who arouses the most complicated feelings, far more elusive ones than her father does. Like my own, Lisa's mother was in many ways a model of self-sacrifice, but she was also a complex, rather angry woman who, not uncharacteristically, put her career on hold until her kids were in school, who never felt sufficiently recognized herself, and who always resented—in a vague, rarely articulated way—Lisa's accomplishments, which (Lisa suspects) have evoked her own sense of failing and unsatisfied ambition. This has put Lisa in a most delicate position, for she has come to understand that the satisfaction of her own appetites might incur a cost, perhaps the highest interpersonal one: Indulged or relished, they might threaten her connection with her mother.

And yet this awareness is not entirely conscious, Lisa can hardly name the feelings it arouses. She calls her mother on the phone to deliver good news about a television pilot she's just completed, and she hears something hollow in her mother's voice, a tone just slightly edged with disappointment or haughty disregard; she feels as though she's broken some unspoken rule, and while there is no overt expression of negativity or transgression ("That's great," says her mother, then moves on to to something else), the conversation leaves a knot in Lisa's stomach, an acid sensation that feels partly like longing, partly like rage.

The sensation, if I understand it correctly, is guilt, and it is the most painful variety, each step away from the prescribed path a step away from mom, each success a possible slap, each appetite tinged with the possibility of betrayal. It is a subtle, pressing feeling, deeper than the garden-variety guilt a woman experiences when she breaks one of the more tangible sanctions against appetite (goes off her diet, takes the last pork chop) and considerably more wrenching.

When you ask women what they learned about gender as kids, and how their sense of what it meant to be female was shaped by their mothers, you don't just hear black-and-white stories about muted maternal desire and the division of personality traits, mom as soft and self-sacrificing, dad as autonomous and strong. You also hear—and with much greater specificity—stories about divisions in value, stories about frustrated desire, dawning awarenesses about power and worth. You hear stories about conflicted mothers, depressed mothers, mothers perpetually tormented by the bathroom scale, mothers whose sense of competence emerged only in the kitchen or at Bloomingdale's or in front of a vanity table, mothers who never had the time or opportunity to consider their own hungers or ambitions. You hear painful stories, too: phrases like "belittled by my father" and "cheated on." You hear a woman talk about watching her mother lose her hair during chemotherapy, her mother weeping into the mirror and saying, "Who will love me now?" You hear a woman describe the first time she saw her father hit her mother, the mother pressed up against the kitchen wall, her face a portrait in terror. You hear about mothers like my own, whose passions were

consistently minimized, buried under heaps of laundry and grocery lists, frustrated by unhappy marriages.

These are the images that seep into the bones, a slow accumu-
lation of data about female value and power or lack of them. A
mother is the all-nurturing center of the universe to a little girl,
her power seemingly boundless; in the absence of a father figure
to connect with deeply, an available model of hunger and striving, she is also a girl's necessary fallback, the woman who will
form the essence of her selfhood. So what happens if a girl grows
aware that this figure is actually perceived in the household (by
the father, the older siblings, the extended family) as a nag or a
glorified maid or a powerless servant? What happens if she comes
to understand that her mother is articulated quite differently
than her father, that she's seen not as active, desiring, and powerful but as voiceless, dependent, and submissive? Even if her
own mother is a strong, respected, confident woman, what happens if she learns that this is an exception, that out in the rest of
the world women are not nearly so powerfully defined, that violence, oppression, and poverty remain fixed parts of women's
lives across the globe, that true gender equality remains a stub-
bornly distant dream?

For the generation that came after me, women now in their
teens and twenties who were raised in a more egalitarian and feminist climate, the images of motherhood may be different but not
necessarily any less problematic. What happens, for instance, if
your mother was a feminist powerhouse, a woman who marched
for women's rights, fought her way into a male-dominated career,
had kids in the midst of it, and then spent the next two decades
dancing the frenzied dance of the working mother, ten balls in the
air at all times? This may be a more empowered picture than the
one I grew up with, but it can be every bit as disconcerting and
every bit as enlaced with questions about divisions in social value;
a model of appetite is not necessarily the same as a model of satiety, and while a contemporary mother may have the freedom to
hunger, she may not always have the resources to get fed. Most

women still have primary responsibility over the domestic sphere; the struggle to find support (good subsidized day care, flexible schedules, partners willing to pick up fifty percent of the work at home, and workplaces willing to let them) remains epic; the image of thwarted ambition I grew up with has become an image of frayed nerves and sleep deprivation, which presents its own challenges to a daughter's conception of appetite. A twenty-three-year-old woman I know, a consummate underachiever, grew up with a mother who ran a successful law practice, worked twelve-hour days, raised three kids, never had five minutes to herself, and made the world of hunger and striving look, in her daughter's words, "like a constant battle, completely overwhelming." Syndicated columnist Ellen Goodman writes about this phenomenon, observing the emergence of a generation of women in their teens and twenties who see in their mothers "the stressed-out, sometimes burned-out front line of the women's movement" and who turn away with the disgusted refrain, "If that's having it all, I don't want it." My young friend extends this argument—her mother's high-achieving stance feels intimidating to her as well as exhausting, she doesn't see how she could possibly measure up, and she's not sure the personal costs would be worth the effort—but she agrees with the sentiment. As she puts it, "If that's having it all, I'd rather be napping."

Every generation measures itself against the one before; every daughter's experience of hunger will be shaped to some extent by that of her mother: what she had or did not have, how much it cost her, how much she herself wants or can allow herself to want in contrast. It is this—this comparison between self and other, this data bank of images, these memories of unfulfilled or undervalued or strung-out mothers, this articulation of women as less entitled, less powerful, less sexual and ambitious, less supported and recognized in the wider world—that so complicates the matter of appetite for women, twists it into a hard knot. Feminist mothers or nonfeminist mothers, devalued mothers or burned-out mothers—a mother's choices, her frustrations, her constellation of limits and constraints become for a daughter both paradigms of hunger and potential sources of difference and rebellion, and this can muddy the waters at the deepest level, it can make a girl's feeling of identification and sameness with her mother feel both risky and at risk. It can also pair hunger with rage—rage at the mother who didn't stand up for herself, or who didn't teach you how to stand up for yourself; rage at the mother who tried to do too much, who never squeezed out pleasure for herself; rage at the mother who can't quite see the person you're trying to become, or the person you have become, or the person you don't want to become; rage at mothers whose difference leaves you feeling confused and pained and disconnected. This is grueling stuff, it's enough to make your stomach tighten into a knot when you talk to your mother on the phone, it's enough to make you storm into a 7–Eleven and steal something.

For that matter, it's enough to make you starve, and to tear off your sweatshirt in the kitchen in a blind attempt to make some agonizingly complicated statement. I was twenty-two at the time of that episode. I'd left my deadly-dull university job for a far more promising position as a newspaper reporter, a job that unleashed a lot of hope but also compounded the more wholesale anxiety I felt during that time. Despite my mounting obsession with food and my increasingly fragile appearance, I was ambitious and hell-bent on succeeding, and this required cultivating qualities that felt not only unfamiliar but also decidedly non-mom: autonomy, a certain fearlessness, a journalistic thick skin and sense of entitlement. My mother found this thrilling, her daughter the reporter; she read and clipped every last article I wrote, no matter how tiny or inconsequential; she got a vicarious charge every time I interviewed someone important; and she could not have fathomed how much strange, conflicted feeling her enthusiasm evoked. When we talked on the phone, she'd ask me about my work with an eagerness that always made me wince, always kicked up an impulse to minimize my efforts, always left me with the most uncomfortable, squirming sensation, a feeling I can only identify in retrospect as a shadowy blend of guilt and disconnection, something a kid might feel if she ran away from home and turned back to see her mother standing in the driveway, blindly cheering her on.

Identifying yourself in opposition to your mother can be such a secret and necessary torment. Several women I've spoken to have evoked the image of driving with blinders on, or navigating without a map, the excitement of charting an independent course compromised by a sense of imperative disidentification: You move on, you leave your mother behind, she can't quite appreciate where you're going or how you'll get there, and all at once you're terrified of the change, guilty about it, thrilled by it, and furious at her for letting you go off without any directions, for letting you go at all.

In *The Hungry Self*, Kim Chernin notes that as a daughter, a woman understands that her life will invariably reflect on the life of her mother. If her mother has been unfulfilled, powerless, robbed of an identity beyond her role as mother or wife, or leveled by stress or frustration, the daughter faces an intolerable conflict as she contemplates her own choices in a shifting world; she's torn between loyalty to her mother on the one hand, and commitment to the "new female being" she is struggling to become on the other. "Suddenly," Chernin writes, "in coming of age and entering the world, she is in danger of calling up [her mother's] envy and resentment, and even worse, more painful and disturbing to consider, she is now in a position to remind her mother of her own failure and lack." She sees this dilemma as central to eating disorders, a woman's attack on her own body hiding "a bitter warfare against the mother: it's the guilt we feel and the hidden anger we can't express."

Precisely. Behind that skeletal display in the kitchen that day, I suspect I was describing in flesh a pain I could not communicate in words, the malnourished form expressing a profound alignment with my mother (*See? I'm as self-depriving and unfulfilled as you are, we are still the same*) and also a hiss of fury, each protruding bone a visible rejection of that alignment, a rejection of all that food—and by association a mother—stands for: female caretaking, the (limited) sphere it represented, the female form, my mother herself.

Guilt is a powerful motivator, and also a sly one. It lacks the shrill, whirring insistence of anxiety; instead, it presses and weighs and whispers, it crops up in odd, indirect ways, and it almost always demands restitution. In a weird, symbolic way, I suspect this was at work that day in the kitchen, as well, the body offered as payment for a perceived betrayal, atonement scored on bone. *I'll leave you*, I might have said, *but I'll starve, I'll hurt, I won't be able to get too far.*

This is a more common phenomenon than I could have known at the time, a way of exchanging growth in one sphere for turmoil in another, and I've seen it expressed by dozens of women, both in and beyond the realm of food. A former compulsive shopper tells me she managed to distance herself from her mother and simultaneously cling by racking up $14,000 in debt within a year of landing a job at an ad agency, a profession her mother disapproved of and a sum that forced her to give up her apartment and move back home. "How's that for a mixed message?" she says. "'I'm completely different from you, I'm moving in.'" A former compulsive overeater describes her binges, not atypically, as a way of fending off sexuality in her twenties. "I think I could allow myself to be better educated than my mother, and more ambitious, and more independent," she says, "but I could not for the life of me have all that and be sexual, too." Between the ages of twenty-one and twenty-five, she acquired an MBA from Harvard, a high-paying job with a venture capital firm, a fabulous apartment, and an extra sixty-five pounds, atonement scored on flesh.

For Lisa, restitution has taken material form, manifest as an inability to indulge in things, a sense that pleasure-seeking and self-pampering are somehow illegitimate and undeserved. New clothes? Off limits. Lovely furniture? No. Vacations? Forget it.

She describes this as an almost consumerist version of anorexia, as "some way of getting off on deprivation," and the parallel is apt; she describes a similar compulsion to stamp out need, to prove to herself that she can outlast desire, transcend ordinary human wants, not cave in. But this brand of self-denial and restraint differs from the anxiety-fueled variety; it has a guilty edge, an undertone of penance. Lisa spent years, she says, "acting in ways that were not aligned with who I was" in order to placate her mother, attending a mom-approved college (Swarthmore) instead of the college she wanted to attend (University of Michigan), beginning a mom-approved career (teaching) before abandoning it for television. Her difficulty with indulgence emerged as the placating behavior began to ebb: the more respect and recognition she accumulated at work, the more she began to deprive herself of luxuries at home, as though her ambition required payment in some other realm, power at work in exchange for disempowerment in her personal life. The clearer she became about her professional identity and goals, the more fearful she became about money, as though to take charge of her finances—and by association her adult life—was impermissible. The more she freed herself from her mother's grip on her choices, the more compelled she seemed to feel to offer compensation. The swaps: *I can have success, but not material comfort. I can be independent and strong, but only if I cling to a piece of childhood dependency. I can seek the recognition and satisfaction that eluded my mother, but I must pay for it.*

We grow, we leave people behind, we make restitution. One of the most common manifestations of this drama involves the smart woman and the man who mistreats her, a Women-Who-Love-Too-Much story line that tends to get explained away in simplistic, somewhat demeaning terms (women have bad judgment and low self-esteem), but that's always struck me as more demonically purposeful, shades of penance in the plot, mothers lurking in the wings. I see it in a woman named Karen, who spent years bitterly obsessed with a very powerful, utterly withholding, not-quite-divorced lawyer, a man to whom she surrendered "every ounce of ego." I see it in a woman named Sarah, who sold her apartment, quit her job, and moved halfway across the country to be with (or, at least, near) a man who made her feel worthless, needy, unattractive. And I see it in a woman named Elena, who threw an enormous, lavish wedding at which all of her friends stood and quietly murmured words of doom: He's such a bastard. What does she see in him? It'll never work.

All of these were—and are—smart, ambitious, strong women. Karen is a speechwriter whose work was capturing national attention during that time in her life. Sarah is a physicist, one of a handful of women at the top of her field. Elena is a professional chef, who'd opened a catering business the year before her wedding to uniformly positive reviews. In steering their lives in such directions, all of these women, too, have made serious departures from their pasts, particularly their feminine pasts. Karen's mother was a housewife in New Jersey who'd grown up poor, married at twenty-two, and spent her adult life in the service of her husband and six children. "Don't expect too much out of life," she used to tell Karen. "That way, you won't be let down." Sarah's mother admonished her about intellect: "Don't be too brainy," she'd tell her. "Always let the man think he's smarter than you." And Elena's most vivid memories of her mother center around the kitchen of her home in Queens, New York: mom literally on hands and knees at the end of a full day of work, scrubbing the linoleum, scrubbing the oven, scrubbing the wainscotting.

This is restitution of the highest order; by day, each of these women constructed a kind of parallel universe, an almost covert realm created out of her own blood, sweat, and talent where she felt successful, autonomous, in charge. And each paid for this in her private life, inhabiting a separate realm of deprivation and belittlement that re-created a deeply unfamiliar unhappiness, a mother's unhappiness, her powerlessness, her despair. Deal struck, penance made. *I can have the independence and freedom that eluded you, but not the love. I can be sexual and ambitious, but not happy.*

Psychiatrist Louise Kaplan describes this kind of bargain as a "pay-as-you-go plan," a reaction to the barely conscious, whispering sense a woman may have that her hungers and strivings are impermissible, indulged at a high cost. "All the time she has been suffering," she writes, "she has been making lots of money in her business, or becoming a successful MD, or preparing hundreds of paintings for an exhibition, or delivering lectures on microbiology. These powerful masterful activities would arouse massive conscious anxiety if she did not do something to appease the gods. . . . If the slave pays by surrendering her soul to her master, then she can continue with her forbidden occupations until the next bill comes. One forbidden occupation is her sexuality; the other is her intellectual ambition."

This makes perfect sense to me; it explains the kind of cruel logic at work behind a destructive romance, misery invited in the door as a way of balancing the psychic budget, stamping the invoice PAID. If your own mother slaved her life away in the kitchen, you surely aren't supposed to march out into the world and make a name for yourself as a master chef. If your own mother kept her sanity by lowering her own ambitions, driving her creative or intellectual strivings underground, you are not supposed to emerge at the top of your craft, to become a highly regarded writer or a scientist. And if your own mother existed within the family as a desexualized servant or a case study in overburdened working motherhood, if every scrap of her being was channeled into her job and her children and husband, if she did not appear to actively desire pleasure for herself, then you are most certainly not supposed to become a picture of loving partnership or self-seeking indulgence or strong, assertive sexuality. Or, if you do, you'd better be prepared to pay for it.

I was blessed with a mother who wanted good things for me, who was unequivocal in her support for my work, who never tried to steer me toward any traditional model of femininity. No diets, ever. No nagging about wardrobe or appearances. Not a single suggestion that the path to self-definition lay solely in marriage or motherhood. She was eager on my behalf, and she delighted in my successes, and yet when I recall those images of her—mom abandoning her studio to fix us lunch, mom lugging in the groceries and making pâté, mom self-sacrificing and frustrated about it, and loving and angry, and full of passions that were never permitted to flower in full—I still feel a pang of the most intricate complexity: a blend of uncertainty and sorrow, some dark fear of betrayal, and a single, guilty question: How can I allow myself to have what she never had?

Each step away from a mother, no matter how deliberately taken or how roundly supported, can be bittersweet, painful in a barely discernible way, and I imagine this is true for many women, in many different circumstances: women who are torn between family and career, women who've chosen careers over children, women who are struggling to balance many competing hungers, their own and those of their families and friends and co-workers, women who are struggling to tease their own hungers out of a knot of need that may include the hungers of ten or fifteen other people. If your mother didn't work outside the house, if she was always there for you, if family defined her core being, how can you help but feel a failure or a traitor if you've compromised family life by comparison, or ditched it entirely, or dared to want more? Alternately, if your mother worked twelve or fourteen hours a day at her career and also managed to run the household, help you with your homework, drive you to and from soccer games, and pay the bills, how can you help but feel selfish and inadequate if you want *less*, if you want something easier? No doubt one of the reasons that television dramas like *Judging Amy* and *Providence* have been so successful, and so cozily appealing, is that they depict women in high-powered careers (a judge, a doctor) who nonetheless live at home, their mothers, living or imagined, always at their elbows, always there to dish out love and ice cream and advice. To a generation of women trying to carve out new paths without a map, these are deeply reassuring pictures. Sure, they suggest, you can have ambition and power and beauty and acclaim, but you don't have to pay too high a price; your youthful helplessness and your dependency and your femininity can remain intact and so, too, can your deep identification with mom. No betrayal necessary; she'll be with you always.

And what of women whose mothers don't harbor lofty ambitions for their daughters, who won't beam with pride at their accomplishments or greet them in the kitchen with fresh-baked cookies at the end of a tough day? What of women, like Lisa, whose independence and hunger and strivings really do involve a kind of psychic betrayal, reminding a mother of her own failings and thwarted ambitions?

In her collection of essays, *The End of the Novel of Love*, Vivian Gornick describes an autobiographical novel called *Mary Olivier*, which details precisely this scenario. Written by May Sinclair and published in 1919, the novel concerns a young protagonist named Mary, an intelligent and precocious girl whose mother resents her budding skill and independence. This conflict puts both mother and daughter in an impossible bind, a Gordian knot of attachment: Mary, who's devastated by her mother's disapproval, understands that she cannot truly leave home and follow her own dreams without sacrificing her mother's love; her mother, who can't bear such a separation, understands that in order to hold onto her daughter, she must continue to withhold her affection. In a poignant passage about how this kind of attachment, with its threats of jealousy and betrayal, can compromise a young woman's ambition, Mary, who has particular talent as a pianist, sits down at age sixteen to play Chopin:

> She exulted in her power over the Polonaise. Nothing could touch you, nothing could hurt you while you played. If only you could go on playing forever. . . . Her mother came in from the garden. "Mary," she said, "if you play, you must play gently." "But

Mamma—I can't. It goes like that." "Then don't play it. You can be heard all over the village." "Bother the village. I don't care if I'm heard all over everywhere!" She went on playing. But it was no use. She struck a wrong note. Her hands trembled and lost their grip. They stiffened, dropped from the keys. She sat and stared idiotically at the white page, at the black bars swaying. She had forgotten how to play Chopin.

Mary never becomes a pianist, and although she understands her own complicity in this surrender of power and voice (there's "a bit of me," she confides in her brother, "that claws onto her and can't get away"), she never makes the psychological break, either.

We may presume, nearly a century later, that Mary is not alone. The personal accounting that operates in the world of appetite—the internal equations about how much to take in; how to balance longing with constraint; how much to pay, literally or figuratively, for satisfaction—can also become an interpersonal calculus, equations measured and weighed against a second party: a spouse, a child, a colleague, a mother. Mary Olivier framed the dilemma perfectly: If you satisfy your own hunger, will you risk starving someone else?

3

I HATE MY STOMACH, I HATE MY THIGHS

BODY-LOATHING AND THE LEARNED EMBRACE OF RESTRAINT

I REACHED MY LOWEST weight sometime after that day in the kitchen. Eighty-seven, eighty-five, eighty-three. I stopped menstruating. I had no breasts. The body was tight, taut, bolted down. It did not curve or bulge or protrude, it did not bleed.

During this time, I used to walk home from work along a strip of shops and restaurants on the east side of Providence, a deliberate route that took me out of my way and past a great deal of food. I'd pass women with armloads of groceries. I'd see couples hunched over hamburgers through the windows of a café. I'd walk past a delicatessen and a bakery and a Dunkin' Donuts, I'd smell spiced meats and freshly baked bread and the heavy sweetness of honey glaze, and I'd feel virtually transcendent, resisting this bounty while others surrendered. Nothing. No appetite: not for me.

The insidious thing is that this felt like a kind of triumph, victory echoed in the deep steady pressing throb of physical hunger, the stomach pulling inward, inward, inward. That hunger was like air to me, I needed the assurance of will it gave me, and I measured its effects with the quiet astonishment of a scientist whose radical experiment is actually working. At night, I'd stand in front of the mirror in my bathroom and take stock—my hip bones jutted out nearly an inch on either side, my abdomen a concave dip between them; my thighs were so narrow I could ring each one with my hands without touching any skin. I'd hold my arm out in front of me and observe its skeletal outlines: the ulna, a long and tapering bone; the elbow, a distinct flare below the upper arm; the tiny wrist bones, angry little knobs the shape of marbles. I'd stand there and count each rib. I lived and walked and breathed hunger, and although my body felt tight and drawn and pained, although I was so faint my vision blurred if I stood up too suddenly, I also felt driven and strong and focused, unyielding in my control and unwilling to relinquish it. This was the hunger of women, hidden and conflicted and forbidden. This was the infinite hunger for love and recognition, the hunger for sex and satisfaction and beauty, the hunger to be seen and known and fed, the hunger to take and take, and I had conquered it, mastered it, roped it like a steer.

I was ruler of my own corporeal continent, the Queen of Anhedonia.

No fat, no fleshy protrusions.

No blood, no seepings.

No needs.

What an extraordinary sensation: anorexia, the most profound form of antagonism toward body and self, experienced as pride.

More extraordinary, really, is that there's nothing so unusual about this view of the body, nothing remarkable about this scrutiny of form and shape or about the underlying concern with potential excesses. This, albeit in exaggerated form, is part of the female voice: body-loathing as a language, sharp verbs, venomous nouns.

I hate my body, I hate my thighs, I ate too much. I can't believe I spent so much money, I haven't been to the gym in weeks, I shouldn't have said that, I'm such an idiot, I'm such a piece of shit. This kind of internal harangue, which is relentless and cruel and so humiliating a woman would be appalled if the words were spoken by an outsider, can be utterly commonplace, conducted so reflexively it's easy not to notice how harsh it is. It simply pops out: the instinctive "ugh" uttered in front of the mirror, the daily ego-lashing over bad hair and imperfect skin, the acknowledged revulsion in the locker room, *Look at me, I'm a mess*. On a bad day, hatred of the specific (a thigh, a belly) can become indistinguishable from hatred of the self, as though they're one and the same. A women I know describes feeling as though the zipper on her jeans triggers an audiotape in her head; the jeans feel too tight, the tape clicks on: *You're a pig, you're a fucking, fucking fat pig*. Another shares a page of her journal with me, kept while she was abusing laxatives during a bulimic phase. Twenty-two at the time, she wrote: *I don't just do disgusting things, I am disgusting, every fiber of me disgusting. I swallow these pills every night and there I am the next morning: literally just shit.*

Anxiety and guilt are about what we do, or fear doing, or fear we've done to others. Body-loathing is about who we are. Fat. Disgusting. Pig. Out of control, or about to be; too big, too much, *women*. The sensation behind it is slithering, poisonous, laced with self-contempt, and it can hit like a slap, a reflexive, often wholly irrational jolt of self-disgust that rises up from a place so deep it feels like instinct. This is the dieting woman's background music, to be sure, that castigating hiss particularly audible around food and weight, but it can rise up anytime a perceived boundary is crossed, anytime a tacit rule about size or presence or hunger is broken. An editor—very skilled, very confident—describes meeting with a group of educators, who'd hired her to consult on a curriculum they were designing for a course in teenage health. She arrived, performed quite brilliantly—she was articulate, forceful, persuasive—but the minute she walked out the door, she was flooded with shame: She'd been way too pushy, too opinionated, she'd alienated the whole group. She had to call a colleague to ask for reassurance, and it took her days to realize where her reaction had come from: terrible discomfort with her own power, a feeling that some hideous eruption had taken place, the self exposed as domineering, loud, uncontained. A therapist—smart, culturally savvy, deeply self-aware—felt a similar stab to the gut while writing a thank-you note to a former boyfriend, who'd sent her a present for her fiftieth birthday. She knows all about the cult of youthfulness in this day and age, she knows how profoundly insulting and also how ludicrous it is to assign value only to inexperienced, wrinkle-free naifs, she *gets* all this. And yet the simple acknowledgment of those two numbers—5-0—hit her like a fist: Fifty meant *old*, a direct threat to the link between identity and beauty; it meant being ejected from the realm of vibrancy and sexual appeal, a place she'd once inhabited with this old boyfriend; it meant being cast into some other realm of sagging brokenness and loss.

Anorexia took all of this away from me, at least in a superficial, immediate sense. On days when I successfully resisted food and held fast to my 800-calorie regimen, which was most days, that voice of self-admonishment grew thin as a butterfly's wing, it evanesced, and its absence made me feel different and strong. See? See what an iron will I have? One of the most common misconceptions about anorexia is that women who suffer from it actually believe they're fat: They look in a mirror and see imaginary bulges, heft, fleshy curves where there are only bones. This was not my experience. My view of my body was certainly distorted—I could not see how truly grim and gruesome and alien I looked, I had no real sense of the extent of the emaciation—but I knew I was stripped down, spare, angular, I knew I had pared away those bulges and curves, I knew I was winning the war, which was precisely how daily life felt, like a state of siege. Body versus mind, flesh versus the purest will.

Sandra Lee Bartky, a professor of philosophy at the University of Illinois at Chicago, writes about the feeling among women—widespread, she believes—that they are under constant observation, monitored by a cool critical "anonymous disciplinary power" that's so ingrained it almost feels like a second self. Disci-

plinary is an apt word; even now, years past anorexia, that sense
of an independent force persists, as though some judgmental entity—me, but not quite me—lives on in a corner of my mind
where it stands watch, always aware of the body, attuned to
every nuance of shape and heft and contour, always anticipating
the worst, always poised to deliver a slap at any hint of laziness or
sloth or relaxed control. Sometimes its voice is proactive: Don't
eat that brownie, don't take seconds; you'll feel pious, you'll feel
resolute and thin. More often, it's punitive, a voice of sneering
disdain: Look at that stomach. Look at those thighs. You're turning into a *cow*.

I don't think this is something men experience, at least not in
the routine, daily way that women often do. Many years ago, during a meeting at work, a male editor asked me to loan him my pen.
I handed it over, then sat and watched as he took the pen, wrote
something down, then stuck the pen in his ear. Then he twisted
the pen around, took it out, and looked at it. Then he stuck it
back in, twisted it around again, and looked at it some more. I
found this so stunning—shameless is the word—I wrote a column
about it, detailing the kinds of things that men (at least some
men) feel free to do in public that a woman almost never does: ve-
hicular nose picking, Kleenex-free nose blowing, phlegm-hurling,
public belching. I called the column "Gross Men" but it really had
less to do with decorum or manners than with a kind of freedom
from stricture and judgment. Bartky also refers to her "disciplinary
power" as a "panoptical male connoisseur [which] resides within
the consciousness of most women: they stand perpetually before
his gaze and under his judgments." If this connoisseur resides
within men at all, it does not appear to plague them the way it
plagues women; if it sees a man spit some huge specimen of
phlegm onto the street while jogging, it (or the man himself) at
least seems not to care.

But this monitoring presence does care what women do, how
they look, how they behave in public, and its castigating tones
are very difficult to get purchase on because they feel both

deeply rooted and rootless, part of self and also part of the wider world. The other day, I cut a workout short, swam three quarters of a mile instead of a mile, which I understand is absolutely no big deal in the grand scheme of things, or even the small scheme of things: completely inconsequential, completely *fine*. And yet as I got out of the pool and headed toward the showers, I could feel the presence stir, the beast rattling in its cage, even this tiny infraction triggering its contemptuous mutterings about thighs, body fat, potential excesses, you *pig*. This is a holdover from anorexia, no doubt, this feeling that all hell will break loose if the vigilance isn't scrupulously maintained, but I think it's a fairly common sensation and also an extraordinarily far-reaching one. Self-contempt of this sort has a deep, visceral, almost sub-terranean quality—it seems lodged in a woman's soul somehow, its voice of admonishment as real and core as conscience—but it also has a more diffuse character, as though it lives in the air be-yond consciousness and intellect, a kind of emotional radon that leaks its poison perpetually but invisibly. I ignored the voice that morning and went about my business, but I'm still a little awed by its persistence: I can reason with the beast, I can temporarily defuse it, but I can't seem to kill it.

Actually, no individual effort seems to kill it. To a large ex-tent, this castigating beast exists quite independently of con-sciousness; it's part of the air we breathe, part of the earth beneath our feet, a entire universe a woman may come to know simply by being female. In my office is a stack of women's maga-zines: temples of self-scrutiny, bibles of body-loathing. On the top of the pile is a *Shape* magazine, July 2000, its cover featuring a lean, smooth-skinned Elle Macpherson, pictured two years af-ter giving birth to a baby. Elle Macpherson is a modern goddess, stunning to behold: Her hair is shot through with glimmers of blond, her skin is absolutely poreless and smooth, her teeth are so pearly-white they look like they could blind you if you caught them in the right light. She wears a pale blue spaghetti-strapped tank top, which exposes a wide expanse of creamy skin, beautifully rounded and glossy shoulders, the barest shadow of cleavage. Her eyes shine; she is beaming.

Beside Elle's image, several stories are promoted, among them: "Burn 1,000 Extra Calories a Week!," "Weight-loss News: You Don't Need Willpower," "One Great at-Home Pilates Move for Bikini Abs," "SPECIAL: New Ways to Stop Stress Eating," and "We Found the Best 12 Moves for Your Abs, Butt & Thighs."

I look at this and sigh. Weight, weight, weight; abs, butt, thighs. Any woman with a modicum of self-awareness understands what this material is intended to do. It is goddess worship, goddess religion for the consumer age, commandments chiseled on skin and bone, and it's designed to whip us mere mortals into a frenzy of inadequacy so potent it causes us to act, to go forth and buy the magazine and the many products it advertises. Thou shalt be thin, the goddess commands. Thou shalt not have wrinkles. Thou shalt compare and contrast. Thou shalt fail to measure up. Thou shalt beget a child and two years later, when instead of resembling the vibrant and dizzyingly happy Elle Macpherson thou hast become the very picture of exhaustion, with sagging breasts and dark circles beneath thine eyes and not an ounce of energy, thou shalt blame thyself and feel like shit, and then thou shalt go forth and buy *Shape* magazine and learn that great at-home Pilates move for bikini abs.

And yet no matter how objectively you look at it or how efficiently you deconstruct it, this stuff sinks in, it gets to you. When the goddess is not cast in an Elle-like euphoric glow—so happy, so beautiful, so much happier and more beautiful than you'll ever be—she pouts and smirks into the camera, her chin uplifted in a gesture of faint superiority, her ice-princess gaze at once sexy and mocking, as inviting to men as it is shaming to women. The expression here doesn't just trigger a woman's own private denigration about weight and skin and hair; it also externalizes it, gives it a body and a face, provides a constant visual slap to reinforce the internal one. *Look at me*, the goddess says. *You're so fat compared to me. You'll never have hair like mine. You'll never be so desirable*. As Wheelock professor Gail Dines puts it, "To men, the look says 'Fuck me'; to women, it says, 'Fuck you.'"

Constantly slapped, constantly measured against perfection, a woman stops seeing straight; the goddess hammers away at perception. In the course of a week, I might see a half dozen ordinary naked female bodies in the locker room at my gym, usually the same half dozen, and literally hundreds of goddess bodies on TV, billboards, and in ads; over time—weeks turned into months, years, decades—reality starts to erode, the ideal bodies start to look normal, the normal bodies ungainly and aesthetically off, the gap between the beautiful and the ordinary grows wider and more distinct. This is why the simple act of walking past a mirror or catching your reflection in a store window can so easily set off the alarm of comparison and critique: flash, a bulge here; flash, a flaw there; flash, imperfect hair, imperfect skin, imperfect breasts, imperfect stomach, imperfect legs; flash, *not Elle Macpherson*. This, too, is why the goddess has such a simultaneously ego-battering and seductive effect: a mere glance at the cover of *Shape*, and the phenomenon of self-scrutiny can kick in as reflexively as breathing. Hair: *Elle's is so shiny*. Skin: *Mine is awful compared to hers*. Burn 1,000 extra calories a week: *How?*

Something more insidious can kick in, too. Jean Kilbourne, one of the more thoughtful critics of the impact of advertising on women, writes quite eloquently about the way imagery—particularly sexual imagery, which is so coolly passionless and so unequivocally appearance-based—can tamper with a woman's gut-level feelings about what it means to be sexual, numbing thinking about sex, skewing expectations about it, confusing real sexuality with narcissism, fostering a plastic and superficial view that's all about arousing others, never about the emotions that might underlie arousal, like intimacy or connection or trust. "This not only makes real intimacy impossible," she writes, "it erodes real desire. . . . We are offered a pseudosexuality, a sexual mystique that makes it far more difficult to discover our own unique and authentic sexuality. How sexy can a woman be who hates her body? How fully can she surrender to passion if she's worried that her thighs are too heavy?"

And how can she learn to feel sexual—tuned into and comfortable with her own body—when she's swamped by images that fuse sexuality with so many decidedly unsexy things, when so many of the external definitions of desirability around her have little, if anything, to do with her own bodily experience? The other day, I came across three ads: One, for Anna Molinari, showed a woman on her hands and knees, wearing a dog's choker; another, for Versace, pictured a woman collapsed at the bottom of a flight of stairs, as though she'd been hurled down them; a third, for Moschino, showed a woman bound in ropes. These are typical images, standard fare—eroticized women in positions of total vulnerability, eroticized women pictured *enjoying* their vulnerability, turned on by it, or at least utterly blasé about it—and it's taken me years to appreciate how truly alienating they are, how powerfully they can undermine not just confidence in the body but confidence in the truth. Total vulnerability is scary, not arousing, a fact that most women know in their bones. But when you're bombarded by statements that suggest the opposite is true, it's harder to understand that fear as natural and human, harder to embrace it, harder to talk about it. The contradiction makes it harder, too, to negotiate the already tangled lines between looking sexy and feeling sexual: To *look* sexy in the contemporary sense—exposed, submissive, vulnerable, even violated—is to *feel* powerless and afraid, which generally dampens appetite instead of whets it.

But these are the daily leakings of radon, slaps to the ego so consistent and routine it's easy to miss the darker threads that bind them together: a steady lingering antipathy toward women; a core wariness about their bodies; a belief, which is ancient and durable, that there's something dangerous, perhaps even poisonous, about the female form. Misogyny—hatred of women, manifest in particular in fear and mistrust of their bodies—is deeply embedded in the culture's psyche and to one degree or another always has been; it cuts across all ages and almost all societies, Eastern and Western, ancient and contemporary. Describing its historic ubiquity, anthropologist David D. Gilmore ticks off dozens of examples: From the ancient Greeks and Romans to contemporary tribal cultures in New Guinea and South America, men have a long history of perceiving women's bodies as sources of evil, as perilous, disgusting, polluting; the Christian Bible, the Muslim Qur'an, the Hebrew Torah, and Buddhist and Hindu scriptures all condemn women, casting their bodies, particularly their vaginas, as gateways to sin and depravity; virtually all religions associate women's menstrual discharges with uncleanliness and ugliness; currents of dark suspicion about the female form run through mythology (think Pandora, or the classical world's rank-smelling Harpies and Furies), literature and art (traceable from Attic poetry to Western folklore), and Western philosophy (Aristotle and Plato to Descartes); and dualist thought about men and women—the idea that men are defined by the lofty spheres of reason and intellect, while women, with their mysterious biological cycles, represent the base, dark, stormy, unpredictable realms of nature and emotion—has been a cornerstone of anti-woman sentiment for centuries.

It's easy to write off such sentiments as broad, abstract generalizations about other peoples in less tolerant and liberated times, but I don't think you have to search too far to see strains of it in contemporary culture, or to feel its presence at work in your own relationship to your body. Gilmore, among others, argues that men are and always have been profoundly ambivalent about women's bodies, which can evoke powerful and deeply contradictory strains of feeling: A woman's body sparks awe at her life-giving power and also terrible fear of that power; it calls up primal feelings of love and need (for a mother's care, comfort, nurturance) and also infantile feelings of helplessness, dependency, and rage; it generates a longing for surrender, a wish to return to the safe harbor of a mother's omnipotence, and also a deep terror of surrender, which so threatens male autonomy and control. "This multitiered ambivalence," Gilmore writes, "creates an uncomfortable and endless tension at every psychic level, which leads to efforts to diminish the source of the turmoil by attacking its source: women."

In its pop culture manifestation, this is where the goddess comes in. She turns male fear into female fear; she makes us wary of our own flesh; she cloaks old suspicions in new clothes, an ancient ambivalence merely veiled in Versace and scented with Chanel. Look closely. The goddess's shape—not an ounce of fat on it, nothing bulging or protruding or exceeding its limits—presents an ideal based above all on the need for containment, as though something dangerous or repulsive might break through if the female body were not carefully managed and controlled; her beauty—highly stylized, detached, youthful often to the point of prepubescence—is constructed as something that's attained only by eradicating much of what is natural—powerful, ample, generative—about the female form.

What's breathtaking is the inescapability of this idea, the battering quality of the message, which is so easy to internalize and so difficult not to. I like to consider myself a fairly laid-back person on the beauty-and-fashion front, self-accepting enough to enjoy its aesthetic, preening pleasures without feeling oppressed by them, but when I think hard about my daily relationship to my own body—the exercises in maintenance I reflexively carry out every day, the way my eye flits across drugstore shelves and displays—I'm sometimes astonished at the sense of wary imperative at work, the quiet but grinding mandates, *fix this* and *watch that*. Beauty products, feminine-hygiene products, hair- and skin-care products, heaps of cosmetics—this relentless needling exists in my own bathroom, gallons of lotions, dozens of bottles and tubes and packages, all reflecting the understanding that a great deal of vigilance and work is required just to get the body out the door. Its flows must be managed, its odors fended off, its weird hormonal irregularities minimized. Its pores must be masked, its lines erased, its unsightly hairs tweezed and electrolysized and bleached. If the body has curves, they must be flattened; if it has bulges, they must be obliterated or concealed with special clothing; if anything jiggles or sags, it must be strapped down.

Much of this is intensified, in a similarly quiet but pressing way, by a lurking sense of unacceptability, a belief (which Elle Macpherson so radiantly underscores) that the body will be lacking, defective and unpresentable, unless modified, disguised, improved upon. I stand in front of the mirror and take stock. Deficiencies, flaws, each one so very evident. The eyes, too small, need defining. The lips, too bland, need coloring. The hair, limp and stringy (or pouffy and out of control), needs to be fussed over, bound and sprayed, yanked this way and that. And the skin—blemishes here, blotches there, wrinkles wrinkles everywhere, the skin is hopeless, the skin makes the heart sink, the skin is an area so troublesome in its natural state it requires its own vocabulary; it needs revitalizing, hydrating, smoothing, toning, balancing, contouring, firming, plumping, daily defending, shine-controlling, tiny-line-minimizing, anti-aging, antioxidizing, everything but a college degree.

The great irony, of course, is that no amount of effort, no amount of toning and improving and disguising and flaw-obliterating ever quite does the trick: The self-acceptance promised by all that work rarely materializes, never seems to open the door to freedom for more than a minute or two. I passed a newsstand just after *Sports Illustrated*'s 2001 swimsuit edition came out, the cover picturing model Elsa Benitez, a bikini-clad, dark-haired beauty with no body fat and enormous breasts. She was facing the camera, crouched on her hands and knees on a beach blanket, back arched, breasts pressed forward like two ample melons, and the cover line above her read, aptly enough, "Goddesses of the Mediterranean." This is an invitation to negative self-perception, and I know this. I understand that such covers are designed to sell magazines and to titillate men, and I know that no one really looks like Elsa Benitez (including, not incidentally, Elsa Benitez herself, who's a computer-enhanced and possibly breast-implanted, surgically altered version of her original self), and I can carp and kvetch and lob such images right into the great cultural recycling bin marked Unattainable Ideals and Warped Perspectives, where they belong. And yet I react. I looked at the magazine for a millisecond and then turned away, and in the split second before rational thought took hold, I had the fleeting sensation that a door somewhere had suddenly slammed shut, an immediate pang of dissociation—*she is sexy in a way that I am not*—and what troubled me about that response was its knee-jerk familiarity, the way I've become so inured to the phenomenon I barely notice it unless I'm paying the closest attention.

But that slamming-door sensation is key; the door, I think, is the gateway to appetite and to the feeling that appetite may be indulged, freely and without regard to consequences. I look at Elle or Elsa and I think, *That is the kind of woman men want.* I flip through *Shape* and think, *Bikini abs, perfect thighs, that is the route to desirability, oh shit, I ate too much lunch.* At least fleetingly, I think in the black-and-white terms of culture, in wholesale trade-offs, A versus B. If I do not have this—the abs, the breasts, the hair—I cannot have that—the allure, the sexuality, the right to desire itself. I may understand the fallacy of that thinking, but these reactions operate at a very deep level; they touch off feelings I first experienced not as a grown woman with an ability to understand the roots of misogyny or to analyze the links between culture and self but by someone much younger and far less fully formed.

Who has the best features? This was a little game, conducted several times and always with the same results, in seventh grade, the time when so many of life's little horrors begin. A very pretty and popular girl named Jill, a leader of the in-crowd, organized the event during recess, gathering seven or eight of us around her on the steps by the school's entrance and beginning the scrutiny. My friend Jen always got best skin, rosy and smooth. My friend Nina got best hair, thick and blond. Jill gave herself best eyes, I think, but I may just be guessing (she did have beautiful eyes, large and dark and framed with the most naturally thick lashes). Me, I got prettiest hands, which felt bitterly disappointing at the time. Hands? Hands didn't matter. Who cared about hands?

If you could change any one thing about your looks, what would it be? We played this, too, frequently: Oh, I'd have Jen's skin, we'd say. I'd have Nina's hair, I'd get rid of these freckles. Once, I mentioned something about wanting curly hair instead of straight hair, and a girl looked at me and said, "If I were you, I'd get rid of those little nostril veins." I didn't even know I had little nostril veins, but as soon as I got home from school that day, I looked in the mirror and sure enough, there they were: several tiny distinct red squiggles, horrifyingly visible, creeping down the skin from inside my nose to the base of each nostril.

These were early exercises in gaze-training, a way of coaxing the eye outward instead of inward, of learning to experience the body as a thing outside the self, something a woman *has* rather than something she *is*. From seventh grade on, we would hone this skill, breaking the body down into increasingly scrutinized parts, learning to see legs and arms, belly and breasts, hips and hair as separate entities, most of which generated some degree of distress, all of which were cast in hierarchical and comparative terms, viewed in relation to others: my hair versus Nina's hair, my eyes versus Jill's eyes; this needs fixing, that needs hiding. Pore by pore, we learned to take ourselves apart.

There's no question that this way of thinking is reinforced in the world beyond seventh-grade school yards, that the art of self-dissection receives constant visual support, that it's part of consumer culture's lifeblood. Thick auburn tresses cascade across a magazine page, shiny and rich with Pantene shampoo. An enormous Maybellined eye stares out from a TV screen, each lash glossy and distinct. A calf stretches across a billboard, lean and taut in an $800 Jimmy Choo pump. American companies spend more than $200 billion each year hacking women's bodies into

bits and pieces, urging comparisons between self and other, link-
ing value to air-brushed ideals, and as the girls in my seventh-
grade class graduated to high school and beyond, the imagery
around us would only grow more specific, more pummeling,
more insidious. Models would become more thoroughly eroticized, presented in more states of obvious arousal, with more
full-out nudity and more undertones of violence; the ideals they
presented would become more specific and out of reach, with
more and more body parts exposed and subject to critique (butt,
arms, hips, and abs as well as the traditional breasts and legs) and
ever more Byzantine configurations of beauty presented (bodies
with no fat but huge breasts; delicate bodies with muscular
limbs; fifty-year-old bodies that still look twenty-five).

Even more dramatic would be a shift in the pitch of imagery,
the level and nature of the bombardment. Around the time I began starving, in the early eighties, the visual image had begun to
supplant text as culture's primary mode of communication, a radical change because images work so differently than words:
They're immediate, they hit you at levels way beneath intellect,
they come fast and furious. When televisions first appeared in
the 1950s, the image on the screen used to change every twelve
to fifteen seconds. By the eighties, the speed of change had increased to about seven seconds. Today, the image on the average
TV commercial can change as quickly as once every 1.5 seconds,
an assaulting speed, one that's impossible to thoroughly process
or integrate. When images strike you at that rate, there's no time
to register the split-second reactions they generate, no time to
analyze them or put them in their proper place; they get wedged
inside, insidious little kernels that come to feel like truth.

This is the subliminal ooze of culture and misogyny, the source
of its grip. It's hard to talk about the power of imagery and cultural mandate without falling into clichés and generalizations:
Images of beauty and directives about the body make women feel
inadequate, they set up unrealistic expectations, they tell us that
well-being has less to do with what's going on inside, in our lives

and relationships and work, than with what's happening outside, how the body looks, what it's wearing, whether it conforms to rigid cultural standards. All of those ideas are valid, but I think the truly corrosive effects of imagery occur on less conscious levels, on the more private terrain where culture interacts with lived experience. Visuals operate like heat-seeking missiles to the ego, each one homing in on a prior pang of insecurity or judgment, a lesson learned, a school-yard game: Jen's skin, Nina's hair. Who has what; what bestows value and status, what takes it away. These memories endure, they're merely reawakened by the Maybellined eye, poked and prodded by the Pantened hair. Images echo what we already know, what we've already come to fear.

By seventh grade, even in that less visual, less eroticized time, we understood the world as a place of physical haves and have-nots: Beauty, and by extension sexuality, were rooms that only a small, perfectly formed portion of the population could enter freely; the rest of us had to buy our way in, tickets available through better hair and clearer skin. And by high school, we'd begin to develop the internal correlary of this, a world of cans and cannots, where hungers are split off from one another and wrapped in threat and consequence, appetite an either-or proposition. Eating versus thighs. Chocolate versus zits. Indulgence versus beauty.

I spent seventh and eighth grades in a small, all-girl's school, an environment that probably insulated my classmates and me from some degree of preoccupation with appearance. We played those who's-got-the-best-what games, we worried about our skin and hair and clothes, but the freedom from boys also permitted us, at least on occasion, a kind of unselfconscious androgyny. We were a tough lot, or at least we thought we were. We wore tight Levi's corduroy pants and heavy workboots and thick mascara; we snuck off at lunchtime to a nearby pizza shop where we'd sit at linoleum tables like odd clusters of teen-girl-construction workers, wolfing slices and laughing and smoking masculine cigarettes, Marlboros and Winstons and Old Golds. We managed to hold onto a shred of pre-pubescent oblivion about the body during those years, and if our externalizing gazes were in training, they weren't as intently focused as they'd become. But in ninth grade, our school merged with a nearby boy's school. We were taken there by bus every day at lunchtime, after morning classes, and if I had to pinpoint what Carol Gilligan calls the female adolescent "moment of revision," when confidence and voice plummet and concern with appearances and conformity soars, it would be during those early afternoons, when our small pack of fourteen-year-old girls trooped off the school bus and straggled past the cafeteria toward the front door. We were completely on display, stared at, sometimes hooted at, parading past the large plate-glass windows and into the lunch line, and if you'd video-taped us, you'd have seen a distinct shift in demeanor and expression. Eyes downcast now, bodies held stiffly, hands fluttering to hair to smooth it down or fluff it up. At lunch, we'd sit in self-conscious clumps, hunched over our trays. Between classes, we'd stream into the girls' bathroom and stand there fussing over our hair and our makeup, obsessing about how the pants fit, whether the butt looked too big, how the body parts were, or were not, measuring up.

Each piece fragmented and judged and compared, each flaw known and perceived as grotesquely magnified, each part greater than the sum. Practiced over many years, this becomes such a familiar way of experiencing the body a woman may come to take it for granted, may come to hear the internal harangue as perfectly natural, may come to view the constant knowledge of shape and heft—how the body feels, what's wrong with it, what's bloated or flabby or too big or unshapely, how it's moving, what's going into the mouth, what's coming out of it—as a routine and predictable part of daily life, as ordinary as blinking. Small wonder so many women segue instinctively into eating disorders, small wonder anorexia felt like such a natural solution to me: Starving, I simply drew on what I already knew about the body, capitalized on my ability to externalize it, elevated that ability into a kind of cruel performance art. And today, many years post-starving, I'm still a little astonished by the durability of early lessons. Thirty years past seventh grade, I've never questioned the attractiveness of my hands; thirty years later, I'm still self-conscious about those nostril veins.

In contemporary feminist writing about female bodies, you read a lot about the notion of inscription, an idea frequently evoked to explain the shaping of a woman's self-image. Culture is written on the body, in this view, encoded on it. Fat, thin, sculpted, adorned, starved, stuffed, the female body is a kind of text which, properly deconstructed, may tell us a lot about how women are seen in the culture, and what they grapple with.

I find this image useful to a point; the anorexic is, surely, a walking manifesto about constraints on appetite, the bulimic a living testimony to both the vastness of a woman's hunger and the vastness of her compulsion to deny it. The statistics on plastic surgery deliver an even bolder statement. One hundred and forty-thousand North American women had breast-augmentation surgery in 1999, a 413 percent increase from the number in 1992. The numbers on breast lifts increased by 381 percent in the same period. Chemical peels increased by 171 percent, eyelid surgery by 139 percent, tummy tucks by 227 percent, liposuction by 389 percent. This is a perfect example of the body as text, despair literally scored on skin, dissatisfaction etched with a scalpel.

But as convincing as such readings may be, I also find the inscription metaphor a little static, as though women were uniform sheets of blank paper, written upon by a detached third party, this external *thing* we call culture. Philosopher Elizabeth Grosz uses the slightly more elastic image of calligraphy, a process that takes into account not just the act of writing but also the specific materials used to write and the distinctive interactions that take place between them; the final product—a woman's core sense of self—will vary depending on the kind of paper used, its texture

and capacity to resist or absorb messages, the quality of inscrip-
tive tools, the quality of the ink.

This feels closer to the heart of self-image, how it's formed,
twisted, encoded with pride or shame, love or hate. It's so easy,
and so tempting, to lay the blame for women's dissatisfaction
with their bodies squarely at the feet of society and Madison Avenue. But when I think hard about my own anorexic years, when
I recall what felt so needful and seductive about inhabiting that
curveless, bloodless, bolted-down body, and when I think about
the broad spectrum of feeling other women express through and
about their own bodies—healthy feelings and destructive ones,
painful ones and joyful ones—the truth seems to reach way past
culture, past even the most misogynistic ads and images and
mandates, and down into less visible internal corridors in which
much more complicated interactions take place.

We are all inscribed, Grosz suggests, from the beginning. Like
individual sheets of paper, we may be naturally fragile or resilient, naturally heavy or thin, inherently beautiful and distinctive or inherently ordinary and plain. These qualities bump up
against circumstance, family, temperament, transforming us over
time, shaping either resistance to societal mandates or vulnerability. There is fantastic range in this paradigm; it helps explain
why cultural messages about appetite can assume such varying
degrees of etched durability and also why culture is only one ingredient in a much larger soup.

A woman in her forties—quite beautiful, large-boned, naturally voluptuous—describes a typically defining moment from her
teenage years, her mother racing up to her at a bowling alley, apparently humiliated on her behalf, and hissing, "Get a bra with
cotton straps! You're bouncing and your nipples are hard!" She
recounts this, years later, with tears in her eyes, and as she speaks
I think about a fine elegant sheet of paper from thick stock, suddenly, then repeatedly, stained with inkblots of shame, messages
scrawled in anger and fear: Don't take pleasure in the body, don't
show it off, the body is bad, you are bad. Another woman, a

recovering bulimic, recalls a Thanksgiving dinner when she was an exquisitely shy fourteen-year-old, an uncle poking at the flesh near her breasts as she reached for second helpings of mashed potatoes, making a lewd comment about her weight. This is a soft-spoken, sensitive woman with an uncertain, self-conscious air; as she talks, I think of a delicate sheet of rice paper, fragile and absorbent, easily marred by a blunt, insensitive instrument. At a twelve-step meeting for love and sex addicts, I hear an incest survivor sum up the way in which a woman's sense of sexuality can be indelibly etched with violence: "For years," she says, "the only way I could feel sexual was to be in a relationship that made me feel ashamed and violated." Listening to her, I think about how profoundly multilayered a woman's self-image is, its strength subject to so many variables. A good calligrapher—a loving parent, a supportive teacher, a nurturing community—can make something beautiful out of the most ordinary paper, using the finest inks, carefully inscribing early messages about value and respect and loveability. And a bad calligrapher—neglectful, abusive, cruel—can devastate the finest.

My own sense of the body seemed to coalesce out of an odd combination of well-meaning calligraphers and woefully awkward tools. There were certainly no intentionally negative inscriptions: There was no violence in my household, no abuse, no contempt or alarm about my developing body during puberty. And yet something about the corporeal form—the body's sexual power, its stubborn insistence on pleasure—was cast early on in negative, fearful terms, its hungers, its vulnerability, its capacity to be provocative etched as somehow dangerous, uncontrollable, not to be trusted.

I suppose silence was the first teacher, messages written in invisible ink. I once asked my sister what she thought we'd learned about the body when we were kids and she answered in a word: "Secrecy." I nodded. There was almost no talk about the body in our household, no ease or lightheartedness about bodily functions or urges or needs, certainly no sense of bodily pride. None of us ever saw our parents naked, or even nearly naked. No one ever heard a word about sex, or a sound. Just before my sister and I reached puberty, our mother took us aside, one at a time, and gave us the most awkward lectures about menstruation: She delivered mine one morning in the car just before dropping me off at school, framing it around a character from a *Harriet the Spy* novel who'd gotten her period. Did I know what had happened to this character? Did I have any questions? I was so embarrassed by her embarrassment I just muttered a few things (yup, nope) and fled.

I noticed tiny differences in other people's homes, hints of more relaxed relationships to the body. A friend's mother used to wake her up every morning with a backrub, which seemed astonishing to me, so tenderly tactile I could hardly imagine it. Another kept candles by her bathtub, and a whole array of bubble baths and scented soaps, which seemed the most lovely nod to luxury. And once, I saw a friend's parents dancing to 1940s swing music in their living room, the father twirling the mother, then holding her close, the mother tipping her head back and laughing out loud: This was like watching a movie to me, a foreign film. I'd never seen such a display between my parents, never gotten a sense of play about the body, or a feeling that it had special powers: to touch, to soothe, to reassure, to arouse. Instead, I picked up an opposing set of sensations: a kind of don't-ask, don't-tell, don't-touch embarrassment about physical matters; a suspicion— not confirmed for many years—that my parents' unhappiness had a sexual component; and a related idea, faint but pressing, that the body had the power to incite not pleasure but trouble.

From my peers, I learned more complicated lessons, the edgy silence at home complicated in high school by a growing awareness that the body in fact had a great deal of power and influence, that it dictated standing in the social hierarchy, that it factored into one's most basic value, its gain or its loss. As they had been in seventh grade, the sources of gain were clear—beauty, slenderness, rosy skin, and shiny hair as the fast tracks to cachet—but they seemed to grow more tenuous over time: Value and standing, and their attendant feelings of safety, could be lost in a heartbeat, and I can remember with Technicolor clarity what it felt like to walk the tightrope of adolescent self-consciousness, the body a vital commodity that might betray you at any moment; a zit might erupt overnight, a tampon might leak, a flaw might be revealed. Elizabeth Grosz writes, "There remains a common coding of the female body as a body which leaks, which bleeds, which is at the mercy of hormonal and reproductive functions. Women's bodies are seen as uncontrolled, expansive, irrational . . . a leaking, uncontrollable, seeping, dirty thing." This may be an ancient conception, too, a theme echoed repeatedly in Western philosophy, but I picked it up in high school; an aura of tittering embarrassment about the body seemed to hover in the air like a vapor, and so did a low-level worry about its unpredictability, its capacity to ooze, smell, shame. I can remember, too, the fear, which was grinding and perpetual, of being exposed as too much of anything in high school: too loud, too brainy, too large-breasted, too small-breasted, too sexual, too easy, regulations all based on the unstated but clearly understood assumption that there were lines to navigate, controls to be exercised, excesses not to be exposed. And, of course, punishments to be suffered if the navigational systems failed, jeers and eye rolling to be endured, the voice of castigation audible in whispers: She has terrible breath. I'd die if I had skin that bad. Can you believe she went to *third* with him? Are you sure these pants look okay? Are you *sure?* The body could grant standing and value, but only if maintained with the utmost vigilance and care.

Pride, which may be the antidote to body-loathing, is such a slippery sensation; if it's not etched onto you at the core, it's enormously hard to hold onto, and its impermanence leaves you with a wobbling uncertainty, grasping for ballast. Photographs of me in high school show a young girl with an expression of formlessness, no apparent center, a pretty but rather blank sheet of paper that I struggled awkwardly to self-inscribe: eye makeup applied with a self-consciously heavy hand; clothes chosen to model myself on other girls; eyebrows plucked into a look of chronic surprise. I'd become fairly adept by that time at finding ballast in the realms of academia and friendship—I knew what was expected of me from teachers and girlfriends, I responded accordingly—but the more concretely physical realms of attraction and sexuality eluded me entirely. I had no social confidence with boys, no sense that I had anything of innate value to offer. I had none of the personality traits they seemed to find attractive, there was not an ounce of anything chatty or outgoing or perky about me, and so the body—this mysterious, secretive, unpredictable *thing* that boys seemed to admire and respond to nonetheless—became a source of power and also a source of the most profound confusion. It could provoke a kind of interest I wanted but one that also felt unknown and tinged with embarrassment to me, off limits; it could confirm value, but only a particular kind, one that needed to be managed—seized and sexualized—in order to be brought into existence. This is a fearsome combination; power is scary when you don't know what to do with it, scarier still when you're not sure how deeply it runs, when you're not convinced it even exists beneath the thin waist and the shiny hair, when it needs to be constantly reinforced by other people, whose judgment you may not even trust.

And so I was scared. I was scared of my own sexual hunger, which felt so secretive and uncharted, and I was scared of the sexual hunger of boys, which felt so vivid and overt, and I was terribly uncertain of the relationships between sex and power and value, which seemed so merged and hard to tease apart. In the midst of all that, I didn't exactly loathe my body, or feel ashamed of it, but I was deeply ashamed of my fear, which felt disabling and immature and woefully, painfully uncool, a terrible secret, evidence of some profound failing and ignorance on my part. Other girls, or so I imagined, knew what to do, how to use their power, how to derive pleasure from it, and in contrast, I felt not only freakish but isolated, as though I was standing outside a vital, defining loop.

In the pre-starving days (and the post-starving ones, for that matter), I used alcohol to fend off the discomfort, to dilute inhibition and wash away anxiety, and the strategy worked quite well, at least in its limited, situational way. Drunk, I could inhabit the body instead of fearing it, or at least I could pretend to; drunk, I could sidetrack uncertainty, deaden it altogether. What I could not do, drunk, was learn much of anything. My fear and shame of fear, my body, hunger itself— all of these remained relatively unexplored, dots on some distant and foreboding landscape, and I did my best to keep them that way.

Periodically, though, I'd get a glimpse of the landscape, a peek at its complexity. I'd get drunk at a party and wake up in some guy's bed, aware in only the haziest way of flirting the night before, of yielding to that power, hungry for that ballast, and humiliated by it in the crush of a hangover, knowing the validation it gave me was alcohol-fueled and false, its effects transient and tissue-thin. Or I'd realize that someone was attracted to me— usually someone inappropriate, an older man, or a figure of some authority or hero worship —and I'd sink into a kind of terrified ambivalence in the face of it, afraid to respond to his sexual interest but also afraid to reject it, loath to spurn something that seemed at once so tangible and so very precarious. What I lacked, in all such situations, was a gut-level sense of agency and integrity, one that could be expressed through the body because it existed within the soul; the body, my body, was not something I trusted and knew and cherished, because those very feelings so eluded me at the heart, they never felt fully inscribed.

The summer before I began to starve in earnest, my father confessed to a long-standing affair, causing a brief separation between my parents and, for the first time, an acknowledgment to my siblings and me about the depths of their troubles. This was confirming news in some respects—it certainly gave their unhappiness a name and a face—but it was also deeply unsettling. My father had seemed like the most powerful man to me, an idolized figure and also a rather fearsome one, with a brusque manner and a brilliant mind and a piercing gaze that made you feel he could see right through you. I'd always imagined his reserve and acuity and vast intellect to be evidence of the most exquisite control, as though he'd achieved a kind of mastery over ordinary human impulses, and while his confession didn't entirely knock him off the pedestal, it did say something about the explosive power of bodily appetites, their inability to be transcended, their potential to wound.

At almost precisely this time, I had a brief, ultimately unconsummated but agonizing affair with my college thesis advisor, a man (married, many years older than I) whom I'd revered and considered a mentor, and who fell into that category of inappropriate authority figures: someone whose approval I'd coveted, and whose sexual interest in me I'd recognized, reciprocated, and denied all at once. He'd taken me to lunch a few days after graduation; we'd had martinis and wine, I'd been heady with his attention, aware of the sexual charge behind it, aware of enjoying it, courting it, and simultaneously fearing it, and when we got into his car after lunch and he lurched over and started to kiss me, I felt thrilled, horrified, and also completely complicit, understanding in some wordless way that I'd exercised a power I hadn't quite been willing to acknowledge I possessed. He was the first professor I'd had at Brown who made me feel special, a feeling I'd needed desperately, a hunger I'd acknowledged; I'd fueled his interest, and I'd participated in sexualizing it, for the alternative, I felt, was to lose it altogether. And so I just sat there in the car, stunned and paralyzed, feeling his hands on my breasts, his breath on my neck.

Until I worked up the courage to flee, we met half a dozen times over a series of weeks, boozy lunches followed by the most excruciating gropings, almost always in his car. My West Coast boyfriend, a man I honestly loved, was living with me in Providence at the time; I was trying to hide the betrayal from him as well as my sense of appalled complicity about it. My mother briefly left my father, moving out of the house in a rage. The simmering truths boiled over, messages once written in invisible ink became distinct, printed in boldface: Neediness is bad, hunger is bad, the body is bad, it all causes confusion, mayhem, heartbreak, anguish.

I danced around that feeling for a year, eating, starving, binge-ing, dieting, all of it traceable to anxiety and guilt, certainly, but also to that deeper mistrust of body and self, a conviction that something terrible might erupt if the body wasn't roped in and belted down, its hungers locked behind doors. I danced and danced and when I couldn't bear it any longer, I shut the system down altogether.

This, I think, is the soul of anorexia, its fevered core, the body as a country that needs to be subdued, its appetites an enemy force so base and treacherous it must be eradicated entirely. How else to explain that sorry sense of pride? I'd watched women do battle with their hungers my whole life, listened to the ha-rangues, participated in the hate-my-body, hate-my-thighs daily raking of the self over hot coals. I'd shared the horrified sensa-tion of overspilling, needing too much, seeping beyond my pre-scribed boundaries. I understood the wariness with which so many women experienced their bodies and, by extension it seemed, themselves. I'd seen how bound together and twisted a person's appetites could be, validation merging with sex, sex merging with betrayal, needs of body and soul tangled in un-knowable, undoable knots. I'd seen where hunger, controlling or surrendering to it, could take a person.

I just carried this knowledge to its logical conclusion and did what others could not do. I vanquished the enemy and with it, the threat of danger, the threat of consequences.

Over time, unexamined, hatred of the body can assume enor-mous power, even in seemingly inconsequential ways. I know of a woman who will not go camping unless she is equipped with a butane-powered curling iron; she will not travel without it; she literally does not feel she can be in the world—even the natural world, where the only person likely to see her is her husband—

unless her hair is coiffed just so. This behavior may not seem directly related to the matter of body-loathing, or even to the matter of appetite—it may seem just plain silly—but I think it says something about how entrenched a woman's sense of constraint can be, and how much those constraints can affect her experience of desire. When anxiety about the body runs deeply enough, adherence to the rules—don't eat, keep the mouth shut, pack up the butane-powered curling iron, starve yourself half crazy—comes to feel voluntary, the mandates self-generated and freely embraced.

I witnessed a display of this several years ago, in a chic midtown Manhattan bistro, while dining with two women—both thin, although not as thin as they'd like to be—who have given the matter of female bodies a lot of thought. Susan Orlean, a staff writer for the *New Yorker*, and Patricia Marx, a freelance writer, are both veterans in the diet wars. They have both gained weight and lost weight, clamped down and surrendered control, exercised compulsively and slacked off, marched into rooms feeling beautiful and svelte, slunk into rooms feeling porky and grotesque. They have been sufficiently preoccupied with the subject of food and weight and bodies to write a book about it, a cheeky little collection of satirical weight-loss tips and dieting strategies called *The Skinny: What Every Skinny Woman Knows About Dieting (And Won't Tell You!)*, which sprung from a year's worth of anecdote-collecting "skinny lunches," held over salads and steamed vegetables with like-minded peers. And although they both say the worst is behind them (neither is "obsessed" with food today, they both have full, busy lives, they understand that this stuff can take over your whole being if you're not careful), they nonetheless have strong feelings about the subject.

They have particularly strong feelings about the words "fat" and "thin," which generated a good hour's worth of free association.

The word "thin" evoked bright expressions and tones of breathless wonder. Susan said, "When I am thin, I feel quick and light and sprightly."

Patricia agreed: "And you are! I used to swim a mile a day, and when I was thin, it was easier. I was sleeker and faster."

Susan talked about how she felt while training for a marathon, some years back: "I was lean and mean and just—you know, I would run past fat people and just feel so strong, and kind of clean and mean—"

Patricia interrupted: "Superhuman. You feel like a machine."

Susan: "Right. It was just a very particular feeling, and there was a kind of arrogance, like I had all this *denial* and *will power*. And people were jealous."

Patricia: "They are jealous. *Totally.*"

Fat had the opposite connotations, words uttered with pursed lips and scowls of disdain. Susan used the words *plump, matronly,* and (inaccurately, but you get her drift) *lumpen*. At times when she was "a little fat," she felt *unsexy* and *blobby* and *fleshy*. "I didn't like looking at myself," she said. "I didn't want anyone else to look at me."

Patricia said when she first started worrying about weight, in her senior year of high school, "it was a conscious desire to look young and boyish, sporty." Describing her less rigorous approach to dieting today, she used words like *soft* and *lazy* and *undisciplined*.

Later, she added, "There's something very Normal Rockwell about food, do you know what I mean? That's why I hate Thanksgiving."

Susan said, "Yeah, it's all this *maternal* stuff."

Patricia agreed, "Like the term 'comfort food' sickens me."

Susan: "Me, too. Although I like to eat it."

These are confident, accomplished, attractive women who enjoy laughing at themselves, at the hoops they've jumped through in the service of skinny. They like being ironic and irreverent about it, they peppered their book with deliberately outrageous, non-PC quips (sample "oddball tips:" "Travel to a third-world country—you'll lose an easy eight pounds," and "Swallow a whole hard-boiled egg without any other food or liquid to wash it down; if all goes well, it will get stuck in your throat so that you can't eat anything else"), and when you ask them whether they think the female preoccupation with food and weight has to do with self-loathing or shame or internalized misogyny or anything of a sociopolitical nature, their eyes get a bit glazed, as though this is akin to asking if a feminist can wear lipstick. Please: aren't we past that by now?

Is fat a feminist issue? Patricia wrinkled her nose. "I kind of resent that argument," she said, "because I think people have a right to look the way they want to look."

Susan agreed. "The one flaw in that logic is that women are a part of culture. We're part of what drives it. I mean, it's not that culture is being imposed on us by men. We *want* to be skinny."

They dismissed the idea—it seemed passé and irrelevant, skinny is an *aesthetic* matter, not a political one, a choice, not mandate—and ordered lunch. Patricia had an iced tea with five packets of Equal, and an egg-white omelet-of-the-day, which was studded with lox and came with a pile of French fries (she requested it sans lox and didn't touch one fry). Susan had a diet Coke and a salade niçoise, no dressing.

And there you have it. Amid all the skinny wit and egg whites, Susan and Patricia kept articulating precisely how tangled the lines of personal desire and social expectation can be, how merged they may feel. Both women claim to have more peaceful relationships with their bodies than they once did, and to have left behind some of their earlier anguish and preoccupation ("I have a perspective," says Patricia, "that allows me to know that it's not *that* important"). And yet fat—the idea of it, the memory of it, the threat of it—sat at that table like a third person, ominous and stern and warning. Fat jeopardizes social cachet: Susan talked about how much attention a thin woman gets, how people invariably remark on it, how "when you're average, no one talks about what you look like." Fat diminishes sexuality (Susan: "I feel really gross if I'm a little heavy, and really, really unsexy"). Fat even puts identity at risk; describing how it felt to be really skinny, Patricia said, "You had a character, you didn't have to come up with a personality, you had an easy eccentricity and you didn't have to create it."

Fat, fat, fat. Don't, don't, don't. You can almost hear that internalized presence in such sentiments, the omniscient second self issuing its warnings, making its judgments, ordering the hand away from the fries. You can hear, too, the echoes of ancient philosophers, the abundant, natural female body articulated as a base and ignoble thing (blobby, lazy, undisciplined) that grows more worthy and powerful (sleek, clean-and-mean, superhuman) as it's stripped down, whipped into more masculine form. Above all, you can hear strains of the same logic I applied to hunger, in typically inflated style, in anorexia: an embrace of restraint based on a fervid belief in its benefits, many of which *feel* and may actually be quite real, at least in a transient and limited way.

Motives get tied in knots under this thinking. Does a woman work hard to stay thin—exercise regularly, watch the appetite, worry when she overeats—because she'd hate herself if she grew fat, because she'd be ashamed by its associations with sloth or laziness or lack of control? Or is it simply because she feels better when she's slender and fit? Is this effort a form of cultural enslavement, an offering to the gods of patriarchy, who are known to penalize women if they exceed their prescribed limits? Or, as Susan and Patricia might argue, is it a choice, part of an aesthetic that women themselves have cultivated and embraced? I can make either case, I can make both: Yes, a salade niçoise would make me feel better than a fat-spattered cheeseburger (in the interest of full disclosure, salade niçoise is precisely what I ordered, dressing intact) and yes, I can acknowledge culture's influence in the matter, its grip on the subjective experience of "feeling good." The lines between choice and mandate are thin because the lines between self and culture are thin, the internal and the external tightly entwined and difficult to separate. "We *want* to be skinny," Susan says. How can you argue with that?

One place to begin, at least for me, is in a bookstore-café in downtown Boston, a world away from Susan and Patricia, where

I spent some time with a young graduate student named Leslie Kinzel, a woman who has worshipped at the altar of slenderness for many years, as well.

Leslie, twenty-four at the time of our meeting, has chin-length blondish hair, large gray eyes, a low-key, confident manner, and she is fat, her word, 265 pounds. She likes to say it bluntly: I'm *fat*. People are unnerved by this, a response she has come to find amusing. When you ask her how much she weighs, she rattles off the number—two-sixty-five, her tone very matter-of-fact—and then waits for the inevitable pause, a little squirm of surprise and projected discomfort. People always expect Leslie to be embarrassed about her weight, to cast her eyes downward and mutter the number, and when she fails to do this, they're taken aback. So they usually mutter for her: "Really? But you don't *look* that big," they say, and change the subject.

Leslie understands this discomfort. She says, "I am their worst nightmare," and she knows precisely what the nightmare represents: Women look at her and they see a case study in appetite run amok, two-hundred-and-sixty-five pounds worth of evidence about where a woman's hunger might lead her if she let it, an embodiment of shame. In fact, she is an embodiment of power, or of a kind of power, in which the slithering underside of body-loathing has been held up to the light, examined, and summarily dismissed.

Leslie, who has been heavy all her life, certainly knows what it's like to detest her own body, to perceive it as the enemy. She went on her first diet at age nine, dieted all through junior high and all through high school. Like many fat women, she put whole chunks of her life on hold because of her weight, carrying around a laundry list of things she'd be entitled to only if she became thin: She'd see a cute boy in school and she'd automatically think, *Well, if I go on a diet for two months and lose twenty pounds, maybe I can talk to him.* Beautiful clothes: *maybe when I'm thin.* Romance, ambition: *maybe when I'm thin.* Which never happened. Leslie would lose thirty pounds, and then the pounds would come back and they'd bring friends: another ten, another twenty. This is not unusual (the vast majority of people who diet will gain the weight back within five years), and Leslie is quite convinced that dieting—which screws with both mind and metabolism—is the most effective way to pack on pounds. It is also, she believes, "a fabulous way to keep women very, very preoccupied—the side effects of dieting are irritability, loss of concentration, and self-absorption." She, of course, was a case in point, too locked into the cycle of gain-and-lose-and-gain-some-more to think about the larger meanings of body image, too full of self-hatred to address its roots and consequences.

When Leslie was about nineteen, a friend gave her a copy of a book called *Fat!So?: Because You Don't Have to Apologize for Your Size*, by Marilyn Wann, an early pioneer in what's variously known as the "weightism" or "size activism" movement. The book squared with feelings she hadn't yet named—an exhausted sense of self-defeat and futility, an awareness that something was very wrong with her enslavement to the scale—and it had a transforming effect; the light of epiphany went on. She thought, "Wow, there are people who exist who think this is okay, and there are people who exist who know that fat people do not eat more than thin people, and in some cases even eat less, and that this is not a reflection of your character any more than if you refer to someone as being thin." There are people, in other words, who exist in the world with fat bodies and healthy egos and a full range of entitlements, shame-free.

She has not dieted since. She stopped poring through women's magazines for weight-loss tips and dieting how-tos. She gave up the constant vigilance and worry. She began to inhabit her body, instead of fighting it, and to embrace the idea of her own presence. This has been a daunting enterprise in many respects, a coming out of the fat closet. For her, it meant talking about being fat, acknowledging to friends and family the fact of it and her decision to live with it, which generated new forms of criticism, raised eyebrows and skeptical commentary: Oh, she's just angry, she's upset that she can't fit in with the rest of us, she's upset that she doesn't have the will power to lose weight like my mother or my aunt or my sister did. Embracing fat also meant disavowing her mother's worldview, the gateway to guilt. Her mother is also a heavy woman, one who's spent her whole life trying to live up to the slender ideal, and although she's come to accept Leslie's *I'm-Fat* proclamations, Leslie says she found them threatening for some time, as though her daughter were calling into question her lifestyle, her aesthetics, even her most deeply held beliefs.

Which, to an extent, she was. Leslie's stance on fat required a fundamental reframing of values, and a slow stripping away of the most ingrained assumptions behind them. She has been blessed in this endeavor by a very accepting father, who loves women in general and large women in particular; she's also been blessed with the native fearlessness and indignation of an activist, not a shy bone in her body. In the last few years, Leslie has become something of a lone gunman on the weightism front. On occasion, she's formally engaged to speak about the subject to groups of students, but she's more apt to target one person at a time: acquaintances, fellow students, strangers at subway stations, anyone who seems willing or able to hear what she has to say.

Anger is an important ingredient here; directed outward instead of inward, it's what breaks the connections between size and entitlement, size and dignity, size and value; it's what turns body-loathing into pride; it's what defuses that grinding, punitive voice, shuts down its warnings about staying on the diet, shutting your mouth, putting your life on hold.

"When you're fat," Leslie says, "you're constantly pretending that it's a temporary state." In a nod to that, she used to wear her weight like a secret, as though it wasn't really *hers*; her friends never talked about it, nor did she, no one ever used the word "fat." They ignored it the way you might ignore a bad smell in the room; it would go away in time, the real Leslie would emerge. In an allusion to the internalized voice of self-hatred, she says, "It's part of the dieting mindset. There's this whole no-tion that there's a thin person inside who's waiting to get out."

She pauses, then adds: "I like to say I sat on her and killed her."

Leslie threw back her head and laughed when she said this, a vigorous hearty laugh so palpably self-accepting it seemed to linger over the table for several moments like a wisp of perfume. The sound stayed with me for hours, and so did the image: a woman suffocating self-hatred with her own heft. A *young* woman, no less. At Leslie's age, twenty-four, I was in the most acute phases of starving. I was isolated and lonely and weak, I hardly could have suffocated a fly, and I certainly couldn't have understood that anything internal—self-disgust, fear, the in-grained messages of culture—needed to be snuffed out.

Back then, a woman like Leslie *was* my worst nightmare, and that thought stayed with me for a long time, too. The night after we met, I went home and found myself thinking about my peri-odic binges, hideous little exercises in body-loathing that spoke to precisely that nightmare: the appetite unleashed and insa-tiable, the steely will exposed as a lie. These episodes took place every six or eight weeks, when I simply couldn't bear the hunger anymore, couldn't bear the sense of deprivation and longing be-hind it, and they were always meticulously, painfully planned. Typically, I'd invite people over for dinner, and I'd spend all day cooking, making foods I'd dreamed about but wouldn't eat—huge pasta dishes with four kinds of cheese, and loaves of the best crusty bread, and the densest chocolate cakes, with hazelnut buttercream and thick sweet frosting—and I'd anticipate the meal with an anguished combination of greed and abject terror. I'd long ago lost the ability to eat "normally," to gauge with any certainty how much food I needed or when I'd had enough—that capacity had vanished way back at the all-you-can-eat buf-fet, replaced by the knowledge that once I caved in, I'd be insatiable. Which, of course, I was. During the actual meal, I'd pretend to eat casually, trying to mask my preoccupation by imi-tating the others: ignoring the bread basket until they passed it, taking seconds only after they took more, too. But later, after everyone had left, I'd steal back into the kitchen, kneel by the refrigerator light, surrender in full. More pasta, more bread, hunks of the cake. I'd eat and eat and eat, and then I'd reel off to bed feeling stuffed, bloated, dizzy, humiliated. The feeling of self-hatred behind those frenzies was leveling, total, soul-deep, the sense of disgust with my own body as literal and defining as an exclamation point. But this is how body-loathing works; hatred of the flesh gets embedded in the heart, constraint (or lack of it) becomes fused with identity. *This* is bad—this solitary binge; this needy, demanding, hungry body; this flesh—becomes *I* am bad. The master must be obeyed because the master is you.

In an act that seems to cast the matter of choice in a new light, Leslie has reinvented that master, altered its conception of identity, traded in the words *I want to be skinny* for something considerably broader and less enslaving: *I want to be myself, I want to have a life beyond the scale and the calorie counting, I want my sense of dignity and value and strength to exist independently of my weight.*

This is not to say that Leslie's is necessarily an enviable situation. I can't really know how deeply her confidence runs, or how shaken it gets, and I get fuzzy on medical questions, physical and psychological. Is it healthier to stay on the treadmill of constant dieting, gaining and losing the same forty pounds year after year, or to hold steady at two-sixty-five? If the latter cuts a decade off your life, is that a fair exchange for a lifetime of anguished dieting, deprivation, and mangled self-esteem? Over the long haul, where are the lines between physical health and emotional well-being?

Those are complicated questions, personal as well as medical, but the primary differences between Leslie and me at twenty-four are what stuck with me: a fat woman with power, a thin one with no power; a fat woman with confidence and humor, a thin one with nothing but a grimace; a fat woman who'd burst out of her self-imposed exile, a thin one kneeling in front of a refrigerator, a portrait in shame. What's astonishing to me, always, is the level of self-hatred a woman can live with, which is really a way of living with chronic pain. As Leslie and I both understand, from our opposite vantage points, tying self-worth to appearance is painful, a daily tightrope walk that requires constant vigilance. Dieting is painful, the body always resisting deprivation, never understanding why it cannot be permitted that simple baked potato, that pat of butter, that smooth dollop of sour cream. And self-criticism is painful, especially in the merciless way it's practiced by women: the sour, defeated thud of disgust that hits when a woman steps on a scale, or feels her thighs brush against each other as she walks down a hallway, or sees her silhouette in a three-way mirror, butt too wide, belly too big, disgusting, *I'm* disgusting—this can be an excruciating way to think, to feel, to live.

But, untreated, pain lingers. Unchallenged, it may be difficult even to acknowledge. Some time after my meeting with Leslie, I described her to a woman I know, someone who has worried about her weight for most of her adult life and who harbors such strong dissatisfaction with her own legs she has not worn a skirt in forty years. Her reaction surprised me. "You see strength," she said. "I see heart attack, diabetes, and stroke, for starters. It's hard to celebrate that kind of denial and self-destruction."

I'm not so sure about that, not sure our definitions of denial and self-destruction quite match up. I look at the cosmetic surgery numbers. I think about my own slavish and profoundly unhealthy relationship to slenderness. I watch a woman hiss at her reflection in the mirror, grab at her own flesh with revulsion, pour the fifth packet of Equal into her iced tea. And I can't help but see Leslie as the embodiment of a paradigm shift, one that many women could learn something from. She sits tall in her chair, as though proud to take up so much space. She speaks with an authority that belies her age. There is nothing passive about her, nothing fragile or weak or non-threatening or deferentially hesitant. In Leslie, you see something exceedingly rare in this culture: size, heft, and not an ounce of apology.

4

FROM BRA BURNING TO BINGE SHOPPING

APPETITE
AND THE ZEITGEIST

I HAVE BEEN KNOWN TO say I rowed my way out of anorexia, which is partly true. In the summer of 1985, I discovered sculling on the Charles River, a rigorous, insanely exacting sport and an endeavor that very gradually began to coax my sense of the body in a new direction. A skinny woman atop a skinny boat, poised to learn something about strength, and confidence, and the nature of power.

There was nothing the least bit deliberate about this. I'd moved to Boston the previous fall, leaving Providence not so much because I had a clear goal in mind, and certainly not out of any wish to take up obscure water sports, but because I sensed I'd die if I stayed there, the rut of starving had grown so deep, the style so entrenched, the sense of stagnation so oppressive. Anorexia takes on such an airless, empty, mind-numbing sameness over time, life at a flat-line, each hour each minute each breath punctuated by the ache of hunger; each decision dictated by it; each day a grinding replica of the one before, same minuscule breakfast, same tiny lunch, same non-dinner, same cripplingly predictable chain of thought, a closed circle that begins

and ends with no: No no no no . . . maybe . . . will you won't you
. . . how much . . . can't . . . no no no. I put whatever energy re-
serves I had during those years into work. Beyond that, not
much: a lot of TV.

The move to Boston forced a slight loosening of anorexia's vice-
grip, catalyzed tiny changes, all of which I resisted. I rented an
apartment in a western suburb, and I remember trying to replicate
my old rituals from Providence, every detail: I spent weeks trying to
find a deli that sold bagels like the ones I'd eaten daily for the previous three years; I looked for a shop that consistently carried Dannon coffee-flavored yogurt, my lunch of choice; I set up my
bedroom just so—TV here, bed there, close attention paid to every
angle—so that I could sit in the exact same physical position I'd sat
in Providence while I watched TV and ate my apple and cheese.
None of it worked quite the same way; the bagels tasted different,
the stores all seemed to stock vanilla yogurt and not coffee, or
Columbo and not Dannon, the light in my new bedroom was not
the same as the light in my old bedroom, and even these tiny
changes felt unnerving, a jarring erosion of the solace of ritual.

On some level, too, I must have recognized the inanity of the
effort, of trying to duplicate something so profoundly self-
limiting. Within several months of moving to Boston, I got hired
as a reporter for a newspaper that covered the local business
community; the staff was larger than it had been at my old newspaper and I found it harder to cling to my old routines in front of
them: impossible to eat my yogurt in my practiced style—tiny
measured spoonfuls—in the midst of so many people, distressing
to turn down invitations to join the others for lunch or drinks after work, and disheartening to be aware of *wanting* to turn them
down. Ambivalence crept into the edges of my rigor, some wish
to rejoin the world asserted itself, and for a long time, I danced
back and forth across the line of deprivation I'd drawn so deeply
in the sand, clung to anorexia's deep familiarity, then released,
then clung again. I'd join my colleagues for lunch and eat a normal amount (a sandwich, or soup and bread) but return to the

apple-and-cheese for dinner. I'd go out to dinner, eat a regular meal, then eat nothing or next to nothing the following day. As I had in the year prior to full-blown starving, I'd binge here, starve there, a few steps forward, a few steps back.

The impulse to retreat was constant, the simple matter of gaining weight terrifying. Even the most minute shift—the jeans just slightly more snug in the thighs, the face just slightly less hollow beneath the cheekbones—could make me feel panicked and invaded—fat creeping in, I could practically *feel* it, oozing into legs and arms and belly, undoing all that painstaking work, dismantling that carefully constructed temple of angle and bone, leaving me with that old sensation of terrifying boundlessness and self-mistrust. If I let myself go, how unstoppable might I be, how much weight might I gain? And who would I turn out to be? That's what I remember most clearly from those years, the post-anorexic riddle of identity, a sense of wild shapelessness, as though a thousand different questions had been thrown open at once, all of them unanswerable, even the tiniest ones. A work friend would ask me to dinner, and I'd writhe with indecision: Did I want to? And if I didn't, was the reluctance about fear of human contact or fear of food? Often, I honestly couldn't tell.

The one unequivocally bright spot on that horizon emerged, quite inadvertently, over the Charles River. My sister had pointed me in that direction: She'd come over during a particularly bleak period that spring and tried to cajole me into making a list of things that might make me feel better, activities, hobbies, anything to coax me out of my own head. Characteristically, I found the idea moronic (Hobbies? What, like *needlepoint?*), but then one of us hit on the idea of rowing. Sculling: long sleek delicate crafts, skimming across the water like perfectly skipped stones. I'd gone to high school across the street from the Charles, so I'd grown up watching rowers on the river, and the sight of them must have lodged in my consciousness, an image of power and grace and symmetry that held out some deep appeal. My sister mentioned that a local university had a summer rowing program; in a completely atypical fit of spontaneity, I called and signed up; in a slightly less atypical act of determination, I followed through and took the course.

Maneuvering a single shell is like trying to stay upright on a giant knitting needle, and from the beginning I think I was aware that rowing offered an alternative challenge, something to master besides my own weight. A typical boat is twenty-six feet long and less than a foot wide; balance is either assisted or impeded by the oars, which measure about nine feet each. It's like an aquatic version of tightrope walking, a merciless and unforgiving sport that requires nerve and enormous precision, and it captivated me utterly. All summer I watched good rowers glide by on the water, their strength echoed in the steady *woosh* of water against hull, their power seemingly effortless. I watched them lift their single shells out of the water at the end of a row, hoisting them up from the edge of the dock to the top of their heads in a single arcing motion, something as graceful and controlled as a piece of ballet. And I studied their bodies: strong bodies, muscular thighs and ropy arms; bodies that moved with confidence and ease; bodies that seemed to reflect the possession of something unimaginable to me, a deep and hard-won joy.

I was nothing like those rowers for years. I flailed on the water, jerked and teetered, held the oars in a blistering death grip, nearly flipped the boat on every outing. But as it turns out, I had the right personality style (rowers, not unlike anorexics, are a fairly compulsive population) and I stuck with it. I rowed and rowed, wobbled and floundered, hacked my way up and down that river hundreds of times, and very gradually, I learned. The muscles in my arms and legs and back began to do what they were supposed to do; my motions became fluid and smooth instead of choppy and tense. And slowly, over the course of several years, I began to feel something I may never quite have felt as a woman before, which was integrated and strong and whole, the body as a piece, the body as responsive and connected to the mind, the body as a worthy place to live.

Oddly enough, for a woman born and raised in a changing world, a climate in which old assumptions about women were being challenged daily, this may have been my first truly radical-izing experience—perhaps even a feminist one.

Timing, as they say, is everything. I've always considered my-self a feminist and yet in some very defining ways, I missed the feminist boat entirely, missed large passages on what I think of as the truly transformative parts of the journey. This may be a ro-mantic assumption about the heyday of second-wave feminism, but I've always believed, perhaps naively, that if I'd reached my college years in 1968 instead of 1978, I might have turned out quite differently, developed a more radicalized view of myself and other women, found my sense of the personal and the politi-cal more intricately entwined. The second wave, after all, was in so many respects about appetite, about demanding the freedom to take in: sexual freedom, legal freedom, economic freedom, the freedom to be as ambitious or headstrong or entitled as any man, the freedom to hunger and to satisfy hunger in all its varied forms. I am something of a *zeitgeist* sheep, and I suspect this pow-ers my romanticized view. If I'd been twenty-one during the Summer of Love, might I have gone to Woodstock, moved to Haight-Ashbury, marched and rallied my way into a healthier view of my self, my body, my appetite? Might I have fought not against my own flesh but against actual, external enemies, the "establishment," the patriarchy, the Vietnam war?

Such questions may be unanswerable, but I think they're im-portant; they have to do with feminism's reach, and about what happened to that movement on behalf of female hunger, and about how the struggle for freedom did—and did not—transform the experience of appetite for women of my generation. There's no question that I'm a classic heiress of feminism, that second-wave activism shaped my sense of possibilities in countless ways, that it gave me both the intellectual and practical wherewithal to satisfy all manner of hungers. And yet for all that, I remained somehow immune to its transformative potential, some sense of its collective and radicalizing power never quite made it to the gut level. As a journalist in Providence, I was particularly drawn toward stories about women's issues: I wrote about discrimination, abortion, violence against women. I wrote about women's health, sexism in the media, cultural imagery. I even wrote about women (other women) with eating disorders. And quietly, privately, I starved myself half to death. There you have it: intellectual belief without the correlary emotional roots; feminist power understood in the mind but not known, somehow, in the body.

I've noticed this phenomenon, this sense of missing a key of sorts, primarily in contrasts; women friends just ten or fifteen years older than I, particularly those who spent their college and young adult years in cities with large activist communities like Boston, San Francisco, and New York, seem to have absorbed feminist beliefs at an almost cellular level, the internal shifts wrought in dramatic and durable ways, which seems to me the essence of revolutionary change. There's a visceral quality to their accounts that I find deeply enviable: stories of scales falling from the eyes and belief systems up-ended and reinvented; stories about founding feminist presses and women's health care advocacy groups, about rejecting unenlightened husbands and repressive assumptions about female sexuality, about joining women's groups, talking honestly and graphically for the first time about what it meant to inhabit a female body. Context feels vital in such tales—time and place and the power of collective energy—and whenever I hear about a woman's sixties-style personal revolution, the image of an earthquake often comes to mind, a massive tectonic shift that may have altered the landscape permanently but that also affected the women in mid-tremor quite differently from those who arrived on the scene later, after the dust had settled, or who weren't standing directly on the fault lines when the quake first hit.

In the late 1960s, when the earth was rumbling, I was still in elementary school: nine, ten years old. In the mid-1970s, when women ten and fifteen years my senior were talking in earnest about women's health and reproductive freedom and sexuality, I was in high school, not generally the most enlightened period in a person's life; my own feelings about the body were immune to the political climate, defined instead by decidedly non-feminist concerns: zits, breast size, the approval of boys. And by the 1980s, which spanned both my starving and early recovery years, feminism had gone into its long (and on-going) period of re-trenchment, its momentum dwindled, its unity given way to fragmentation and backlash. The tenor of the times had changed dramatically by then—these were the having-it-all years, the decade of *Dynasty* and Reagan-Bush—and so had the dominant cultural constructions of appetite. Feminism defined hunger broadly, its focus encompassing a woman's sexuality, ambition, economic life, legal freedoms. Consumerism, the ethos that washed over the landscape in its wake, defines hunger in the narrowest terms, as the desire for quick fixes, external solutions, things.

This was the mindset that seemed to affect me most dramati-cally, leached into consciousness in a way that feminism hadn't quite had time to. I may have managed to row my way into some sense of personal empowerment during those years. But some of my most essential feelings about appetite—the body, its sexuality and its value, its link to emotional well-being—remained stub-bornly unaffected for a long time, lodged in a past that wasn't quite touched by feminism, and in a present that was guided by an entirely different sensibility.

My formal education about the body took place in 1971, just two years after the Summer of Love and two years before the passage of *Roe v. Wade*, in a sixth-grade classroom in Cam-bridge, Massachusetts. Outside, the world was crackling with activist energy; inside, it was not. Sex ed, for my peers and me, consisted of a single lecture on menstruation given by the school principal, a tall forbidding woman with hair the color of steel wool. Her name was Mrs. Morse. She separated the girls from the boys for one hour, stood at the front of the class, and used a pointer to familiarize us with the female reproductive system, detailed on a large poster. These are the fallopian tubes, she said. This is the uterus. She told us how eggs got fertilized by sperm, and she talked at some length about the lining of the uterine wall, and just before she moved onto cramps and Kotex pads, she spent a few minutes talking about the act of sex itself. This part was vague: a few words about hormones and changing bodily sensations; some cautionary sentiments about boys, whose hormones apparently would affect them more dramatically than ours would; and the briefest suggestion that sex could be an expression of feeling between people who loved each other. I believe she used the word "pleasurable," but she said this with so much reticence and strain she might as well have been describing a periodontal procedure.

This is a textbook example of what some feminist scholars call the "missing discourse of desire" among and in regard to adolescent girls. Girls of my generation did not—and girls for the most part still do not—receive a lot of honest information about the body, particularly the female sexual body and the subject of its arousal. This is an old taboo, culturally and academically. Freud never explored the subject of female sexuality, dismissing it in his infamous phrase as "a dark continent." Most major theories of adolescent development have ignored it, as though sexual feelings don't really play much of a role in the lives of girls. Even feminist theorists have tended to steer clear of the subject, and the silence on all fronts has been both deafening and deeply disconnecting. The French philosopher Michel Foucault first popularized the idea that discourse about sexuality can significantly shape sexual experience, noting that the language and tone we use when we talk about sex, the things we hear or (equally important) do not hear, have a direct impact on the way we register, interpret, and respond to our own bodily feelings. When you hear nothing about the body, he suggests, you stop listening to it, and feeling it; you stop experiencing it as a worthy, integrated entity.

Despite the activism bubbling around us, girls of my generation received a fairly classic education about the body, which is
to say a non-education, not so different from one we might have
gotten in 1950s middle America. Female sexuality, we learned,
was primarily a medical event; new equipment would be required; a fair amount of blood would be involved; boys were the
ones with the big (and possibly scary) drives. Our own drives,
meanwhile, went undiscussed, grade school through high
school. Our teachers did not broach the subject of female
arousal, neither did our parents. No one—adults, peers—ever
uttered the words masturbation, clitoris, or orgasm. Presumably,
this was not necessary information: Girls did not get aroused; we
did not need to learn much about our sexual appetites because
we didn't have them, or, at least, we weren't supposed to.

This is one of the reasons culture would assume such defining
influence in our lives; into that vacuum of information, into the
hole left by the lack of straightforward discussion about what sex
was or could be like, seeped messages from the world around us,
which we could see and hear with increasing clarity. Culture was
poised just then for a major shift in tone and focus, a particularly
visual and intense brand of consumerism gaining prominence, its
tidal wave of high-speed visuals beginning to build, and this is
what we glommed onto. Scrambling to make sense of our bodies,
we absorbed the imagery from ads and movies and TV, which
consisted (then, as now) of visual statements about physical
beauty and sexual powerlessness: young women with immature
bodies and detached gazes, women who appeared highly sexualized but only in the most commoditized and disembodied way.
We paid careful attention to boys, who in turn paid careful attention to our body parts, covertly measured and ranked us by
beauty and breast size. We adopted the equipment and tools of
adult sexuality—the bras, the razors, the pots of lip gloss, the
lacy underwear—but our attention was continually coaxed outward, our early educations in self-scrutiny advanced, our eyes focused on the smooth skin of our calves, the curves of our hips

and waists, the presence or absence of body fat and pimples, deflected along the way from whatever sense of bodily integrity we may have been born with or experienced at younger ages.

We learned, in short, the lessons that imagery would merely reinforce and keep alive over the years. We did not learn how to feel or experience our bodies, how to appreciate our own strengths, how to value or respect or understand the packages we came in. Instead, we learned how to look at them, to pair sexuality with desirability, to measure the worth of our bodies by their capacity to elicit admiration from others. In a word, we learned to dissociate, which is what such an experience of the body requires: Sexuality in this construction is located not within the self—within one's own body and bodily sensations—but within someone else; the ignition must be turned with a key. To *be* sexy is to be *found* sexy, to be permitted to want, you must first be wanted.

I can remember all too well what this felt like, sexuality less a matter of feeling sexual than of being perceived as sexual. My first high school boyfriend was a hockey player named Steve who also played drums in a band, both activities that designated him as very cool, neither of which interested me a whit. No matter. He singled me out at a party and we spent what felt like an interminable evening making out on a sofa in the basement. We were both stoned and I don't remember feeling much of anything except a muted pride over having been "chosen," a tacit understanding that I was to stay there on the sofa with him until he determined it was time to stop, and then some vague embarrassment when I emerged from the basement with my hair a mess and my shirt all twisted. From then on, Steve and I "went out," if you can call it that, for about six months, which basically meant we spent a lot of time making out after school. I felt shy to the point of muteness around him; we'd walk to a nearby cemetery in the afternoons and barely talk, just plod along in a disconnected fog staring at our feet. The silence felt like excruciating evidence of failure on my part: Quite clearly, my job was to be bubbly and outgoing and interesting, to draw him out and make myself alluring, and instead I was deadly dull, a voiceless blob. Making out with him felt like failure, too, because my body seemed so unresponsive. Steve pawed at me, and his mouth was spitty, and his interest—physical or otherwise—seemed to have little to do with me or who I was. So I'd just lie there, not sure which was more oppressive, the making out or the painfully shy silences that fell before and afterward. Not once did it occur to me that we simply had nothing in common, or that he might be the boring one, or that feeling sexual required more than the presence of a hulking, uncommunicative hockey player. Nor did it occur to me to break up with him. I waited for him to do that, which he did in due time, dispatching a friend to deliver the news. When I got the message, I felt like I'd been fired, but I also felt relieved.

This was such a typical scenario in high school, at least it was for me, and such an achingly complicated one, like negotiating the most perilous highway. The hunger of boys was so vivid and clear, expected, accepted as fact, and ours was so dangerous and secretive and fraught with consequence. To give into his hunger would brand us as sluts; to withhold too much would make us prudes. And so, if we were to retain any power at all, we had to master the most delicate balancing act, learning without any in-struction at all to both provoke and control his hunger, to satisfy it just enough to maintain both his interest and our social posi-tion. Our own hunger? Our own pleasure? We didn't talk about it. And if we thought about it at all, its place on the priority list was very low.

Deborah Tolman, a Harvard University psychologist who studies adolescent female sexuality, has witnessed the effects of this silence first hand: A girl's sexual impulses and hungers, she writes, become "the feelings that no one names." She is not taught that it's permissible or natural to have a sexual appetite. She is not introduced to the idea that she has a right to sexual pleasure, nor to the possibility that men and women have differ-ent sexual needs; often, she is not even told about her clitoris.

Without language with which to discuss or understand or question her body, sexuality becomes a puzzle, her arousal a mystery and a taboo. A common response, according to Tolman, is to simply turn the appetite off. "Many girls," she notes, "may in fact solve the dilemma of their own sexual desire in the face of a culture that does not acknowledge their bodies by not feeling those feelings."

I suspect my response as a teenager was a variation on that theme: surges of feeling that often stopped dead in their tracks. I certainly didn't lack erotic sensation in my teens and early twenties; the hormones raged, a boy could hold my hand or touch my breast and my whole body would be flooded by an astonished, tingly wash of feeling, the physical system was intact and operational. But it shut down easily, as though barbed wire had sprung up around the part of the meadow where deep, internal bodily sensation lived, separating sex and eros. The boy's touch would turn to pawing; the balancing act—how much to give, how much to withhold—would begin; the mind would start to take flight from the body, which itself was shrouded in so much silence and mystery. And erotic feeling—this deep, private, magical, gleaming thing—seemed to fly off with it, as though it had woken from a dream and found it had no place to go: no safe place, no place where it was encouraged, understood, held, made to feel special, no place where it was allowed to be talked about or coaxed gently into the room. I could be desired, I could (and did) covet that feeling of being chosen, and I could act the part, making out in boys' cars and in dark corners at parties. But sexuality felt less like a physical pleasure than an out-of-body experience, less like a mode of expression than an award to win, a performance.

Performance, of course, is not the same as satisfaction. Permission is not the same as agency; the ability to say yes is not the same as the ability to say yes, with him but not with him, or yes, like this but not like that. The sexual revolution, in full bloom by the time I hit high school, seems to have given the girls in my circle a half-filled tool kit, an ability to act sexual without much of a corresponding sense of what it really meant to *be* sexual, a door that opened into a poorly-lit room. This may have been a by-product of the difference (which was considerable) between the sexual revolution, which advocated freedom of expression in the most love-the-one-you're-with general way, and the women's movement, where activism tilted toward the more tangible arenas of reproductive freedom and sexual health. In the mid-seventies, women all over the city were actively engaged on those fronts—they were attending conferences on abortion and birth control, they were bringing home speculums and examining their own cervixes on kitchen tables; they were writing *Our Bodies, Ourselves* in an office not two miles from my back yard—and their efforts certainly trickled down to my peers and me. They equipped us with birth control pills and information about sexually transmitted diseases. They gave us gynecologists who would answer questions if we were brave enough to ask them. They gave us at least a rudimentary sense that sex was something we were allowed to do. But they went only so far. What did not trickle down—what may have never quite crystallized within the movement itself—was a deeper sense of empowered desire, a construction of female sexual pleasure as an end in and of itself, a *yes* articulated in our own voices.

What might it have been like to feel that we could do the choosing instead being chosen? How might we have felt if we'd been raised to talk as openly about our sexual appetites as we were about our appetites for food and clothing, if we'd been encouraged to scrutinize and understand our actual sexual bodies—how they worked, what they needed, how they responded to touch—instead of their tangential sexual parts, the shape of the breasts, the size of the thighs? That kind of framework was not in our consciousness—and wouldn't be, for many of us, until we were well into our thirties and forties, a time in a woman's life when the concept of agency, grappled with over many years, finally settles into the bones. But back then, talking directly about our own bodies seemed inconceivable; sexuality was a freedom that terrified as much as it tempted, and so it became a minefield we pretended not to inhabit. We didn't name the mines—this one is fear, this one is power, that one is raw hormonal energy—and we most certainly weren't equipped to defuse them, and what I remember most pointedly from those years is a terrific sense of discord, a feeling reinforced by all those unraised and unanswered questions, as though the sexuality of women, my sexuality, had been left on the back burner somehow, undiscussed and uncharted and ultimately understood to be less important than the sexuality of men.

Which, to an extent, it was. Had any feminist theory about sexual politics reached me during those years, I might have gathered that men's bodies have a long and deeply rooted history of eclipsing women's bodies in the collective consciousness, that for decades both our cultural and medical definitions of sexual "normalcy" have been based exclusively on male sexual function, male needs, male equipment. Feminist sex researchers have argued about the persistence of this thinking throughout the twentieth century: From Masters and Johnson to the American Medical Association, they claim, the dominant research bodies have relied overwhelmingly on the sexual behavior and interests of young, white, middle-class, able-bodied, heterosexual men, a bias that ignores female bodies entirely and frames healthy sexuality in the narrowest possible genital terms, as an ability to achieve orgasm during intercourse. Women have been expected not only to accept that paradigm but also to adjust their own needs and expectations to it: To be sexually "normal," many women learn, is to be as goal-oriented and genitally focused as a man—or, at least, to mirror and amplify his goal orientation and focus. In the prevailing view, writes Lenore Tiefer, a New York–based psychiatrist, urologist, and sex researcher, "normalcy can be easily summarized: men and women are the same and they're all men."

This notion *did* trickle down, and far more vividly than any ideas about female sexual empowerment. Am I acting the right way? Is this what he wants? How is *he* feeling? In the absence of any sense that it was permissible or even possible to focus on my own body and my own hunger, these became the great preoccupying questions, matters of performance that would actually grow more tormenting as I got a little older and *should* have, I felt, become wiser, more confident, and sexually adept. The disconnected gropings in high school were followed by disconnected sexual encounters in college, blank and invariably alcohol-fueled affairs that tended to be high on passivity and need for validation, low on agency and pleasure. There were exceptions to this rule—men I loved, men with whom I felt safe enough to let down my guard—but I certainly didn't outrun the feeling that sexuality had to do with pleasing men, nor did I outrun the feeling that my own body was somehow secondary, that his body—his hunger, his orgasm—was the important thing, that my satisfaction would be or at least should be directly related to his. Men's bodies worked, it seemed, and they worked properly and efficiently and normally, and if mine couldn't work the same way, with the same urgency and focus, that must have indicated some failure on my part.

This is a terrible way to learn about the body, living under a curtain of voicelessness and uncertainty, taking all your cues from boys who harbor their own unarticulated feelings and insecurities and agendas, trying to tap into their hunger while yours retreats to a distant corner. And feminist gains aside, it remains a woefully standard lesson, one that never quite got buried in the earthquake's rubble. A (very) young woman I know, a fifteen-year-old high school sophomore named Jessie, tells me a story about a recent sexual escapade: She'd gone to a party, had a fair amount to drink, and ended up in bed with two boys from the soccer team, one of them a junior. She appears rather nonchalant about this—she uses the words "weird" and "fun"—and her description seems to encapsulate something about the sexual revolution's legacy, how much it's given girls and also how little. Jessie has buckets of permission, far more than I did at her age, and in some respects the freedom has served her well: She's grown up in a climate of vastly increased sexual tolerance; she appears less mystified by her own sexuality than I was at her age, or at least less inhibited; and she seems, to some extent, to have an easier, more natural relationship with her body, courtesy of both a post–Title IX athletic bravado and a slightly solidified sense of female entitlement.

But Jessie also suggests how easily permission can mutate into pressure, and how hollow it can be if it's not bolstered by honest dialogue and wisdom. In her book *The Body Project*, Joan Jacobs Brumberg, a professor of history, human development, and women's studies at Cornell University, describes a fundamental crisis in the most physical aspects of contemporary female adolescent life, with both biology and culture encouraging behaviors and attitudes toward the body that girls may not be emotionally ready for. Girls appear to be physically maturing at earlier ages today, and they are certainly sexualized at earlier ages: Weaned on Madonna, surrounded by sexual imagery, they live in an intensely explicit and visual sexual culture; more parts of their own bodies are adorned and on display; the race to lose virginity is far more heated than it was during my adolescence, with nearly half of all teenagers making it across the finish line by age sixteen. All of this takes place, Jacobs Brumberg argues, in a context with precious few social protections, which leaves girls unsupported in their development and vulnerable both to peer pressure and to the excesses of popular culture. Referring to the repressive but also protective attitudes toward female sexuality in the Victorian era, she writes: "As a society, we discarded the Victorian moral umbrella around girls before we agreed upon useful strategies or programs [to replace it]—a kind of social Gore-Tex to help them stay dry."

Jessie is an example, which is what came to mind when she told me about her night with the two soccer players. A little shocked by her story, I started hinting around about issues of desire and control: Did she do this because she felt she had to or because she really wanted to? Did she know she could say "no" to these two boys? Was the sex about what they wanted or what she wanted?

"Oh, it was what I wanted," she assured me, but I couldn't help sensing an old narrative at work: female desire shaped and defined by male desire; sexual wants linked to pleasing others; the old tyranny of sexual repression replaced by its opposite, a tyranny of sexual permission in which young girls learn to see erotic expression as a personal goal long before they've developed a clear, individual, or even remotely adult definition of the term. A little while later, Jessie told me more about one of the boys, the junior, whose name was Marshall. She'd had a crush on him for weeks. He was "totally hot," a rising star on the soccer field. She hadn't heard from him since the party, but she hoped he'd call ("I'm taking my cell phone *everywhere*," she said, tapping her coat pocket). I also managed to glean that before the party, they'd only spoken two or three times.

I doubt this plot line is unique. Most kids today (about 89 percent) will get some kind of sex education between grades seven and twelve, but in about half the cases, this will consist of a single class, not unlike mine with Mrs. Morse. More often, sex ed gets folded into health classes, where discussion of physical arousal and intimacy is eclipsed (if taken up at all) by talk of STDs, AIDS, or abstinence, currently the preferred approach in more than 4,000 school districts. Not surprisingly, in a Kaiser Foundation study on sex education conducted in 2000, almost half of all teens surveyed said they needed more information about how to deal with the emotional issues and consequences of sex. As was the case in my generation, most teenagers still get the majority of their information about sex from each other and from the media, where the operating definitions of sexuality are as limited and paper-thin as ever.

This is particularly true on the man-pleasing front. *Glamour* magazine runs a feature called "43 'Don't-Stop's He's Dying To Try Tonight." *Cosmo* offers, "Be the Best Sex of His Life—How to Tease Him Mercilessly, Seduce Him Slowly, Then Rock His

World in Ways He's only Dreamed About!" *Redbook*, oddly obsessed with numbers as well as sex, provides, "Six Little Moves
That Will Make Your Sex Life Hotter"; "Five Amazing Sex
Tricks Every Woman Should Know"; "Ten Instant Tips for Better Sex"; and "Thirty-Five Sexy Places to Touch Your Man."
This is standard fare—stories about *him, your man*, what *he's* dying to do—and I suspect they spring from the same river of silence and uncertainty that surrounded female sexual appetite
when I was growing up. Certainly, they propose the same solution: If your own hunger is elusive—unknown, undiscussed, not
quite permitted to exist on its own terms—focus on his: Look
the right way and (more important) act the right way.

Lost in that solution, now as then, is any notion that sexual
knowledge should be mutual, that female pleasure might depend
on more than the ability to incite male pleasure. Lost, too, any
sense of what it might be like to talk about female pleasure in
more complicated or meaningful ways—let alone more helpful
ones. In its 1999 report on sexual dysfunction, the *Journal of the
American Medical Association* cited lack of interest in sex the
most common problem among women: About a third of respon-
dents in the *JAMA* study said they regularly didn't want sex,
twenty-six percent reported they regularly didn't have orgasms,
and twenty-three percent said sex wasn't pleasurable. Right
around the time that report came out, *Glamour* magazine's cover
featured a story called "Fifty Tricks for Outstanding Orgasms,"
which turned out to be a rundown of directors' cues, lighting
tricks, and sexy soundtracks filched from Hollywood movies. For
"raw, rip-off-my-clothes-and-take-me-now sex," the magazine
advised, simply pop in a tape of Prince's "Purple Rain." If you
need a good "'do-me' costume," try a skin-tight tanktop and pair
of pants made from the same material used to make garden hoses
(Carrie-Anne Moss wore one in *The Matrix*). And if you're feeling shaky about your allure, just lie on your side; according to director Steven Soderbergh, women look better that way: "The
S-shape curve of the body is the most erotic line."

Whether such techniques do anything to advance a woman's satisfaction is unaddressed, presumably because it's beside the point. As *Cosmo* so aptly summed it up, the goal is to be the best sex of *his* life.

If sex, in my teens and early twenties, felt like an increasingly complicated game with daunting rules and no meaningful instructions, anorexia took me off the playing field altogether. Extremes of fat and thin have this effect: It is profoundly desexualizing to pare away curves or bury them under flesh, and this may help explain why eating disorders are showing up in girls at younger and younger ages—there's something deeply self-protective about walking away from the sexual game, and no doubt something deeply tempting about doing so when the stakes feel so high and pressure-filled.

Fearful and disconnected from my body to begin with, I suspect a part of me welcomed this aspect of anorexia, needed and fueled the sense of cool metallic asexuality it offered. I used to run during those years, two- or three-mile stints that had the quality of forced marches, mandatory and punitive. I'd lace up my sneakers with dread, and I'd set out through the streets on the east side of Providence, and I'd *push*, each step a contest of will, the whole body tense and resisting, the matchstick legs wanting so badly to stop. The neighborhoods I ran through were lovely—serene and leafy and lined with elegant Victorians—but I didn't really notice them, or take any pleasure in them. I focused on my feet, and on those skinny thighs, pumping pumping pumping, and I thought about calories: 100 burned per mile, the equivalent of half a container of yogurt; 200 for two miles, lunch. The body was a machine, or at least I wanted it to be: a system to be scrutinized and tinkered with, its input and output to be measured and controlled, its pain to be considered collateral, its capacity for pleasure irrelevant. The libido vanished along with flesh; sensuality became a distant memory, something other people experienced. I lived in my head, and only my head.

Very slowly, rowing began to alter that paradigm, which is why it seems radicalizing in retrospect, a first step toward a working relationship with my own body, instead of a battle. It changed me. Over time, I developed arms, strong and capable ones. My forearms grew firm and sinewy. My upper arms became toned, then defined, my shoulders round and strong. Rowing is actually considered a leg sport—a lot of the power of the stroke comes from the large muscles of thigh and butt—but the changes in my upper body were more visible to me, and in many ways more important, each sign of physical strength both correlating to and fueling a sensation of internal strength. That first summer, my own personal Summer of Love, I used to slip into the ladies' room at work and secretly flex my biceps in front of the mirror, and the little thrill this gave me (muscles!) was utterly distinct from the thrill I'd once felt at my own emaciation, as different as self-care is from self-destruction, as giving is from withholding. The shift was indeed dramatic; since I'd begun obsessing about food, this was the first physical transformation I'd not undertaken in the service of slenderness.

Which is not to say that rowing single-handedly propelled me out of anorexia, or that it filled me with unconditional love for my own body, or that I burst forth from the river with strong arms and a newly feminized heart. Hardly. Recovery from eating disorders is an inherently murky and nonlinear process, motivation hard to assess, progress hard to quantify, and relapse hard to define. You can't simply "stop" being anorexic or bulimic the way you quit drinking or give up drugs; you remain in constant and necessary contact with food, you have to make choices about it every day. Not atypically, there was nothing deliberate about my own path away from starving. I had no moment of sudden clarity or grace, no blinding transformation in which the wish to starve was replaced by the wish to change, I never woke up one day and said, *Enough,* nor did I outline or follow any specific post-anorexia program: Eat that amount of food, gain this amount of weight. Instead, the obsession with food loosened by slight degrees. I rowed. I went into therapy. I ate a tiny bit more, put on a pound, two pounds, five. Over time, the old system simply fell apart, eroded, became too stultifying and oppressive to maintain, and I recall the sensation of watching this happen, knowing I no longer had the will or energy to starve or the commitment to self-destruct but not really knowing how to live differently, how to make choices, how to define and respond to hunger.

This was deeply destabilizing, a gradual untethering of identity, like realizing your boat has come loose from its mooring and is drifting out to a dark sea. I spent a lot of time clinging to past behaviors and groping blindly for new ones, a puzzle in search of a grid. Who was I? What did I want? If starving didn't fix me, what would? To an extent, this wild, grasping sensation goes with the addictive territory: Anorexics, like all addicts (and to some degree like most humans), are masters at seeking external solutions to internal sources of emptiness and distress, their lives dictated by a grand, encompassing hunt that revolves around a single phrase, *if only*. If only I lost another pound, and then another, and another. If only I ate a little less. If only I grew thinner. If only, if only, if only. This is useless thinking and I knew it—even mid-anorexia, I understood that the weight itself was essentially inconsequential, that I'd hideously inflated its importance, that the loss of a pound here or a pound there would not leave me with beauty or happiness, or protect me from anxiety or sorrow. But it is powerful thinking, too; the words beckoned with terrible force—if only, if only, as though this futile pursuit might actually take me somewhere I wanted to go, or yield a reward, a victory at the finish, a pot of gold at the end of that thin, thin rainbow.

What seems poignant to me today, and also deeply unfortunate, is the way in which that central addictive feeling—that sense of ravenous displaced need—not only lingered within me as I began to eat again, but also dovetailed with the times. If only, if only: By the mid-1980s, this had become a cultural mantra, as well as a personal one, the deflection of hunger writ large and etched on plastic. Forget about the feminist sisterhood;

by the time I began to re-enter the human social world, women were connecting not over politics and placards but over Prada and Evan Piccone, shared visions suddenly less cementing than shared aesthetics ("*Love* your shoes!"). Forget about activism: The impetus for social change began to vanish during those years in a haze of self-help workshops and how-to books, the long social view supplanted by the quick-fix tweaking of the inner child. And forget about such thorny issues as female sexuality and empowered desire: Bra burning, such as it was, gave way to binge shopping.

But isn't this what Americans do best, the pursuit of happiness reconfigured as the pursuit of *stuff*, the diet, the toys, the boys, the magic bullet? And isn't this what women, in particular, are encouraged to do? Find it, buy it, marry it, change it, hunt it down, wrap it in a pretty package and take it home: *It* may be a mirage, vast and ungraspable as mist, but the reach for easy solutions is in many respects the American way, our culture's instinctive response to discomfort, and this form of displacement reached a stunning peak, and unprecedented intensity, in the eighties and nineties. In the last twenty years, Americans have become the most consumer-oriented population in modern history, spending three to four times as many hours shopping as Western Europeans, consuming more than $5 trillion worth of goods and services a year (more than double the consumption rate in the 1960s) and racking up a staggering amount of credit card debt (60 percent more than we incurred ten years ago). Behind such numbers, of course, is the very sense of wild need that so persistently drove me: a constant push to externalize, a clinging belief in the idea that every problem has an immediate solution, that every void can be filled with a product, a substance, *something*.

As a culture, we may have hit the wall on spending, or at least *a* wall: The fat, complacent America of the mid-1980s has vanished to an extent, the fantasy of instant millions as bankrupt as a dot.com start-up, the notion that every generation will fare better than the one before as battered as the Dow Jones on a bad day, our historic sense of invulnerability largely buried in the rubble of the World Trade Center. But we have not hit the wall on displacement, and perhaps never will. Whether we're in the middle of a recession, a war, or a decade of Wall Street decadence, Americans have a long history of casting desire in the most tangible terms, well-being viewed as a commodity that can be bought, built, even medicated into existence, threats to well-being always (and in some respects increasingly) identified as starkly external. Depression is the problem; we have a drug for that. Fear is the problem; we can name the enemy (Soviet one day, Middle Eastern the next) and we can root him out.

As for murkier problems—emptiness, alienation, frustration, insecurity—we have a store for that, many stores, each one of them bursting with balm. This is the seduction, the velvety promise of consumer culture—*fix what ails with a product; look outside the self*—and if our spending power is somewhat diminished today, our tendency to transform emotional longings into material ones is not. We now live in a country in which four billion square feet of the total land area has been converted into shopping centers, about sixteen square feet for every man, woman, and child. We are awash in easy credit, eternally tempted by plastic apples: In 1995 alone, financial institutions sent out more than two and a half billion preapproved credit card applications, which means that if you're an American between the ages of eighteen and sixty-four, you received seventeen of them in the mail. And we live and breathe information, consumer culture's courier, its steady whispers of promise so integral to day-to-day living and so mercilessly reinforced it's easy to forget where the word "consume" comes from (once upon a time, the verb meant "to waste, to eat up, to destroy"). It's easy, too, to forget how efficiently a consumer mindset can imbue objects with meanings and capabilities far beyond their essence (Zest, in our world, can be lathered on with a bar of soap, empowerment swooshed on with a pair of Nikes), easier still to forget how much it can both feed and shape one's baseline sense of hunger. I want becomes I *want*. And then I *want* becomes I want *that*.

In some critical respects, the very definition of satiety has changed in the last few decades, as well, I *want* gradually mutating into I *need*. The gap between the haves and the have-nots began to widen in the eighties (it's a chasm today); middle-income workers like me suddenly found ourselves looking at a landscape populated by extremely high earners within more and more occupations (finance, real estate, sports, advertising, and media); the sudden visibility of the super-rich, paired with growing insecurity in the middle class, raised the bar on well-being, ratcheting up the collective sense of what it meant to be successful and satisfied and secure. Working at a business publication during those years gave me a close-up look at this shift: I both worked for such high earners and spent most of my time interviewing them—rich, middle-aged white guys who drove Porsche 911s and wore made-to-order Italian suits and drank $400 bottles of Chateau Latour—and I could almost feel the concept of keeping up with the Joneses begin to wither and die. People like me no longer measured ourselves against the folks next door. We looked at people at work, who often made two, three, or ten times as much as we did, and by portrayals, real and fictionalized, of people on TV and in magazine profiles.

I remember writing a profile of the president of a very hot little advertising agency on the North Shore of Boston in the mid-eighties. A proud member of the suddenly super-rich, he lived in a converted Japanese tea house by the ocean, perhaps the most exquisite home I'd ever seen, with a panoramic view of waves crashing on the rocks and a huge marble table that rose up from the middle of the dining area at the touch of a button. He had beautiful artwork, the most elegant furniture, the finest tailored suits. I felt so lacking, looking around at all his things, and so shabby and miniature by comparison, me, a speck of a person with a paltry $18,000-a-year salary and a ratty attic apartment and scuffed pumps. I developed a crush on him in about three seconds, which suggests just how seductive such pictures can be, how deeply the *if onlys* can grab you: If only I had that house, that artwork, that taste, that man, *that* would do it.

Things—identifiable objects, products, goals with clear labels and price tags, men you've known for five minutes—make such a handy repository for hungers, such an easy mask for other desires, and such a ready cure for the feelings of edgy discontent that emerge when other desires are either thwarted or unnamed. A woman I know—thirty-seven, independent, smart—is making herself crazy over real estate, wanting to buy a home, lusting after a home, driving to open houses at places way out of her price range, gawking at elegant vestibules, high ceilings, polished wood floors. She understands that this search is more metaphorical than real, she understands that moving from her perfectly fine apartment into a house would give her little more than a cosmetic upgrade and a monthly mortgage payment, and she understands that a geographic move would not fill the other holes in her life, which she admits are considerable: It would not fix her relationship or her career, both of which are stalled; it would not make her feel safer in the world or more optimistic about the future; she'd lug every ounce of her current dissatisfaction right into a new place. And yet the fantasy can render her powerless: If only she had those oak floors and those pretty bay windows, if only she had a sun-filled porch, and a fireplace with a marble mantle, and a kitchen with exposed brick, something fundamental about her life would be altered, improved, validated, massaged into the proper form. Identity bought and paid for; sense of belonging secured.

"Shopping," a friend says, "is the five-pound bag into which we pour fifty pounds of insanity." This is a woman who owns at least forty pairs of shoes, an entire rack of linen jackets, more makeup than an Avon sales rep. She is sick to death of shopping, sick of her own possessions, sick of how crazy-making the whole activity can be. And yet she acknowledges that in a very real way, shopping is at least an option: It's available, it's there, it's an outlet for the confusing range of hungers she often denies herself

in the rest of her life. Eating too much is taboo. Sex is complicated. The body's strange pairings of physical urges and psychic
longings are mysterious and scary. But walk into a store, and suddenly nothing is forbidden or out of reach, the intangible is rendered clear and vivid and attainable. There is abundance in
shopping instead of taboo, and so it's no wonder a woman can go
mad with acquisitiveness. The mathematics of desire is different
in the world of things, the exchanges are direct: Take all those
hidden, private longings related to food and sex and the body,
bring them out into the marketplace to get them fed, bring them
home in boxes and bags.

Fixing the outside, of course, rarely fixes the inside, but this
was lost on me for many years. If anything, the consumer mindset that so powerfully took hold in the eighties merely mirrored
and magnified what was for me an already potent sense of disconnection. I'd long ago learned, as a teenager, to see the body
in external terms, to divorce its worth from the heart and mind;
as an anorexic, I'd elevated that skill to an art form. And by the
time I began to creep out of my anorexic cage, the ostensible
merits of that skill were being preached from every mountain-
top—or, at least, every billboard and TV screen. Steer the appetite away from the heart and out toward the world of products.
Separate sexuality from warmth, passion, intimacy; fuse it even
more thoroughly with appearance and desirability. The body—
accessorized, well-dressed, beautified—is the ticket to well-
being, sexuality, confidence, success; the soul is not.

In the midst of the consumer din, feminism became something
of an echo, a distant tick on another generation's clock. By the
time I moved to Boston, the word itself had lost its revolutionary
sheen, acquiring instead the eye-rolling associations that still
linger in some circles: extremism, humorlessness, a shrill, man-
hating stridency. A Time/CNN poll conducted mid-decade
found that only thirty-three percent of women called themselves
feminists, only sixteen percent of college-age women. Membership in the League of Women Voters began its precipitous de-

cline in the eighties (it's now half of what it was in 1970). The
number of women running for state legislatures began to level
off, then decline; the handful of women who made it to Congress stalled at a handful. The earthquake, it seemed, had passed.

I certainly called myself a feminist in those years, but I did so
in a rather reflexive, ill-considered way, and I can recall quite
clearly the creeping feeling of irrelevance, the sense of something being over and done with. This was true of political activism in general, which began to give way to apathy and
disenchantment in the wake of Vietnam and Watergate, but it
may have been particularly true on the feminist front, its urgency dampened not just by backlash but also by the movement's very success. Women of my generation were no longer
armed for battle; we'd never had to face the front lines. We
hadn't had to muscle our way onto athletic fields or into universities or job interviews. We paid our own rent and bills, we got
abortions if we needed them, we had what felt like the ultimate
freedom, which was the freedom to be oblivious about history, to
take our rights for granted, to forget how hard-won and new they
were, to look back at sixties-style feminism with a yawn and a
shrug, as though it were all somewhat tedious and dramatic.
Consciousness-raising groups? BYO-speculum parties? Please.

This, I think, was a powerful combination, and also a powerful
loss, the explosion of an externalizing consumer mindset—buy,
shop, spend—in lockstep somehow with the diminishment of
feminist visibility and momentum. It made the air even heavier
with false promise, it skewed definitions of desire in the most intractable ways. It also warped perspective, that thick fog of feminist forgetting obscuring the bitter fact that the struggle to feel
entitled and whole was by no means over. Recalling that period,
I'm reminded of how profoundly unsettling it was to try to give up
the structure and control of starving, how unfamiliar my body began to feel, how daunting it was to re-enter the world, where
questions about desire and need arose at every turn: employers to
be negotiated with; men to be intimate with, or not; a lifetime of

baggage about appetite to unpack. How to appear professional and serious in front of a boss instead of young or nervous or *cute?* How to tease out sexual desire from the desire for validation? How to tackle or even frame questions about female authority, size, agency, ambition? The world had so recently opened its doors to women, it seemed, and then so suddenly stopped talking about what that meant, how it felt, what challenges it presented, and when I paged through the lifestyle sections of the newspapers or the women's magazines for guidance, I found only the thinnest dribs and drabs of advice, most of it summed up in that pat and deflecting and woefully inadequate bit of eighties-speak, *dress for success.* Forget about the tricky emotional landscape. Forget about the relationship between head and heart. Forget about the professional world, with its looming issues of power and compensation. Try this power suit with the forty-inch shoulder pads. Try control-top panty hose. Externalize the problem, go shopping.

Of course, this has been the solution to distress—particularly female distress—for centuries in Western culture, well-being linked to externals then gift-wrapped and tied with pretty bows. Karl Marx first wrote about the phenomenon of displacement 150 years ago, describing the ways in which commodities become substitutes for "real human and natural faculties," such as power and talent and ambition. And as any good feminist economist will tell you, the deflecting power of consumerism has a long and well-earned reputation for serving men, and serving them quite effectively: They control the marketplace, and they permit women to be in charge of the goods, an activity that fills up lots of time, steers energy in limited and specific directions (toward decorating, adorning, pleasing the eye), and also has a marvelously mind-numbing effect. In the world of things, there's not a problem—not a thwarted ambition or an itch of longing or a hot surge of rage—that can't be renamed and soothed away with a product.

Second-wave feminism, very briefly, blew open that paradigm: It gave women an entire vocabulary of desire, their own linguistic take on the subject—broad constructions instead of narrow ones, social visions instead of material ones, words like "rights" and "entitlements" instead of "lipstick" and "floor polish"—and it gave them a megaphone with which to broadcast it. This is what seemed to go missing in the eighties, the power of that language, and the connective tissue of female indignation and focus that formed it, and the thick sense of community and sisterhood it produced. By the mid-eighties, the refrains of female strength and unity had become the cant of salesmanship, put through Madison Avenue's mill and duly commoditized, diluted, and trivialized in so many Virginia Slims campaigns ("You've come a long way, baby"), maxipad commercials ("Get the power!"), and hairspray ads ("New Freedom"). This, too, is what I have in mind when I say I missed the boat on feminism: By the time I came out of my self-imposed exile, I associated the letters ERA with the laundry detergent, not equal rights.

I also developed, I think, a fairly flat and limited view of this new post-feminist terrain. The ad I remember most clearly from that period was for Enjoli perfume, a TV spot that featured a power-suited woman clutching a frying pan in one hand and a briefcase in the other, a voice-over of lusty confidence crooning, "I can bring home the bacon, fry it up in a pan, and never let you forget you're a man." This was the prototypical having-it-all superwoman, equally at home in the bedroom, the boardroom, and the kitchen, and while I didn't take the ad particularly seriously, I can't entirely say I rejected the ideal it held up, either. Ads tell us who we are supposed to be, and this one—ludicrously, perhaps but very efficiently—captured some coveted combination of beauty, power, and confidence, then wrapped it up as a done deal. Case closed, end of struggle, a woman's triumvirate longing—for ambition, family connection, and sexual expression—available not through the grueling work of social change but through perfume, smart suits, leather accessories. I suppose this is why I remember it all these years later; on some level, the image must have seemed legitimate. At that point on the continuum of cultural history, several degrees removed from active or meaningful talk about what beauty and power and confidence actually meant, I thought I should know, intuitively, how to *be* that woman, how to combine sexuality and ambition, how to navigate all those fuzzy lines between femininity and authority, relationships and autonomy. And not knowing these things intuitively, I thought I was missing something, or had missed something, or (more hopefully) might acquire something if only I looked in the right places . . . if only, if only. This is what's insidious about consumerism: It's not that it encourages us to shop but that it encourages us to forget, not that it sparks need but that it dilutes it, shrink-wraps it and flings it into the handiest and most tangible containers.

Very gradually, almost seamlessly, I yielded to that press; the old hunt morphed into new hunts: If being thin didn't give me beauty and power and confidence, maybe this would, maybe that would. This is fairly typical of recovery from eating disorders—modifying the behavior doesn't necessarily end the hunt; the *if onlys* often change primarily in name—but it was typical of the times, too, each inchoate longing piloted toward something, someone, the next great elixir. I fell quite naturally into the consumer frenzy, racked up an obscene amount of credit card debt in the eighties, spent more time than I care to admit pawing through department store racks, shopping in that greedy, disconnected way that almost always speaks to a hunger for something more complicated than the objects at hand: for identity, confidence, a persona magically crafted out of fabric and thread. Obsessions with men loomed large in those years, too, particularly with men who seemed to possess qualities I coveted but felt I lacked, men who might imbue me by association with power and competence, as if such attributes were contagious. These relationships were uniformly destructive (at least for me) and uniformly consuming, such an edge of desperation to them, such a compelling need to have someone fill in the blanks where anorexia used to be—tell me who I am, tell me who to be—and such a powerful *if only* behind each one: If only I could get this man to love me, then I'd be safe, then I'd be proven worthy, then I could land. And alcohol loomed large, an almost seamless segue from eating too little to drinking too much. This, of course, was the simplest of external fixes, a concept advertisers reinforce to the tune of $1.1 billion a year. Alcohol was golden and available and marvelously effective, the word *proof* on its very label, fear washed away in fluted glasses of Chardonnay and tumblers of Scotch, confidence bottled and bought, the object of the hunt—if only I felt more relaxed, more attractive, more self-assured—temporarily but very efficiently achieved. Consumerism thrives on emotional voids; that externalizing press is very seductive if you feel empty and ill-defined and wanting, and I was perfect bait for its lure: young, uncertain, desire an unsolvable riddle. I bit and bit and bit. A decade of displacement, hunger chasing its tail.

A sense of possibilities atrophies without outrage, vision withers without unity, the language of desire grows hollow when it's not spoken from the heart.

Leafing through some women's magazines not long ago, I found a number of stories that seemed to be heralding a revival of vision, the beginnings of a new, more accepting view of self. In *Shape*: a feature called "How 25 Women Got Over Their Bad Body Images." In Oprah's magazine, O: a piece called "Hey, Gorgeous! (Yes, We Mean You): The Art of Loving Your Looks." In *Glamour*: a story called "Love Your Butt, Chest Size & Belly Bulges."

I flipped through. I read. My heart sank. *Shape*'s story turned out to be a feature on a four-day "Body Positive" workshop held at the Canyon Ranch Spa, in Tucson, Arizona—quite nice for the twenty-five women who could afford the $1,650 price tag, but not exactly a ticket to self-esteem for the wider public. The subtext of O's piece could be summed up in two words: new makeup. And *Glamour*'s prescription for body-love turned out to be a four-page spread exhorting women to *act* sexually enthusiastic no matter how they feel about their bodies, a piece that managed to be both ego-boosting and condemning in the same breath. "Before you start blaming your satisfactory-but-hardly-stellar sex life on a bad boyfriend, bad timing, or bad feng shui," the author quipped, "consider that a more obvious culprit could be coming between you and the spectacular sex you deserve: *you*."

I laughed out loud at that *Glamour* magazine, and then I hurled it across the room, but as absurd as I found it, the piece stirred something in me, some memory of the anorexic loneliness and isolation and self-centered fear, some awareness of its persistence as a female state, and some sense of the cost of our diminished outrage. I suppose it's the circulation numbers that get to me—the image of 2.1 million young women, anxious about belly bulges and hunched over *Glamour*; 2.6 million with *Cosmo*, trying to figure out how to "Drive Him Loco with Lust"; 2.2 million with *Redbook*, wondering if there really is such a thing as a "Better-Orgasm Diet." Perhaps many of those women are also hurling the material skyward in an offended snit, but I also know that this stuff can suck you in against all better judgment, that it can tap at a lingering suspicion that you've missed something along the way, or might miss something if you don't pay close attention: some key information, some instruction in the art of femininity and self-improvement, some easy way to leapfrog into the land of beauty and sexual prowess, which can look so very much like the land of bliss.

I also know how numbing this mindset can be, how easily it can derail a woman's anger, which is generally the most efficient catalyst for change, if not the only one. Several months ago, I spent some time talking to a forty-three-year old woman named Francine, a full-time secretary at a law firm, mother of two, and a textbook example of contemporary female burnout, the kind that by all accounts ought to foster outrage. Francine—exhausted, eyes hollow with dark circles—is the having-it-all Enjoli powerhouse mutated into the icon of doing-it-all isolation and fatigue. Despite the presence of an able-bodied husband, a commercial contractor, she does all the cooking, all the cleaning, all the grocery shopping and laundry, and the bulk of the child care, which remains, four decades of social change notwithstanding, par for the course. (Women today still spend on average about twenty-five hours a week doing unpaid household labor; although that is quite a bit less than the thirty-nine hours that women in 1968 logged on average, if you factor in the increased hours today's women work at outside jobs, the figures show how burdensome having it all and doing it all has become.) Francine's father died recently after a four-year battle with cancer; she bore the bulk of responsibility for caring for him and still maintains primary responsibility over her aging mother, who lives a forty-five-minute drive away. This is also standard: More than half of all women and nearly two thirds of women with children expect to be responsible for caring for an elderly parent or relative in the future. Because she has health insurance, Francine is on slightly safer ground than many working women (about one quarter have no employee-sponsored health coverage at all), but like a full third of women like her, she has almost no control or flexibility over her work hours, and no paid leave to care for a child or an ill family member. In response to an AFL-CIO survey of working women conducted in 2000, more than half of all mothers with children under six said they found it harder to balance family and work than they did four years earlier; thirty percent said they found it much harder. Francine puts herself in the latter camp without hesitation: "It gets harder every year."

When Francine gets distressed and overwhelmed by all of this, which is often, she eats and she shops, and then she berates herself for eating and shopping. We sat in her kitchen, drinking tea, and she pointed to a heap of publications on a counter: beauty and fashion magazines, clothing catalogues, home and garden catalogues, catalogues with kitchen equipment and athletic gear, dozens of yellow Post-It notes sticking out from the pages. "I can be so *bad*," she said. "I'll stay up until one in the morning going, 'Oooh, I want that; oooh, I want *that*.'" This is not a superficial woman. She is acutely aware that the eating is about anxiety, the shopping about a need for solace, and that both are misguided approaches, or at least limited ones. She also understands the need for more comprehensive and complex solutions, ones that might tackle her brand of burnout and frustration head-on. We spent several minutes talking about subsidized child care, family-leave policies, changes that might make workplaces more compatible with family life, the wish for a more woman-driven and woman-friendly political and corporate climate; Francine nodded and nodded, but then she seemed to grow weary of the subject and shrugged the matter off, as if to say, Oh, well, nice pipe dream. She said she's "just not much of a fighter" these days. She says she's "lost faith" in feminism, and that she's grown pretty apolitical over the years, disenchanted, cynical, frustrated by the sense that no one in Washington really has her best interests at heart. Asked if any of this makes her angry, she smiled a little wistfully and said, "I don't really have the energy to get angry. I mean, what good would it do?" Then she added, rather brightly: "I guess that's why we shop; it's a whole lot quicker to get new curtains."

Francine, of course, is quite correct—curtains can be had in a mouse-click or a phone call—and this is an understanding that consumer culture is all too willing to support. In its hands, a woman's distress—her unhappiness, stress, unsatisfied hungers, fears—is presented as an individual problem, not a social one; its solution must be worked out in isolation, with assistance, of course, from MasterCard and Visa. Collapsing under the super-human weight of caring for kids, spouse, parents, and self? Order this "stress-busting" exercise video, send away for those curtains. Carve out ten minutes for yourself at the end of the day and light an aromatherapy candle, take a bubble bath. Better yet, go buy yourself something pretty, which is still the assumed hunger, even when women themselves are doing the assuming. What do women really want? Log onto iVillage.com, one of the new breed of Web sites designed "by women, for women" and find out. In iVillage, they want "Three-Hundred-and-Sixty-Five Answers to

Women's Everyday Problems" (#123: 'Lose Those Love Handles!')." They want quizzes ("How Sexy Are You?"). They want shopping guides and shopping tips, and so they turn to "Della, the Gift Expert" and "Missy, the Shopping Expert." Presumably, they want to keep their credit card numbers handy, too: The site offers links to sites like Nordstrom's, Spiegel, and Origins.

This is a cut-and-paste approach to appetite, hungers and strivings not only displaced but also boxed up and segregated into distinct compartments, as though they're self-enclosed entities that can be experienced and managed on an as-needed basis, one-appetite-at-a-time: For career advice, click here; for tidbits about food and diet, click there; for tips on how to feel sexy even after you've worked a twelve-hour day and taken the kids to soccer practice and grocery shopped for your ailing mother and mopped the kitchen floor, turn to page eighty-two. *Sexy?* How about brain-dead?

Or, alternately, how about mobilized? How about infuriated? This is what saddens me when I think about my own grasping reach for externals over the years, and about the fervor with which I rerouted so many longings—for connection, for validation, for identity, for relief—away from food and into the worlds of men and things and substances. I can't say with any certainty that following a more politically enlightened or activist path would have made me a dramatically different person, that it would have guaranteed me a healthier relationship with my body or dampened the allure of false gods. But I can say that in leaving anorexia behind, I didn't find much of a cultural nature to replace it, the *if onlys* were not naturally coaxed in non-material directions, either in toward the deeper emotional world or out toward the wider political one. If something was missing in the air back then, if something's missing still, it was a sense of broad alternative vision, a language that might have encouraged women to talk not about new *things* to want but about new *ways* to want.

These are the *if onlys* I did not consider twenty years ago, ones that still seem so terribly difficult to imagine, or even talk about:

If only we lived in a culture in which internal measures of satisfaction and success—a capacity for joy and caring, an ability to laugh, a sense of connection to others, a belief in social justice—were as highly valued as external measures. If only we lived in a culture that made ambition compatible with motherhood and family life, that presented models of women who were integrated and whole: strong, sexual, ambitious, cued into their own varied appetites and demands, and equipped with the freedom and resources to explore all of them. If only women felt less isolated in their frustration and fatigue, less torn between competing hungers, less compelled to keep nine balls in the air at once, and less prone to blame themselves when those balls come crashing to the floor. If only we exercised our own power, which is considerable but woefully underused; if only we defined desire on our own terms.

And—painfully, truly—if only we didn't care so much about how we looked, how much we weighed, what we wore. This one was brought home to me with particular clarity after the terrorist attacks on the World Trade Center and the Pentagon. I was in my office the morning of the 9/11, working on this very chapter, when my cousin phoned with the news. It was about nine-thirty by then. I rushed downstairs to the TV and, like the rest of the nation, spent the rest of the day glued there in horror and then the next several weeks in a state of mild shock, some rock of stability and permanence having turned to shifting sands, the familiar suddenly eerily unfamiliar. For a long time, my normal opiates (TV, crossword puzzles) seemed ludicrously ineffective. My concentration withered. And work—in particular this work—felt hopelessly irrelevant.

"Women and their thighs," I sputtered to a friend. "Who cares?" It took me quite a while, many weeks, not just to feel reengaged by the subject of appetite, but also to link that specific question—who cares?—to broader questions about female power, energy, values, to that whole wide spectrum of *if onlys*. The years I spent obsessing about weight were also years spent

not obsessing about the wider world, not considering alternative
visions, not appreciating how deeply and fully this merciless,
nagging distress can obscure the larger picture, with all its horrors and injustices. In the aftermath of the terrorist attacks, I was
struck by many feelings, but one of the more bitter and lingering
was a kind of deep embarrassment about my own complacency:
my blindness to the depth of hatred harbored in other parts of
the world toward the United States; my ignorance about our role
in fomenting it; my eminently comfortable remove from the circumstances in which so many others live, the poverty and desperation that drives women to madness and men to homicidal
rage. I'll put it this way: In the late 1980s, when American
troops pulled out of Afghanistan, leaving legions of Afghanis in
the sea of chaos that would give rise to the Taliban, I was worrying about whether my jeans were too tight.

I *care* about women and their thighs for precisely this reason:
because so many women care, and because that care is so devas-
tatingly blinding.

About a year ago, Carré Otis, one-time cover girl of *Vogue* and
Harper's Bazaar, abruptly ended seventeen consecutive years of
dieting after taking a charitable trek through Katmandu with an
organization called Medicine for Nepal. "I was in an orphanage,"
she told *The New York Times*, "and there was an infant that was
totally swathed in cloth; it was dying. There was absolutely
nothing anyone could do. No medical attention, no doctor, no
food. Mothers are crying, mothers can't feed their babies. And
it's just like, Whoa! All this time I've been spent being unhappy
with my precious human body and it gets me where I need to go,
it doesn't break down, it functions perfectly. I've spent a lifetime
being upset with the way I look. That experience was key." At
five foot ten inches, Otis now weighs 155 pounds, a thirty-pound
increase over her *Vogue* days, and wears a size 12. She says she's
never been happier or healthier.

It is so difficult to wrest the focus away from externals: It can
take bombs, and starving infants, but it can happen, and in the

aftermath of September 11, I briefly entertained the possibility of a major zeitgeist shift, our grab-it consumer mentality and quick-fix approach to problems detonated along with the twin towers. No one can say precisely how (or how permanently) the events of September 11 will alter the national psyche, but a chunk of that fantasy went out the window within a week of the attacks, when shopping was neatly recast as a patriotic act, when I started seeing Web sites advertising "red, white, and blue sales" and American flag T-shirts, when a major department store left a prerecorded message on scores of local answering machines, intoning with great gravitas that the company's heart went out to the victims of the attack but that its fabulous fall sale would go on, some tiny percentage of the proceeds to be donated to relief organizations.

We may be a more sober nation than we were in the binge-happy eighties and nineties, a warier, less indulgent and less jaded one, but wariness does not always go hand in hand with depth, fear does not always pave the way to change. And so we muddle along, many of us, stumbling toward private solutions to pain, worried about the world *and* our thighs, eyes opened but vision still easily blurred.

Mid-row the other day, a bright fall morning just this side of crisp, I found myself thinking about a conversation I'd had with a friend, who'd stated rather bluntly: "I think the gym has done more for women than forty years of feminism." This is not entirely accurate: Women wouldn't have access to gyms today without those forty years of effort; nor have gyms done much to liberate women beyond middle-class America. Then, too, exercise has its dark side, serving in its less healthy incarnations as a substitute addiction, or a way to stay in battle with the flesh, or yet another consumer experience, the body a commodity that must be wrapped in Lycra, properly accessorized, and meticulously maintained.

I'm not unaware of those tensions in my own life—I am nothing if not compulsive—but as I moved across the water that

morning, the boat balanced and the muscles strong, I appreciated my friend's sentiment. Rowing is the most rhythmic of
sports, exhilarating and also deeply calming, and when it's working smoothly, you feel like some kind of prehistoric water bird, a
creature designed to skim across the river's surface, oars like ex-
tensions of your own arms, the boat moving through the water in
a steady balanced rush of exertion, each body part—legs, back,
shoulders, abdomen, even wrists and fingers and thumbs—following a set of learned rules, reaching out to catch the water and
pull through in a way that comes to feel as ingrained as instinct.
This is where the world began to open up for me. It was on the
river, in that daily repetition of physical motions, that I first got
a glimmer of what satisfaction felt like when it came from
within: The sense of mastery I'd sought from starving, the confidence I'd tried to eke out of clothing and men, the release I'd
found in drinking—all of this came to feel possible, and available and known, as visible as the concentric circles of water that
form when the blades break through the surface of the water. It
was there, too, that I began to redefine words like power and
strength, to understand and experience them as qualities that
existed within my own musculature, to re-write the rules of triumph. Building up versus paring down; taking in versus taking
away. Starving had been about what I could do *to* my body,
sculling about what I could do *with* it.

This thought led, oddly enough, to a memory of a woman I'd
heard at a meeting of Overeaters Anonymous several months
earlier, an earnest, dark-haired young mother who'd stated, very
simply and clearly, *I know if I don't speak, I will eat.* She was talking quite specifically about her own life, her understanding that
she over-eats in order to stuff down the rage and disappointment
she feels when she is unable to tell the people in her life what
she needs, but I interpreted her words more broadly, as a reartic-
ulation of what second-wave feminists understood so well: the
power of language. I suppose that's why they came back to me at
that moment: They reminded me of those early lessons on the

river, of words gradually redefined, truths gradually gleaned, new paths painstakingly made as a result.

Pain festers in isolation, it thrives in secrecy. Words are its nemesis, naming anguish the first step in defusing it, talking about the muck a woman slogs through—the squirms of self-hatred and guilt, the echoes of emptiness and need—a prerequisite for moving beyond it. This is what I admire about twelve-step groups in general, OA groups in particular: Like the gym, they've supplanted the sixties consciousness-raising group as a locus of self-radicalization; unlike the gym, where the lines between health, compulsivity, and narcissism can blur, they focus quite deliberately on mind and spirit, the body's shape and well-being conceived as a reflection of state of mind rather than a specific target. They are places where women can talk as freely and fervidly about anxiety and turmoil and sorrow as they once talked about appearance and weight, where knee-jerk self-reproach and self-destruction can be replaced by honest conversation about pains, joys, risks, ordinary human struggles. In a culture so doggedly oriented toward quick fixes and immediate gratification, their very existence can seem extraordinary.

This struck me, too, as I rowed along: the similarities between an open river and a church basement, the myriad ways in which women learn to talk differently about themselves and their bodies, and the ways in which this powers change. I thought about a woman I'd heard in a meeting of Sex and Love Addicts Anonymous, an incest survivor, who told a hushed crowd of twenty about her efforts to feel safe in her own skin: years of therapy, years of meetings, and now a long stint with yoga, meditation, massage, all efforts to help her feel connected to her body, which she needed to do long before she could contemplate sharing it with someone else. "I couldn't have done this work without all of you," she said. "I was so isolated with all this pain before I started coming here, it would have killed me if I hadn't found other people who really *got* it." I thought about a conversation I'd had with an artist named Diane, from Los Angeles, who described redefining the word *wealth* in meetings of Debtors Anonymous, slowly coming to see that she'd understood it for most of her adult life in the most passive and external terms— the right job would come along, or (preferably) the right man with the right job, she'd glom onto him, he'd rescue her from her mountain of debt, all would be well. She couldn't unlock that mindset until she'd sat and listened to dozens of other people, all of them struggling to break free of the allure of fantasy, all of them trying to face instead their own very ordinary strengths and limitations. Wealth, today, means something very different to Diane. She is far from rich, but she has a decent job, some pride in responsibility, and a sense of well-being that utterly eluded her five years earlier, the inside at last aligned with the outside. Just the other night, she told me, she sat down to make a list of things she'd really like in her life and to her great surprise, there wasn't much on it she didn't already have. Connection, check. Loved ones, check. A sense of belonging to a community, check. All that and enough money. She felt infused with hope, looking at that list. "That's where real meaning comes from," she told me. "It's better than any shopping spree, better than any picture you see on the cover of a magazine."

Steering hope away from false gods, shepherding the focus back toward the heart, learning to see one's private pain in a larger context, coming to link body with spirit: This, of course, is the essence of revolutionary work, and it always requires the re-framing potential of language, the ability of words to fuel insight, rearrange facts, break down old paradigms. A psychiatrist tells me about her efforts to get women to think differently about sexuality, which is often a battle fought with words: Her patients get terribly hung up on language; they hear the word *sexy* and they think, *a black garter belt that you never wear*; they hear the word *masturbation* and they want to run screaming from the room. She is forever steering her clients away from imagery, forever telling them, This is junk, forget about it, this is a bubble-gum fantasy dreamed up for men, it has nothing to do with reality, all it does is keep you disconnected from your own body. She tries to use different language instead: She talks about sexuality in terms that evoke its internal nature, a man's native level of desire as "sharp and daily," a woman's as more "hidden and complex." She uses food metaphors to describe differences in need and satisfaction—the sexual ideal for a man might be quick and frequent and focused, the equivalent of grabbing a bite to eat; the ideal for a woman might be more leisurely and indulgent, a gourmet meal in a restaurant instead of a sandwich on the fly, an encounter preceded by a lot of thought, a lot of planning and preening and fantasizing during the day, a lot of warm-up time, no distractions, no work to get done or bills to pay or piles of dishes to wash. Her descriptions are peppered with words you rarely hear applied to female sexuality—"dark" and "glittery" and "mysterious"—and when I listen to her, I'm impressed by the power of even those hints at a reconfiguration, a word like "glittery" so much more apt and evocative than a word like "sexy," its path so clearly headed inward instead of outward. She understands this: "We *have* to find new ways to talk about sexuality, to describe who we are and what we need," she says. "It's the only way to break free of this ridiculously narrow, disconnecting, image-oriented *crap*."

Even the smallest steps toward change involve linguistic shifts, gateways marked with nouns and verbs. Toward the end of my row, I remembered a young woman, a recovering anorexic, who'd told me about writing down three words in a notebook, *shells, blankets, cat:* They referred to a list she made during the earliest stages of her recovery at the urging of her therapist, who asked her to write down things that had given her pleasure in the past, memories of simple tactile sensations that once soothed her, activities and behaviors that once intrigued or engaged her. And so she recalled searching for sea shells on a beach with her brother as a child, the feel of sand beneath her feet, the smell of salt air. She recalled how pleasant it felt to lie under a great pile of blankets in the middle of winter, the weight and heft offering a sense of shelter, a safe woolen harbor. She recalled a cat she had as a teenager, the feel of its silky fur, the low rumble of its purr. This, she told me, was her "reintroduction to the world of sensuality," a place from which she'd become utterly detached and to which she's become gradually reacquainted, in part by rediscovering those lost pleasures: walking on the beach again; trading in her electric blanket for a new heap of blankets; acquiring a kitten.

I steered the boat into the dock and sat for a moment looking out at the water, a wide ribbon of blue, glassy as a mirror in patches, rippled and glinting with diamonds of sunlight in others. I thought about that young woman with her cat and her pile of blankets, and I thought about how sculling had served a similar purpose, reintroducing me to beauty and grace, re-framing the body as a source of pleasure. Defining desire in new ways is achingly complicated, painstaking work; it requires de-veloping a vision that runs counter to consumerism, counter to a corporate and political culture that's still tightly structured to meet male needs, perhaps even counter to one's own deeply-ingrained assumptions. That vision may be elusive and under-discussed, it may not exist in *Glamour* magazine or *Redbook*, and it may be difficult to discern in the externalizing clatter of cul-ture. But new visions do get forged, and if they're not political in a large social sense, they certainly involve shifts in personal poli-tics, in defining what works, what fits, what matters. A group of women in a church basement reconceiving hunger and satiety; a fashion model redefining starvation; a therapist and a client in an office carving out a path toward sensuality; a solitary sculler on a river learning to see strength in a new light. The public bat-tlefields may be private ones today, but the dynamics are largely the same. Anything that connects you—to the body, to the self, to other women—can free. Anything that frees may also feed.

5

BODY AS VOICE

THE HIDDEN
PANTOMIME OF SORROW

BUT BEFORE THERE IS FOOD, there are tears. Before the pound can lose its power, something ancient and equally potent must be felt.

I remember grieving anorexia quite distinctly, weeping over the loss of that predictable futile safety, which was really a way of weeping over the self, the poor scared self who needed that safety and felt there was no other way to attain it. This must have taken place in therapy, although I can't quite retrieve a specific memory. Instead, I have a sense memory of it, several years in which that initial post-starving frenzy gave way to a quiet, persistent sadness, an emptiness I could neither identify nor shop nor drink nor obsess away, as though a heaviness had crept into the edges of things and refused to budge.

Once, right around this time, I told the therapist about what may well have been my worst anorexic day, a Sunday afternoon in August in the very thick of the starving years, when my parents had arranged to come visit. They'd been in southern Rhode Island for an event of some kind early in the day, and they'd planned to stop in Providence to spend some time with me before heading home. I'm not sure we made an actual plan, but I'd assumed dinner would be involved, and I'd hungered for that dinner for weeks: fantasized about it, worried about it, and

planned for it with a vengeance, sticking fast to my 800-calorie-
a-day diet for three straight weeks prior, not one variation, running extra miles, *earning* that meal, every bite.

They arrived mid-afternoon, around three, and I took them to
a little café near my house for tea, figuring we'd pass some time
there, perhaps take a walk, then go out to eat. I'd already picked
the restaurant, already memorized the menu in the window, already decided which salad I'd order, which rich pasta dish, which
dense chocolate dessert. But my parents left after the tea. I suspect there was a marital explanation for this (they both seemed
depressed and preoccupied that day), but they didn't share it
with me, just said something vague about needing to get back,
having things to see to, calls to make. I remember feeling absolutely crushed—no meal? no reward? all that effort in vain?—
and offering no protest. I walked them out to their car, said
good-bye, then came upstairs to my apartment. It must have
been four-thirty by then. The afternoon sun was still bright, I
had hours to fill before darkness fell, hours to fill before I could
allow myself to eat the same tiny meal I'd eaten every night for
the past twenty-one nights, hours.

Anorexia is primarily a state of denial—denial of hunger, denial
of pain, denial of emotion—but every so often the denial cracks
and you feel the full force of your hunger, the depth of your emptiness and despair, the enormity of the ache. Recounting the story, I
wept over that sensation, the chasm in my life where food and
love and people were supposed to have been, but mostly I wept
over my reaction to it. I did not cry that afternoon. The time
passed like molasses. I clenched my teeth and waited for nightfall.
I slogged through each minute, I ate the apple and the cube of
cheese with my usual numb focus and then went to bed, and the
memory of this filled me with an aching tenderness for that sad
stoic creature, and also the most puzzling feeling of loss. Certainly
it felt scary to give up that steely defense, the capacity to muscle
through no matter what, but it also felt oddly *sad* to give it up, as
though in leaving starving behind, I was saying good-bye to a kind

of bitter and necessary consolation, a form of self-protection that had been painful but also deeply deeply reliable.

The therapist asked, What did it protect you from?

That, I answered, meaning: that very emptiness, that very level of despair and disappointment, those tears, which always managed to be unwept, denied, starved away. In a word: sorrow.

He nodded, and we both fell silent for a moment, lost, I suspect, in a complicated set of shared responses: a respect for the sorrow of that specific day, and an understanding of starving's seductive but wholly illusory protection from it, and also an acknowledgment of sorrow's larger reach, its durable place in the psyche. The ache I felt that afternoon—loneliness, emptiness, yearning—predated anorexia, coexisted with it, persisted in its aftermath, and no doubt always will; it was the simple ache of being human.

Sorrow is stubbornly resistant to insight. I can put together the puzzle pieces of anxiety and guilt and self-hatred, I can draw neat lines between culture and alienation from body and self, I can trace pieces of my anorexic history to this moment and that one, this lesson and that message. Sorrow is what runs beneath all that, a more mysterious pull that seems at once deep as earth and free-floating, and that casts the matter of appetite in a strong and singular light, all individual and known longings blurred and indistinguishable beneath its glare. Anorexia did not protect me from this feeling, nor has recovery from anorexia. It simply makes its presence felt, periodically and without obvious cause on a sleepless night or the first waking moment of a bad morning, a sudden pang of hollowness and yearning that seems wholly unrelated to any specific want, that seems instead to speak to a deeper variety of hunger, an oceanic brand from which other appetites merely split off, diverge, reveal themselves to be smaller rivers and tributaries of feeling that always, somehow, lead back to this. When the feeling hits, I'll lie there and try without success to trace its roots, and only the tiniest, most steadfast comforts will seem to ease it: I'll reach for the dog on the bed beside me and hold her paw in my hand, I'll scratch her chest, listen to her deep, peaceful breathing.

Something is missing: that's as close as I can come to naming the sensation, an awareness of missed or thwarted connections, or of a great hollowness left where something lovely and solid used to be. This, I think, is the coarse grit at the bottom of the ocean, the floor beneath appetite's sea: simple human sorrow.

"Desire," said the French analyst Jacques Lacan, "has indestructible permanence. Desire is inextinguishable." There is something, he suggests, fundamentally insatiable about being human, as though we come into the world with a kind of built-in tension between the experience of being hungry, which is a condition of striving and yearning, and the experience of being fed, which may offer temporary satisfaction but always gives way to new strivings, new yearnings. Once satisfied, the goal always leads to another goal, and then another and another.

Paul Hamburg, a Boston psychiatrist who specializes in eating disorders, describes this tension by recalling the image of his daughter when she was an infant, nursing. For a very brief period, early in her life, she'd look utterly "narcotized" while breastfeeding, completely at peace, as though there was nothing else at that moment she could possibly want. But that period, he says, was relatively brief, and when he thinks about the nature of desire and appetite, Hamburg always returns to another image, not much later in his infant daughter's life, when she'd be nursing and then she'd hear something, a sound from outside the window or elsewhere in the room. She'd want to see where the sound came from, and so she'd turn away from the nipple and not be able to nurse anymore, and in that instant you could witness the beginning of a central edginess or dissatisfaction, appetites emerging in competition with one another: The infant's literal hunger for food pulled her this way, and her hunger to see more of the world pulled her that way, and there, in the conflict between those urges, was the nascent sea of frustration that comes from always wanting more. If there is an infantile experience of pure perfection—nirvana, utter contentment, all needs met—it is woefully short-lived; as Hamburg says, "It's never going to be quite so simple again."

Freud wrote about the human "death instinct," a phrase that has less to do with an actual wish to cease living than with the longing, likely embedded in all of us, to recapture that early state of narcotized bliss, a place devoid of the tension between wanting and being, a condition of complete calm and release. Some of us do get back there from time to time—it's where we go when we're lost in music or rhythm or work or sex, or when we do drugs or drink alcohol, or when we give ourselves over to prayer, or when we lie awake in a half-sleep, curled against someone we love—but as a more permanent state it is lost, its memory folded into the soul, blended and paled and diluted with the passage of time until it's no more than an echo, a whispering ache, that inarticulable sensation that something—something—is missing.

And yet it's a powerful, haunting sensation, the ache behind it all the more pressing because its roots are so difficult to trace. Freud himself, along with most of his contemporaries, didn't really attempt to locate it. In his view, infants were essentially narcissistic creatures—bundles of instincts, centers of their own need-driven universes, their relationships with others characterized entirely by physical dependence—and (to grossly simplify) the truly defining aspects of development didn't really emerge until the child hit the Oedipal years, roughly ages three to six. Like many of Freud's ideas, that conception of infantile life— passive, orally driven, essentially non-relational—has been criticized and extended, and if you were to plot the focus of post-Freudian thought on a graph, you'd see an increasing emphasis—from Jean Piaget and John Bowlby to Margaret Mahler, D. W. Winnicott, and Daniel Stern—on the earliest stages of life, a reach back to the baby at eighteen months, the baby at six months, the baby at three months, torn between the breast and the sound coming from elsewhere in the room, the baby reconceived as a profoundly relational creature who's primed from the very first days and weeks of life to recognize, connect, and engage with others.

Mothers have emerged in post-Freudian theory as much more complicated figures as well. Freud, among others, viewed the mother in rather static terms: a largely passive and stationary player in the baby's world, a figure the baby reacted *to* rather than *with*, took from rather than engaged with—a bit of a vending machine with breasts. More recent work has viewed the mother in much more human terms, a dynamic, subjective, fallible, and complex individual whose earliest interactions with a baby can echo through a lifetime. What kind of dance did these two creatures dance? How much comfort was there? How much pain? How much consistency, how much hunger? "Each of us," writes psychiatrist Polly Young-Eisendrath, "spent some time as an overwhelmed, enraged, unattended little bundle of nerves." Each of us, she suggests, inhabited a land of squalling infantile need, cold or terrified or hungry, inevitable moments of pain experienced as absolute, moments of panic so intense they set the heart pounding; distressed, an infant's heart revs up to 220 beats a minute. Each of us knew, too, the experience of relief from that state, which must have felt like an act of magic. Pain is aroused, registered, intensified, and then, just as suddenly, pain is eased; the nerves are soothed, the hunger is allayed, the mouth closes upon a nipple and begins to suck, the fearful moment is interrupted as a baby is picked up, held, contained in the vast warm universe of its mother.

Temperament, to be sure, affects the intensity of this experience, some babies naturally calm and sunny and resilient, others jittery and high-strung and fragile, the individual capacity for contentment in some respects a neurological gift, granted or withheld in utero by the gods of serotonin and dopamine. But environment affects its texture, too, its shape and resonance, for that dance of need and relief is negotiated, inevitably, by the caretaker, usually a mother, who sets the tempo and choreographs the steps, who either responds or does not respond, who soothes or smothers, who begins to stamp the world from the outset as safe or unsafe, others as caring or unreliable, hunger as fundamentally satiable or fundamentally insatiable. Mothers give us our first terrible instructions in giving and withholding, and I suspect these early experiences of need and provision become braided through the individual experience of appetite, that they form a kind of baseline sense of what it means to hunger.

Mothers, too, give us our first lessons in the complexity of appetite, its intrinsic links to relationships and love and nurturance. Lacan talks about this connection by describing the difference between infantile need and demand. Need, in his view, has to do with the requirements of brute survival: food, shelter, warmth, freedom of movement, a minimal amount of contact with others. Need is innate and instinctual and it requires real, tangible objects—the mother's breast, the soft blanket, the clean diaper—for satisfaction. Demand takes place as a child enters more consciously the world of relationships and begins to develop language, a shift that fundamentally alters need by connecting, immutably, the thing that's needed and the person who either fails or succeeds in providing it. Hunger, in turn, becomes (and remains) a much more loaded experience, relational as well as physical, forever yoked to the people who either do or do not respond to it. Bound up in the symbolic order of language, a child's basic survival needs for food and warmth and shelter split off from their instinctual origins and take on multilayered social and interpersonal meanings. *I am hungry* begins to mean: *I am hungry and my mother is (or is not) responding. Feed me* not only expresses a physical need for food; it also begins to mean: *Love me, take care of me, show me that the world is a safe place, heed my will.*

This, I think, is the stuff that lasts, these frayed threads of original fear and original rapture, of huge hunger and hope, provision and failure. And however the story turns out—whether it ends in a happy childhood or a sad one—it seems that sorrow is an inescapable chapter in the narrative, the urge to reach back inevitable, the sense of something gone missing unavoidable. The fortunate among us may spend a lifetime longing for that early bliss, which we found in the arms of calm and consistent mothers but could not hold onto if we were to separate and explore and grow. The less fortunate may long for a bliss that was never ours to begin with, that was kept out of reach because we were colicky or irritable babies, constitutionally incapable of knowing solace, or because we had mothers who were too depressed or nervous or unavailable to soothe us, or because we grew up in chaotic or violent families. Felt and lost; never felt and yearned for—whatever paradigm inspires it, the sensation whispers and tugs, it keeps you up at 2 A.M. on a bad night, it compels you to reach for things, for food, for objects of comfort, for the dog beside you on the bed, a creature of heartbreakingly satiable needs.

Some of the saddest women I know, women who seem particularly prone to fits of sorrow and despair, are the ones whose relationships with their mothers felt somehow compromised or distant or tinged with resentment, who grew up with the feeling that their mothers didn't really like them. I am one of these, although my own mother would have been horrified to hear me say that: I know that she *loved* me, and in the years before her death I also came to feel as though she liked and admired and felt close to me, but for much of my life I felt as though some early wires between us had been crossed, a pivotal connection never quite made or sustained. She and my siblings had a more natural, easier rapport; I was constitutionally and temperamentally more like my father, somehow more aligned with him, and I suspect this left me feeling out of the loop in some critical respect, outside the maternal circle, never quite sure how unequivocal or stable my mother's attachment to me was. My conversations with her were strained in a way that my sister's conversations weren't; there seemed to be the slightest edge of wariness between us, as though neither of us felt truly attuned with the other, and for years I felt like a stormy adolescent in her presence, withdrawn and angry and dark. I'd walk into her house and regress within five minutes, as though some oppositional cloud had descended from the heavens and followed me inside.

Anger is easy to identify; it makes your heart race, your teeth clench, your blood run hot; it makes you want to rage and spit. I knew for many years that my mother made me *angry*, that whatever its origins, the distance between us made me edgy and restless and full of bile. What took much longer to understand, or to tap into, what I didn't really begin to unearth until I reached back toward times like that August afternoon in Providence, was the deep current of sorrow beneath that anger, a yearning for connection so acute it defied ordinary words; voiced, it would have come out as a howl, the longest and loneliest keening.

Is this why I starved? Perhaps in part, but only in part: Starving sprang from many more sources and served many more purposes than ones related to my mother; to throw all the blame in her direction would be as one-dimensional and simplistic as to point the finger solely at culture or the media. But I do think my relationship with her left me with a particular kind of emptiness, a sorrow-laced brand that's by no means unique to me. The wounds of childhood, deep and pre-verbal and way beyond the grasp of memory, are like footprints covered by new snow; they get hidden with time, sealed over, the traces of felt anguish difficult to perceive, even harder to access. And so the sorrow behind hunger tends to be acted out, described in symbol and code instead of nouns and verbs, a woman's body and behavior communicating what words can't quite capture.

For instance, a woman I'll call Suzanne, now in her midforties, used to steal things. She never took anything she really needed, nor anything major or even particularly memorable, but periodically, during her teens and twenties and even into her thirties, she'd find herself in a store fingering a sweatshirt or walking past a cosmetics counter or standing in line by the candy rack, and she'd be overcome with the compulsion to take something and stuff it into her pocket or her bag: a scarf, maybe, or a pair of gloves, or a Clark bar. Later, she'd feel guilty and deeply perplexed—Clark bars? she didn't even like Clark bars—but at the time the activity gave her an odd sense of power and satisfaction, as though she'd taken something she deserved, something essential.

Janet, also mid-forties, used to cut herself, still does on occasion. She was twenty-one the first time she did it, alone in an apartment she shared with two roommates, and although she can't recall the precise circumstances that motivated the behavior, she knows she walked into the bathroom, looked through the medicine cabinet, and happened upon a pair of nail scissors, which she picked up. Then she stood there for a long time, looking at the scissors, and then she opened them up and ran one pointed edge very slowly against the soft skin on the underside of her forearm. A long, red scratch appeared, and she observed this in a rather detached way. A moment later, she ran the scissor along her arm a second time, same spot, and watched as a string of tiny red beads dotted up along the scratch line, her blood. She had no name for this behavior—articles in the mainstream press about self-cutting were at least a decade away—but it gave her a sense of necessary release and she continued to engage in it for twenty years.

Kathleen, late twenties, has engaged for nearly fifteen years in bulimia, behavior that has ebbed and flowed depending on her state of mind, relative level of anxiety, circumstances. At the moment, she's in a prolonged ebb, in which her symptoms have become, in her words, "manageable." But in her teens and early twenties, she threw up once, twice, sometimes three times a day, the cycles of bingeing and purging organizing her life, dominating most of her waking thoughts, landing her twice in the hospital. Today, she is far more controlled. She follows a meticulously planned diet, exercises regularly, and binges rarely, maybe only a few times a year. She continues, however, to throw up, once a month or so, when she is plagued with an old sensation of horror about the shape of her body, a feeling so deeply ingrained by now that it's nearly immune to rational thought.

Behaviors that appear disparate and unrelated—compulsive shoplifting, self-cutting, bulimia—nonetheless share a profound reliance on symbols to communicate what words cannot. Suzanne's history of stealing—stealthy, bizarre, provoking both satisfaction and guilt—says something about a central feeling of deprivation, one she can't quite describe in ordinary words or address by ordinary means. "I've never been able to explain it in a satisfying way," she says, "but the word 'deprived' gets at it: some feeling of missing something, and of being really pissed off about that. The feeling is about being entitled to *have* it at that very moment, even if 'it' turns out to be a stupid lipstick or a candy bar." Janet's self-mutilation—violent and needful—communicates an opposite sensation, which is a basic lack of entitlement, and a deep distress at feeling unentitled. When she describes the mindset that leads to a cutting episode, she uses the image of a balloon: "It's as though my whole body is so swollen up that it's about to burst, literally about to explode, and the only way to relieve that feeling is to cut. Bleed it out." The swollen sensation, of course, is about emotional rather than physical weight: "Need, want, anxiety, I don't know—*feelings*, the whole nine yards, you name it," she says. "I think cutting is probably a lot like throwing up. The compulsion is huge—to just to get rid of it, get rid of whatever the hell you're feeling because it's unbearable." Kathleen, who is well aware that her bulimic episodes have less to do with food and weight than they do with emotion, would agree. Vomiting, she says, is always preceded by the sensation that she is "holding too much inside," that she needs to "get it out," and that—at least at that moment—there's "no other way to address it."

Transcribing the interviews with these women, I was struck by the use, by all three, of the word *it*. Suzanne is "entitled to have it." Janet is compelled to "get rid of it." Kathleen needs to "get it out." *It* is no doubt shorthand; the word may refer generally to the galaxy of feeling that surrounds female appetite, to the blend of longing and constraint that underlies it, but I suspect it also refers to that ocean of sorrow, to a woman's awareness of its depth and her horror at the volume of need it inspires. All three women come from troubled backgrounds, histories punctuated by maternal loss and failure. Suzanne grew up as the ordinary girl in a family of beautiful sisters, her mother a woman who highly valued appearances, who lavished her other daughters with pretty things, and who left Suzanne feeling "like a mistake, a blob, an object of contempt." Janet's mother was an active alcoholic who alternated between periods of neglect and periods of raging, bitter resentment toward Janet, her only child, whom she referred to as "a pariah who sucked me dry." Kathleen's mother was more generally erratic and withholding; she favored Kathleen's brothers, her attitude toward Kathleen was critical and belittling, and she had a violent, unpredictable temper.

How bearable were the losses of childhood? How tolerable the hunger? How laced with confusion or rejection or hurt? And then: How deprived, how unentitled, how full of sorrow and self-hatred did the essential self become? The answer to these questions—and the difference between those who steal compulsively or cut themselves or force themselves to vomit and those who engage in less extreme versions of cruelty to the self—is essentially one of degrees. Suzanne grew up with both a particular sensation of hunger—a girl who never quite felt full enough, never quite felt as worthy of being fed as the others—and a particularly clear mode of expressing it: Take what was never given to you, take it in a way that mocks the happy, open exchanges of ordinary consumerism, take it in a way that says, essentially, *Fuck you; I got ripped off, so I'm going to rip you off in return*. Janet and Kathleen use different vehicles to express the same feeling: a sensation of being too full of emotion, too hungry, too needy, too large for their own bodies, and an attendant compulsion to release those feelings and to punish the self for having them in the first place.

There is anger in all these behaviors, certainly: rage at the mother who ripped you off, rage at the mother who inspired so much need and failed to meet it, rage at the self for needing anything at all. But underneath the anger is the most powerful sadness, too: the sadness of children who feel unloved and unlovable, who blame and hurt themselves because of it, who remain speechless in its presence, who engage, instead, in a pantomime of sorrow, a shadowy acting out that can be seen everywhere if you look through the right lens. On the day I met Janet, in an ordinary Starbucks filled with ordinary men and women, I overheard a young woman behind the service counter complaining to a co-worker about the buttermilk-cinnamon rolls: They were "too good," she said; she'd already eaten two, which was "two too many." She hissed, "I'm such a pig." Several tables away from us, a pair of high school girls were putting on makeup, passing a compact back and forth, worrying over their lips, skin, hair. "I look like *shit*," one of them said, and snapped the compact closed. Before meeting Janet, I'd seen an anorexic jogger, a woman I see almost every morning while I walk my dog—skeletally thin, she runs in rain and snow and heat, her face drawn and tight, her legs so heartbreakingly thin her Lycra tights literally bag at the knees.

Women wanting to eat and slapping themselves for giving in. Teenage girls mastering the art of negative self-scrutiny. A skeletal body forcing itself to run and run. An arm with more scars on it than you can count. This is endlessly sad, this steady, quiet pummeling of the self, women borne along on a river of unwept tears. What does it feel like to lose control in a shopping binge or an eating binge? Desperate, panicky, frightening, to be sure, but then, way beneath those sensations, is an ancient, aching emptiness, a gaping hole so vast you think it could kill you, a longing for comfort that you know, even as you buy and eat and eat and buy, cannot be filled with food and objects. What does it feel like to lose yourself to an obsession with a man who treats you badly? Again, scary and consuming and profoundly destabilizing, but there, too, is the desperate, driving sadness that comes from feeling unloved, the longing it evokes to be *fixed*, to be held and needed and valued, to be proven lovable at last. And what does it feel like to starve? I have to reach quite hard to get at the sorrow there, for my primary emotional memories have to do with anxiety and isolation and a kind of cold leaden endurance. But starving is a state of sorrow, it is necessarily so, if only because it feels at the time like the only available option, the only possible way to cope, the only way to express how empty and hungry and fearful you truly feel, the only way to make yourself known.

Being known. This, of course, is the goal, the agenda so carefully hidden it may be unknown even to the self. The cutter cuts to make the pain at her center visible. The anorexic starves to make manifest her hunger and vulnerability. The extremes announce, This is who I am, this is what I feel, this is what happens when I don't get what I need. In quadraphonic sound, they give voice to the most central human hunger, which is the desire to be recognized, to be known and loved because of, and in spite of, who you are; they give voice to the sorrow that takes root when that hunger is unsatisfied.

All children will experience rage and helplessness and the terrible pain of unmet need. The luckiest among them, the ones cared for by mothers who were sufficiently attuned and responsive enough of the time ("good enough" mothers, in analyst D. W. Winnicott's phrase), will learn to manage these feelings, to develop a sense along the way that there is some intrinsic goodness and safety and care in the world. If you grow up with the feeling that the source of this goodness exists within you—if your mother's care and attunement has been sufficiently internalized, if it has sparked the confidence that your needs can be safely communicated to and reliably met by someone else—then hunger becomes bearable, rage and helplessness easier to tolerate. You feel, in a word, safe, known, or at least able to *be* known. If, on the other hand, that early attunement and comfort eluded you, if you never internalized that sense of safety and recognition, then hunger becomes more problematic, rage and helplessness move closer to the surface, the ocean grows wider and deeper.

The pantomime begins when the hunger overwhelms, when it exceeds the organizing capacities of language. When words fail, you fall back on the body, you permit its behaviors and compulsions and urges to say what you feel and need, to explain the inexplicable. And so a woman closes her hand around a candy bar. She draws blood on the delicate skin of her arm. She inserts a finger into her throat. Hidden in the symbolically recast worlds of things and body parts and food—worlds, not coincidentally, that are assigned particular meaning to women in our culture—is an entire language of female sorrow, one that serves as a substitute for ordinary language and also reveals a kind of despair about ordinary language, as though there are no words, have never really been words, to describe how we feel.

The philosopher Hegel posited desire as a lack, an absence, an idea also developed by Lacan, who described desire as a longing for something previously experienced as pleasurable or gratifying and then lost. An inherent part of desire, both believed, is a fundamental sense of incompleteness, something missing, some early division that was never quite repaired, and whether that "something" is a buried memory, or a lost experience of love or recognition or safety, or a never gratified wish for such an experience, it haunts us, tugs at the psyche's sleeve, creates an eternal loop of hunger in which every new incarnation of want (that man, that apartment, that pared-down body) is yet another stand-in for the more visceral absence. And the story of appetite becomes, essentially, a story of substitutions, or a chain of substitutions, in which each failed attempt to fill emptiness leads to another attempt and another: longings in search of replacements, forever attaching themselves to things, to people, to behaviors which then take on lives of their own, become organizing principles, fragments of hope that always promise transcendence over pain and longing and always disappoint.

This is not a particularly cheerful philosophy—it suggests that human beings are essentially sorrowful creatures, wounded, eternally fated to seek fulfillment from dislocated and impossible sources—but a dash of Hegelian despair can be a useful thing, a check against consumer culture's blaring strains of false promise, and also fodder for a deeper kind of acceptance. To know that hunger is an essential part of what it means to be human, that it's possibly epic and anguished and intrinsically insatiable, is at least to muffle the blare, to introduce a sense of proportion.

And yet proportion is hard to hold onto, and may be particularly hard for women. During an interview on National Public Radio's *The Connection*, conducted following the publication of her 1999 book, *The Whole Woman*, feminist Germaine Greer described something she sees with increasing frequency: the weeping woman, the woman stopped at a traffic light with tears streaming down her face, or exiting a stall in the ladies' room with red-rimmed eyes, or slumped in her seat at the movie theater, clutching a handful of Kleenex. The weeping is always private, indulged on the sly, and Greer sees the sorrow behind it as a cultural phenomenon as well as an individual one, a reaction to the lingering understanding among women that despite several decades of social change, the world remains largely indifferent, disdainful, even hostile to their most defining qualities and concerns.

Women weep, Greer believes, because they feel powerless, and because they are exhausted and overworked and lonely. Women weep because their own needs are unsatisfied, continually swept into the background as they tend to the needs of others. They weep because the men in their lives so often seem incapable of speaking the language of intimacy, and because their children grow up and become distant, and because they are expected to acquiesce to this distance, and because they live lives of chronically lowered expectations and chronic adjustment to the world of men, the power and strength of a woman's emotions considered pathological or hysterical or sloppy, her interest in connection considered trivial, her core being never quite seen or known or fully appreciated, her true self out of alignment with so much that is valued and recognized and worshipped in the world around her, her love, in a word, unrequited.

In a nod to the diminishment of outrage that began to take hold in the eighties, Greer told her interviewer, "We tried to mobilize women's anger. We spent years telling women to get in touch with their rage, and I think I've come to the conclusion that there's just not enough rage to go around. Women don't get angry enough. What women do is get sad."

This sentiment stayed with me for a long time. I was driving from Boston to Rhode Island while I heard it, to visit a friend for the weekend, and I spent much of the trip thinking about the steady press of sorrow in a woman's life, the feeling of discord that may run through her days, the singular loneliness of living in a world that emphasizes and rewards so many qualities that may run counter to her central humanity: independence instead of interdependence; distance instead of closeness; self-seeking instead of cooperation; the external world instead of the internal world; glamour and wealth and celebrity instead of kindness and generosity and warmth. I thought about the private pain of women, expressed with so much wordless anguish: the anorexic, isolated and terrified and working so relentlessly to starve away her own hunger; the shoplifter, trying to compensate for what she never had with a Clark bar; the self-cutter, lashing at her own skin instead of out at the world; the bulimic, hunched over a toilet bowl, retching out a river of need. I thought about thwarted connections—a girl's from her mother, a woman's from her culture—and then I did something I almost never do: I pulled my car over to the side of the road, and I sat there, and I wept.

6

SWIMMING TOWARD HOPE

FAITH, AGENCY, AND THE REACH FOR SATISFACTION

FOR THE LAST FEW YEARS, when people have asked me what I've been working on, I've trotted out an ironic little capsule statement: "Oh, a book about women and appetite—you know, anxiety, guilt, self-hatred, alienation, and sorrow." The response has worked, at least insofar as it's seemed to freak people out and grind further questioning to a halt (I hate talking about my work in mid-project), but I got tired of repeating it after a while, largely because the answer sounds so dark and cynical, more so than I actually feel. Appetite—naming it, satisfying it— *is* a monumental struggle for many women, a long-distance swim against a current of painful feeling, but I don't think I could have tackled the subject if I didn't feel the presence of some other current, moving in an opposite direction, if I didn't feel some hope.

And so for all my dark irony about the subject of appetite, and for all my conviction about the number of obstacles a woman may face as she slogs toward satisfaction, my desk is also littered with little totems of hope: scraps of paper, interview notes, folders and computer files, offerings from women who have swum against that current of pain and finally made it to another shore, new altars of desire built on the banks.

Margaret Bullitt-Jonas, a fifty-one-year-old Episcopal minister, inspired the first of these folders, which is labeled "Spirituality." Margaret and I first met on a Sunday afternoon in autumn, just after she'd returned from a weekend in the country with her son, ten-year-old Sam. Her counters were strewn with goods—fresh corn, late-summer tomatoes, strawberries, oranges, pita bread—and when I walked in, she was bustling about in a faintly distracted way, cheerfully purposeful. The weekend had been good: While away, Margaret began to think in earnest about buying a horse, which is a childhood dream, and she fairly glowed with the idea, her smile so authentically radiant it seemed to color the whole room.

There was something wondrous about this picture, a woman smiling in her kitchen. Twenty years ago, Margaret used to steal into grocery stores like a thief. She'd fill her cart with lemon crullers and loaves of bread, and then she'd shut herself in her car and begin to eat, vast quantities, one doughnut after another, she'd eat until she ached. She lost a good decade of her life to the obsession with food, dieting, bingeing, loathing herself through all of it, and so to see her now, amidst strawberries and a full life and a flowering dream, was akin to a miracle: This was an image of possibility.

And an image of hard-won change. The path here, to hope, is rarely sudden or dramatic, the fixed self—new-and-improved-and-sated-at-last—never as neatly achieved or fully realized as we might like it to be or as consumer culture suggests it can be. Hope is about willingness and persistence and faith; it's about personal and social shifts so incremental they're often hard to discern; it's about daily human struggle, in all its banal and brutal glory. On the day we met, Margaret ushered me into her living room and spent some time talking about that struggle: her relationship to food; the despair that led her to Overeaters Anonymous in the early eighties; her long, finally successful effort to make peace with her appetite, which she subsequently detailed in a memoir called *Holy Hunger*. She is not casual or cavalier about food today—no one I know who's dealt with a full-blown eating disorder has ever fully reclaimed that particular gift of lightness—but she does know the difference between physical hunger and emotional hunger, she does catch herself when she starts obsessing about food and rationalizing about when to eat and what and how much, and she has learned how to eat sanely, how to take care of herself, how to set the obsession aside, making some room for joy.

This conversation segued almost seamlessly into talk of Margaret's prayer life and her relationship with God, the development of which was and still is conjoined to her recovery from food addiction, both cause and effect. I tend to dissociate just a tad when people start to talk about God and prayer—having had little in the way of a religious education myself, my own sense of the spiritual is profoundly vague, and so I usually react with a feeling of detached envy when people describe their spiritual lives, and also bafflement, as though they've stumbled upon something literal and deeply consoling but also alien to me, a ghostly presence that I can't quite make out. And yet the bafflement eased in the presence of Margaret's clarity, and the sense of shimmering serenity beneath it. She described believing in the existence of a kind of love that can't be satisfied by people, places, or things, and a need both to feel that love and to offer it in return. This love, which she understands as the love of and for God, is bigger and more encompassing than anything the concrete earthly world has to offer, and although it can be elusive and fleeting, she does find it in moments of prayer, which are often so intense they literally make her weep, so vivid is that feeling of love and so palpable her sense of connection to it. And in the aftermath of these moments, she feels an enormous proportion and calm, the inevitable frustrations and disappointments of daily life not only surmountable but also acceptable, as though they reflect an emptiness that can, finally, be filled.

In those moments of prayer, Margaret has that rarest of human experiences, satiety.

It is probably no surprise that the most consumer-oriented society in modern history has also turned into the most oddly soul-
searching one, a world in which day traders log off and head to
meditation workshops, in which books about angels and past
lives vie for top spots on best-seller lists with books about mil-
lionaire entrepreneurs. Nor is it any surprise that spirituality has
emerged as a solution to the troubled appetite, which, after all, is
such a close cousin to the troubled soul. A Christian weight-loss
program, the Weigh Down Workshops, boasts 30,000 chapters
nationwide; First Place, a similar program, is taught at an estimated 12,000 churches across the country. As is the case in
many Twelve-Step programs, the purpose behind these approaches is simple. They aim to replace the hunger for food with
the hunger for God, which may sound black-and-white but is really a version of what anyone who grapples with a compulsion
around appetites must learn to do: Direct the focus inward (or, if
you choose, heavenward); still the self; learn to grasp the true
source of hunger rather than merely reacting to it. And, in the
process, learn to fill some of the emptiness with more nourishing
things: connection, beauty, God, whatever fills you, however you
define that.

The totems of hope on my desk speak to such lessons; they
have to do with leaps of faith, with tiny shifts in perspective that
yield to larger shifts, with the messy business of muddling
through, reaching for that shore of contentment. Some of them,
like Margaret's, are spiritual in the strict sense, stories about dis-
covering a religious connection, or sense of belonging through a
spiritual community, or a path to joy in prayer. Others defy easy
categorization but nonetheless involve the spirit, the effort to
hear its whispers and to heed its directives and to move, step by
painful step, in its direction.

A line from a transcribed interview reads, cryptically: *Exercises
in pleasure*—this from a woman with a long history of compulsive
promiscuity, a woman whose need for validation and worth were
so inextricably linked to male sexual approval that she'd put

even her most basic human needs on hold in order to secure it: If she was on a date and she had to go to the bathroom but the man in question was in a hurry to get somewhere, she'd wait; if he was ready to have sex and she wasn't, she'd go ahead and have sex; if he had a need, she'd ignore her own: "If I put mine first," she says, bluntly, "he'd leave and then I'd die." Getting beyond this mind-set has involved redefining pleasure in the most elemental ways, detaching it from men and from sex, coming to believe that she can experience pleasure—and deserves to experience pleasure—on her own terms, without the defining presence of a man. Hence the exercises, which she developed with the help of a sponsor from Sex and Love Addicts Anonymous. They include activities: bowling, hiking, swimming, all of which have reintroduced her to the concept of nonsexual physical pleasures. They include people: friends to join her in these activities, to help teach her that it's possible to have fun and to feel connected with others without the stamp of sexual validation. Celibacy has been an exercise—dating, she had to learn to believe that she could go out with a man and be liked without sexually pleasing him, that he might actually call her again if she didn't sleep with him, that she might not even *want* him to call—and so has masturbation: She had to learn, too, that she could feel good physically by herself, that pleasure could originate within her own body, that her own desire did not depend on male desire for its satisfaction.

"I'm much more sure of myself today," this woman says. "I have a much stronger sense of self. I'm able to walk away from a relationship and not have that fear that I'll die without it. I feel . . . I guess the phrase is spiritually grounded."

A line from another transcript reads, *Let the body decide*—this from a woman who's battled with weight for most of her life and who, in her mid-forties, is just learning to tune out the voices of self-recrimination in her head, to tune into her own body instead. She often has to take concrete action in order to do this: If she finds herself engaged in some twisted debate over a piece of cake, she'll literally walk out of her kitchen, go into another room, sit down, close her eyes, *breathe*, a kind of adult time-out in which she tries to locate the source of the discomfort, the nature of the hunger, the real need, which may or may not involve the piece of cake. If the debate involves a more substantive question about desire, like a job change, she heads to the natural world: the woods, the ocean, places where the voices of obsession and anxiety can be eased by sound and smell and touch, where the physical calm can clarify the puzzle, make the voices of spirit and truth more audible.

Another woman, whom I'll call Natalie, has found hope—and satiety—in her daughter, a Chinese baby girl whom she adopted after a long struggle with infertility and a subsequent divorce. Natalie called me up about a year after she'd returned from China with her daughter and told me she'd been thinking about me all summer, and about the whole matter of appetites and where they come from and where they go when they're unsatisfied. "I'll tell you," she said, "this is the first time in my life I've really felt liberated from all that." Natalie is a woman who's always worried about food, who's both loved food and overused it, long relying on it in order to satisfy other hungers. Since the adoption, she said, that whole roster of concerns—what to eat, when, how much, how much is too much—had fallen away, as though she'd simply shed a skin and stepped gingerly away from it. Part of this, of course, had to do with being otherwise consumed: not only a new mother but a single mother, Natalie didn't have time to think about food, or worry about it, or even *eat* it during much of the day. For the first time, food became stripped of its multiple meanings and became, simply, food: fuel, nourishment, something her body needed in order to function properly. She says, "I remember standing in front of the refrigerator one day and thinking, 'God, I better eat something.' And I reached in and took out two ice cream sandwiches and just kind of gobbled them down because I felt like I'd faint otherwise. Food as basic sustenance: That has never been my experience."

Her other appetites, and difficulties with them, went through a similar transformation. Work? Years of concern and confusion over ambition and anxieties about being adequately recognized just sort of fell away. Shopping? Sex? Who had the energy? Who *cared*? Natalie would lie on her sofa in the den and cuddle the baby, feel the baby's soft warm heft against her chest and neck, and she'd feel completely filled, completely at peace, as though the whole constellation of needs and hungers that once dominated her daily life (need a new man, a new body, a new couch, a new job) had been miniaturized, down-sized, stowed away in a cupboard marked *not really so important*.

What we want, of course, what lies in the cupboard marked *important*, is connection, love: If the deepest source of human hunger had a name, that would be it; if the boxes of constraint in which so many women live could be smashed to bits, that would be the tool, the sledgehammer that shatters emptiness and uncovers the hope buried beneath it. Love—the desire to love and be loved, to hold and be held, to give love even if your experience as a recipient has been compromised or incomplete—is the constant on the continuum of hunger, it's what links the anorexic to the garden-variety dieter, it's the persistent pulse of need and yearning behind the reach for food, for sex, for *something*. We may come to understand the vastness of this sensation as a buried hunger for a mother's love, or we may accept it as an inevitable part of the human condition, or we may see it as a form of spiritual yearning, or we may dismiss it as an unsolvable riddle, but in the end, understanding only takes you so far. You can't curl up at night with understanding, you can't feed on it or hold its hand or share your secrets with it; knowing a hunger is not the same as satisfying it. And so it persists, for many of us, hunger channeled into some internal circuitry of longing, routed this way and that, emerging in a thousand different forms. The diet form, the romance form, the addiction form, the overriding hunger for this purchase or that job, this relationship or that one. Hunger may be insatiable by nature, it may be fathomless, but our will to fill it, our often blind tenacity in the face of it, can be extraordinary. We long, we aim for the safety of the shore, we stay afloat, often clinging to nothing but the smallest buoys of hope. And sometimes, if we are very lucky, we find the right form, the right kind of satisfaction, one that feeds us, at least for a time, in a way that's so deep and true it seems to take place at an almost cellular level, a need stamped, finally, *met*. *This* is it, Margaret feels, emerging from prayer; *this* is it, Natalie thinks, holding her child; *this* is it, I am home.

The tough part, of course, has to do with finding love, and then taking that sledgehammer and breaking out of the box long enough to hold onto it, which in itself is no small feat. That job involves naming desire, and it involves understanding what stands in its way, and it involves mustering the strength and courage and self-acceptance to smash through the constraints, consequences be damned. The key—the bridge to the shore—is agency, a feeling (almost always hard-won) that marries entitlement with power: I *deserve* to be filled becomes I *can* be filled, I can make it happen. Margaret spent years feeding her ravenous soul with food, Natalie spent years clinging to a bad marriage hoping that at least it would yield a child. At some point, both simply stopped, said, Enough, this road is fruitless and unbearably painful, I want something else, I need something more. And then, equipped with little more than faith, they changed direction, started swimming against the current. The satiety they describe is the result, fought for and finally attained and deeply fulfilling.

Daughter of a psychoanalyst, I was raised under the Gospel According to Freud, so it's no surprise that my own feelings about faith and hope, ill-defined as they may be, have been shaped in fifty-minute bursts, in a therapist's office. *Know thyself. Our father who art in analysis, hallowed be thy name*. Some fathers want happy marriages for their daughters, or professional victories or healthy babies; mine dreamed of a *successful transference*. Unresolved conflict was the great barrier to peace and satisfaction in his view, self-knowledge the gateway: I grew up on these tenets, believing in my heart that analyzing problems would solve them, that talking about feelings would cause them to go away.

It was my profound good fortune to end up with a therapist who saw self-scrutiny as a rather dubious goal, or at least an incomplete one, who focused so doggedly on those odd concepts of his: "fun" and "joy." Of course, it took many years for me to understand what he was talking about. Fun? Feeling good? For years, eating (or not eating) had been my primary link to feeling and passion, if not the only link, and so words like "joy" and "delight" seemed mysterious and rather alien to me, if not altogether irrelevant. I didn't want to have "fun," or even talk about it. I wanted (at worst) to stay thin and (at best) to stop worrying about staying thin, and his insistent focus on the world of pleasure made no sense to me, as though he were talking about some other patient, or speaking in tongues. He is a very goal-oriented therapist, a man who believes in action, and this baffled me, too. Suppress the instinct to understand every nuance and source of feeling, he'd urge. Experiment! Try something *new*. I'd look at him blankly. Huh?

I suppose I suffered from the form of delusion that always accompanies obsession, which is to view the object of desire as the solution rather than the problem: If I could get weight and eating under control, the rest would follow, I'd find peace, I'd feel if not exactly "fed" than at least free to be fed. And then . . . if I could get the right man to love me, *then* I'd find peace; if I could *look* sophisticated and mature and composed, then I'd *be* sophisticated and mature and composed; if I could shoehorn my life into a shape and form that looked normal, then I'd feel normal, problems solved. Add drinking to this stew, which minimized both clarity and the possibility of change, and you get a whole merry-go-round delusion, years of spinning in an endless sad circle.

What a Sisyphean task that poor therapist faced. Every week, he pushed the same rock up the same steep hill, the rock being my intractably externalized focus, the hill being reality itself, with its inevitable pains and its moments of peace and its limits and its essential mystery. I droned on and on: weight, men, work, drone, drone, drone. I periodically worried aloud about drinking but showed no inclination to address the magnitude of the problem, let alone do anything about it. Instead, I bitched and moaned: if only this, if only that. And he chipped away at the rock: The struggle is not *about* food, he'd say; it's not about the boyfriend, it's not about the problem-of-the-week or the fantasy-of-the-week, which are no more than red herrings and false hopes, and the solution is not going to reveal itself in external form, in a new man or a new job or a bottle of Chardonnay. The real struggle (chip, chip, chip) is about *you*: you, a person who has to learn to live in the real world, to inhabit her own skin, to know her own heart, to stop waiting for her life to begin.

He chipped and chipped; the rock grew smaller by degrees, which is something that happens not in moments of blinding insight or revelation but in much more gradual and less dramatic ways: baby steps; tiny moves in this direction or that; experiments that seem so petty and small it's almost embarrassing to claim them as victories. The therapist pestered and nudged. *Eat an entire meal; now eat another:* See how that feels, see how scary it gets to surrender some of the control, see what comes up. *Don't call the ex-boyfriend:* See how *that* feels, try to feel what's underneath all that need. *Have you ever thought about getting a pet?* He asked me that question about five years into therapy, and I looked at him like he had two heads. A *pet?* What is this, play therapy? Could he *be* any more dense?

Baby steps, no matter how tentative and seemingly beside-the-point, lead you if not toward change than at least toward information. They are painful to take. You eat the entire meal and you feel like a blob, a cow, worthless and disgusting, but you're also left with something to look at, feelings to examine instead of merely fear. You don't call the boyfriend; you sit alone in your apartment instead and you feel desperate with longing and fear, but you learn that you can tolerate the discomfort, that it passes.

You try things, and some of them backfire, and some of them lead you nowhere at all, and some of them make you stronger—certainly, quitting drinking was a powerful step for me, chipping several hefty slabs away from the rock of delusion and denial and warped perspective I'd been living under. And so it goes, the pace of change glacial and the effects rarely dramatic. If you are fortunate and sufficiently supported, you move incrementally onto slightly different terrain, a landscape that inch by inch grows less harsh.

The key, I suppose, has less to do with insight than with willingness, the former being relatively useless without the latter. Left to my own devices, I would have talked in therapy until I was ninety, yammered on about the family and the past: this need to please and that need for approval, this little hurt and that little disappointment, who, what, where, when, why, *why me*. But without willingness—willingness to experiment, to take risks, to pick up a chisel and join in the chipping of rock and resistance—that kind of talk can get pretty hollow, a narrative with no action, not much conflict, only the faintest outlines of a plot. Willingness is grist for the mill of insight—it's what gets you off the sofa, out of your own head, out of the paralysis of obsession long enough to view the self in different lights, and to begin filling in the narrative, or coaxing it in new directions. Willingness is also the antidote to helplessness and, as such, the kernel of a kind of faith. You take one baby step, then another; you leap off this tiny cliff and that one; you keep it up long enough, and somewhere along the way you begin to understand that moments of emptiness and despair can be survived, that pain can be offset by pleasure, that fear can give way to safety. Whether you choose to define that faith as spiritual, whether you call it an emergent belief in self or in a benevolent universe or in a higher power or in God is in some ways beside the point: By any name, faith refers to the mysterious reservoir of feeling that helps you tolerate the bad nights and savor the good ones; it's what lets you believe in your heart that your hungers won't kill you, that you can, in fact, find the succor and nourishment you need, that you'll be okay.

My great terror during the early years of therapy concerned the opposite belief, namely, that if I escaped the anorexic prison and truly surrendered all that hard-won control over appetite, two things would happen: I'd be so consumed with need and desire that I'd never stop eating; and I'd find this so horrifying I'd have no choice but to lock myself back up, this time in a maximum-security unit with an even harsher warden. At times today, when I'm feeling particularly pessimistic or grim, I still invoke that image, moan to the therapist that all I've really done is build myself a more spacious cell with slightly prettier things in it: nicer furniture that merely dresses up same internal structure. There is a grain of truth to this: I'm still prone to periods of isolation, still more fearful of the world out there and more averse to pleasure and risk than I'd like to be; I still direct more energy toward controlling and minimizing appetites than toward indulging them; I am one of the least spontaneous people I know. But the landscape is indeed less harsh than it once was; at times, it feels veritably lush. There are people in it: a man I'd trust my life with; a few cherished family members; a handful of close friends who make me feel known; the therapist. There is food: meals shared and delighted in, desserts indulged without anxiety. There is an animal on the landscape, too, a dog who has taught me volumes what it means to love another being unequivocally, and there are woods to walk in, and long, flat, beautiful bodies of water to swim in and scull on, all activities in which I can lose myself in the sheer physicality of rhythm and beauty. And there is work, which engages the heart and mind and, at least occasionally, lends a sense of purpose to my days.

I no longer fear sliding back into the anorexic prison, but I am somewhat stunned, and a little rueful, at how arduous it all is, how long it can take a woman to achieve a degree of balance around appetites, to learn to feed herself and to understand and honor the body, and to hunger for things that are genuinely sustaining instead of hungering for decoys. In a cruel twist of irony, the diminution of physical appetite appears to be a by-product of at least two things that can liberate it emotionally, antidepressants and aging. The Zoloft that can free you up enough to explore the world may also kill the libido; the Sisyphean terms of therapy that can help you understand your hungers may last straight through menopause. So the prison fear has given way to the fear of the ticking clock: Will I get the right emotional balance—the right combination of joy and entitlement around the vast blend of human hungers—at the same time the body starts to lose interest? Will I feel truly entitled to be fed only to find myself staring at a bowl of oatmeal in the nursing home?

Granted, that's a rather ageist fear, and it's not one that really keeps me up nights—given the emotional contexts in which physical appetites always exist, I'd like to believe that time will do more to encourage than dampen desire, at least in my own foreseeable future. What plagues me more is the matter of "getting it right" in the first place, as though there is some achievable balance of hungers and satisfactions, some place of repose where the struggle finally ends, the battle is won, you have enough.

Enough. Now, there's a word that can keep you up at night. What, finally, is enough? Ask me this question on a bad day and I'll probably shrug. Maybe this little landscape I've created isn't enough, and never will be enough; maybe there's no such thing. I once maintained in a column that there were three ingredients to a woman's true happiness and that most of us never have all of them at once; two were destined always to be missing. The three in my assessment were a joke—a woman, I wrote, needs a good mechanic, a good gynecologist, and a good therapist—and I've toyed with the equation over the years, recasting the three ingredients as a good job, a good boyfriend, and a good apartment, which can be an equally evasive combination. Levity aside, I think there's some truth behind both equations. The mechanic represents freedom and mobility, the gynecologist physical health, the therapist emotional well-being, all defining characteristics of appetites that are healthy and freely expressed; the job-boyfriend-apartment combo is a similar construction—to get all three down requires a rare combination of self-determination, self-knowledge, and good fortune. And it does seem, in either case, that achieving all three is woefully difficult. Perhaps there's emotional freedom and poor health. Or a great job and a disappointing boyfriend. Or a promising love life but no real sense of home. On my bad days, my worst days, I can see something missing in any realm: The boyfriend is getting on my nerves, the words won't flow, the paint is chipping on the psychic walls. But even through the periodic haze of despair, I can shift the kaleidoscope a little, long enough at least to understand that a certain degree of emptiness and dissatis-faction is not only an inevitable part of life but also a useful one: Hunger, no matter how uncomfortable, is like fuel; it's what keeps you striving, it's what powers those baby steps, impels you in fits and starts onto new terrain.

So is this enough? Ask me on better days, on the best days, and I'll count the blessings, I'll talk about the hard-won intima-cies and the minor victories over fear, about the friends and the dog and the woods and the work, but I still won't answer un-equivocally. For there is no unequivocal answer, no final resting place, no pinnacle reached, all appetites understood and sated at last. Instead, there are moments of contentment, moments of sudden alignment between body and mind and spirit, moments of feeling fed that arrive unexpectedly, like gifts from the uni-verse. These come in the simplest packages: in a look of love from the dog, a joke shared with a friend, a spark of affection here or understanding there. They come in the morning light, which hits the water just so as I set off for a row; they come in a perfect meal, a perfect sentence, a touch, a glance. There are moments, which in the end may be the best you get in this life: flashes of satisfaction, glimmers and tastes of hope, fleeting mo-ments that you have to relish and eat up like pie.

EPILOGUE

THERE ARE FEW THINGS like the sight of a woman in labor to shake up your perceptions of the female body. Last December, at age forty-one, my sister gave birth to a baby girl, using a system of natural delivery called the Bradley method. She spent a good portion of her labor in a chair, flanked by her husband, Jim, and me, and when a contraction came, she'd lean back, shut her eyes, and focus on relaxing as much of her body as possible. She'd breathe very deeply and evenly, and she'd try, as she described it, to dive down into the pain rather than flee from it, the idea being that if she could get out of her own way—calm the muscles, resist the urge to fight—her uterus would do its job.

Which it did, brilliantly. My sister had labored at home for the better part of the afternoon and evening, contractions mild-to-somewhat strong, and then arrived at the hospital around nine that night, contractions stronger and more regular, her cervix dialated to about six centimeters, past the halfway point. At about 10:30 P.M., with contractions coming every three minutes or so, she was wheeled into the delivery room, and as the intensity increased, she asked Jim and me to help her stay relaxed by evoking images of her favorite beach on Martha's Vineyard. When a contraction came, we imagined them as waves, using as our guide a monitor, affixed via suction cups to her belly, which recorded both the baby's heartbeat and tension in my sister's abdomen. Between contractions, the tension numbers stayed very low: eight, nine, eleven. When the numbers started to climb—twenty-eight, thirty-five, fifty-four, eighty-two—we'd see her close her eyes and lean back, poised for the pain, and we'd describe the wave building: *You're half-way there*, we'd say, *this is a big wave, you're almost at the top* . . . The contractions seemed to reach peak intensity at about 127, and then they'd gradually ease. *Okay, we'd say, you're coming down, three quarters of the way down the wave, halfway down, it's over.* And she'd exhale, and sigh slightly, and say, *Okay.* Periodically, she'd comment with a kind of awe and wonder at what her own body was doing, at the sheer power of the uterine muscle and the sense of independent drive it seemed to possess: She could have been in a coma, she said; she could have been completely unconscious and her body would still be doing this work, this miraculous and innate system having kicked in and rolled up its shirt sleeves and begun its job, operating on its own timetable, equipped with its own tools.

This was astonishing to watch. At about 11:35, contractions coming more rapidly and with greater intensity, my sister moved from chair to bed, and the room, relatively quiet and dim until then, sprang to life: urgency in the air; obstetrician, medical student, nurses suddenly present; bright lights flooding the room. My sister began to push at this point, and when the baby came she came fast: five contractions, a set of pushes with each, a great deal of vocal encouragement from the obstetrician—*that's it, that's it*—and then, amazingly, a tiny human, the abstract suddenly rendered tangible and extraordinary. I was standing by my sister's left knee, holding her foot so she could push against the palm of my hand. I looked down during the last contracted push, and there, within a matter of seconds, was the small round curve of an infant's head, and then suddenly shoulders, and then an entire miniature body, curled in the fetal position still, eensy fists against an eensy chest. A human, attached to mother for only seconds more by the umbilical cord, and then snipped apart, and breathing on her own, mouth open in a first choking sob.

Later, I would describe this experience to friends as a cross between a breathtaking miracle and an episode of *The X-Files*, there being something almost inherently cinematic about such a literal expulsion, and about the sight of blood, and about the eerie gray cast of a baby's skin before it begins to pink up. Given our distance from the natural world, these are the kinds of things most of us only witness in horror movies or on TV, and during the actual delivery, I had a momentary flash of such cinematic detachment, a sense of visceral shock paired with a split-second inclination toward disbelief, as though I were watching something at the local multiplex: great movie, amazing special effects. *Wow*, I said aloud, eloquently.

The next split seconds, though, are the ones I want to remember, for a birth really is the most extraordinary feat of nature, and I'm not sure I've ever felt such profound respect for the female body or such awe in its presence. A body creating a body; a woman's body, equipped with this exquisite knowledge and stunning capacity to create life, and then to house it and protect it and nurture it through its own web of cord and fluid, and then to bring it into the world, producing human life itself. To watch my sister deliver this creature with such focus and grace, and to see that baby in its first instant outside the womb—a perfect replication, with tiny perfectly formed ears and fingernails and toes—and then to grasp in the same instant the reverberant power and potential of that new life, which is the potential of humanity itself, the potential to go out in the world and develop a cure for cancer or to set a new world record for the hundred-yard dash or to simply live as humans live, a life of joy and sorrow and intimate struggle, each one of us touching and shaping irrevocably the lives of countless others—this is quite truly the stuff of miracles, and it begins in the body of a woman, and it springs from the body of a woman, and it takes your breath away.

This birth had its moments of particular meaning for me, given my immersion at the time in the world of women and their bodies and appetites; it also had its moments of particular irony. In an almost perverse testimony to the extent to which we are creatures of culture, inhaling media and imagery like air, there are TVs everywhere in hospitals, affixed to the walls in the waiting areas, in the maternity triage areas, even in the delivery rooms themselves, some of them blaring, some muted, but all of them on. After the delivery, after the dust had settled and the nurses were busy weighing and measuring and swaddling the baby, I happened to glance up at the TV screen above my sister's bed and noticed that a PBS station was rerunning a documentary about anorexia that had debuted the night before. The show opened with images of fashion models, their beauty typically cool and frightening and seductive, and it went on to images of anorexic women: a teenage girl as skeletal as a concentration camp victim; a compulsive runner, who'd realized she had a problem when, twenty-three miles into a marathon, she found herself obsessing about when she'd next get to the gym; a retired ballet dancer in her fifties, anorexic for decades, hobbling across a street on a walker, her bones as brittle as those of a woman in her seventies.

So the birth of this child was punctuated by imagery and omen, body-loathing and self-contempt almost literally written on the walls. I stared at the screen for several moments, dumbstruck by the sense of discord. On one side of the room, the shockingly familiar: the cold, angular ideal, the attendant press to whittle the body down, pare it away, attack it at the core. And on the other, this shining truth: a mother's body delivering life.

Late that night, driving home, I thought about the world this new baby had just come into, which seems to me a place of such mixed and partial blessings. Several months before her birth, I'd spent an evening with a group of high school girls, eleven in all, sophomore to senior years, whose feelings about appetite seemed to hint at what lies ahead, a strange combination of promise and peril. The promise comes from the landscape they inhabit, a vastly altered world where girls are entitled to every opportunity boys are, where parents share child-raising responsibilities, where confidence and voice and entitlement are neither as elusive nor as rare among girls as they once were. The Family and Medical Leave Act passed while these girls were in puberty, a feminist was named to the Supreme Court, a woman was appointed to run American foreign policy, and if this group didn't particularly like the label "feminism," they certainly shared feminist principles and they have certainly benefited from feminist values. They are products of supportive families, of a liberal pro-woman community, and of a suburban Boston school system that works particularly hard to embolden girls.

All of this is good news, its effects clear. This was a confident bunch and I could hear genuine strains of agency in their voices: an ability to think critically about media and culture; an aware-ness of choice; a basic acceptance of their own intelligence. But there were familiar undertones of anxiety and strain in their voices, too: worries about weight and fat and control; an ac-knowledgment of the profound link between appearance and self-esteem; anecdotes (everybody seemed to have one) about this bulimic friend and that anorexic one; hints of the pressure—considerably heightened since I was their age—to act and feel sexually mature long before they were ready. Will he hate me if I'm fat? Will he dump me if I won't sleep with him?—if any-thing, such questions have grown more tyrannical in our hyper-sexualized, hypervisual culture, the mandates about sexiness and body shape more rigid, the stakes higher. Even this group, who in many ways represent the best, the brightest, and the savviest, is nowhere near immune, and the bright picture of promise they present begins to dim considerably when you move beyond their relatively well-insulated circle.

A March 1999 study in the journal *Child Development* reported that boys continue to have higher estimations of their academic abilities than girls do and that girls tend not only to underrate their achievements but also to suffer in greater numbers from poor self-esteem, anxiety, and depression. Eating-disorder statis-tics continue to climb, with experts in the field treating girls at younger and younger ages. In one study, forty-two percent of girls in grades one through three reported wanting to be thinner; in another, thirty-nine percent of girls in grades five through eight said they were on a diet; of those, thirteen percent had already binged and purged. Thirty-one percent of ten-year-old girls say they're afraid of being fat; more than fifty percent of adolescent girls think they're overweight. Sexuality among adolescent girls seems to translate less frequently into personal gratification than into high-risk behavior and hurt: The earlier a girl begins to have intercourse, the less likely she is to use birth control; girls under the age of fifteen in this country are at least five times more likely to give birth than girls of the same age in any other industrialized nation. And even if it's entered into freely by some, the sexual world is a dangerous place for many others; if current statistics hold true in the future, nearly two out of every five girls will be physically or sexually assaulted in their lifetimes. So for every girl with a liberated, healthy appetite, there's a girl on a diet, a girl slashing her skin with a piece of glass, a girl having drunken, unprotected sex. The battle to produce girls who feel as strong and entitled as they ought to has hardly been won.

My new niece is entering what journalist Peggy Orenstein calls "a half-changed world," a place where appetites may be psychically liberated but socially and institutionally unsupported, and where the social movement that fueled the first half of the change remains in the slumber that first took hold in the 1980s, the fog of forgetting. Feminist momentum ebbs and flows, tending to crest and then recede in cycles of thirty years or so, which means we may be due for a revival. But that forgetfulness worries me, in part because it seems so persistent and in part because progress is so entwined with women's level of awareness, our political and historical sense of how good or bad our lot has become. Will this new child, my niece, grow up in a world where women are so tired, or so inured to half-changes, that they choose to remain in a slumber? Or will she witness, perhaps participate in, a new tide of agitation? She was born in the midst of what feminist historians call an "open moment," a period in which women will either forge ahead or stand still, deciding that a half-changed world is insufficient or learning to live within its confines. That choice is far beyond her control, but its outcome could shape her life—her view of herself, her relationship to her body, her capacity to make choices—irrevocably.

The female body may represent one of feminism's least-touched frontiers, perhaps one of its final frontiers; a woman's appetite, and her ability to indulge appetite with freedom and entitlement and joy, is both a mark of progress and a metaphor for it. How hungry are we? How filled? How conflicted? I thought about this, too, as I drove home: I thought about my sister, whose body had just delivered this new life and was now prepared to feed and soothe it, and I thought about women and their bodies in general, about how many of us view the body as an enemy and a locus of shame instead of a blessing or a gift, about the despair and loathing that greets so many of us as we wake to the feel and sight of our own hips and thighs and breasts, about the extent to which the astonishing capacities of those bodies are minimized, forgotten, disregarded, turned into sources of the most cruel contempt.

The road before me was empty at 2 A.M., the sky black but starlit. I pictured that tiny infant, nursing hungrily at the body that created and sheltered her and will now guide her into the wider world, and I said a prayer for her, I prayed for change. I whispered to the universe, Let her be filled.

NOTES

Prologue

ix   Renoir once said that were it not for the female body...: Götz Adriani, *Renoir* (Cologne: DuMont Buchverlag, 1996; distributed by Yale University Press), p. 270.

Introduction

15   ... some twelve billion display ads, three million radio commercials, and 200,000 TV commercials flood the nation on a daily basis: Harry Flood, "Manufacturing Desire," *Adbusters: Journal of the Mental Environment*, no. 28, Winter 2000, p. 20.

15   ... most of us see 3,000 ads a day: James B. Twitchell, *AdCult USA: The Triumph of Advertising in American Culture* (New York: Columbia University Press, 1996), p. 2.

16   Nearly 30,000 women [said] they'd rather lose weight than attain any other goal: "Feeling Fat in a Thin Society," survey by Drs. Susan and Wayne Wooley, University of Cincinnati College of Medicine, *Glamour*, February 1984.

16   More than half of all Americans between the ages of twenty and seventy-four are overweight, and one fifth are obese: Sheryl Gay Stolberg, "The Fat Get Fatter: Overweight Was Bad Enough," *The New York Times*, Ideas and Trends, May 2, 1999, p. 4.

16   Cost of obesity-related illness is expected to reach into the hundreds of billions within the next twenty years: Greg Critser, "Let Them Eat Fat: The Heavy Truths About American Obesity," *Harper's*, March 2000, p. 42.

17   Obesity also appears to be a class issue: Ibid., pp. 41–47. Also see David Barboza, "Rampant Obesity, a Debilitating Reality for the Urban Poor," *The New York Times*, December 26, 2000, p. D5.

20   Five million women in the United States suffer from eating disorders: National Institutes of Mental Health, *Eating Disorders*, NIIH1 Publication

No. 943477, Rockland, Md., 1994. See also "Dying to Be Thin: Desperate for a Better Body, More and More Americans Are Taking Bigger Risks— and *Paying* with Their Lives," *People*, October 30, 2000, p. 109, and Jane E. Brody, "Exposing the Perils of Eating Disorders," *The New York Times*, December 12, 2000, p. D8, both of which put the figure at about seven million.

20   **Eighty percent of women report that the experience of being female means "feeling too fat":** C. Steiner-Adair and M. Purcell, "Approaches to Mainstreaming Eating Disorders Prevention," *Eating Disorders*, vol. 4, no. 4, Winter 1996, pp. 294–299.

20   **More than forty percent of women between the ages of eighteen and fifty-nine report some kind of sexual dysfunction:** Edward O. Laumann, Ph.D., Anthony Paik, M.A., and Raymond C. Rosen, Ph.D., "Sexual Dysfunction in the United States: Prevalence and Predictors," *Journal of the American Medical Association*, vol. 281, February 10, 1999, p. 537.

20   **Estimates on compulsive shopping range from two to eight percent of the general female population, fifteen to sixteen percent of a college-age sample:** Juliet Schor, *The Overspent American: Upscaling, Downshifting, and the New Consumer* (New York: Basic Books, 1998), p. 159.

Chapter 1: Add
Cake, Subtract Self-Esteem

23   **Eating disorders are the third most common chronic illness among females in the United States:** Steiner-Adair and Purcell, "Approaches to Mainstreaming Eating Disorders Prevention," p. 296.

23   **Fifteen percent of young women have substantially disordered attitudes and behaviors toward food and eating:** L. B. Mintz and N. E. Betz, "Prevalence and Correlates of Eating Disordered Behaviors Among Undergraduate Women," *Journal of Counseling Psychology*, vol. 354, 1988, pp. 463–471.

23   **The incidence of eating disorders has increased by thirty-six percent every five years since the 1950s:** Brody, "Exposing the Perils of Eating Disorders."

30   **Weight of the average model or actress or beauty pageant contestant has dropped to twenty-five percent below that of the average woman:** Terry Poulton, *No Fat Chicks: How Big Business Profits by Making Women Hate Their Bodies—And How to Fight Back* (Secaucus, N.J.: Birch Lane Press, 1997), p. 13.

31   **By the late 1970s, doctors were handing out some ten billion appetite-suppressing amphetamines per year:** Ibid., p. 47.

31   **Weight Watchers had spread to forty-nine states, its membership three million strong:** Ibid.

31   **The diet-food business was about to eclipse all other categories as the fastest-growing segment of the food industry:** "The Food Giants See the 'Light,'" *Business Week*, June 1, 1981, p. 112.

31   **"The female body is the place. . . ":** Rosalind Coward, *Female Desires: How They Are Sought, Bought and Packaged* (New York: Grove Weidenfeld, 1985), p. 60.

32   **Sixteen percent of adults would choose to abort a child if they knew he or she would be untreatably obese:** Carey Goldberg, "Fighting the Stigma: Citing Intolerance, Obese People Take Steps to Press Cause," *The New York Times*, November 5, 2000, p. Al.

35   **Forty-three million women live independently today:** Tamala M. Edwards, "Flying Solo: More Women Are Deciding That Marriage Is Not Inevitable," *Time*, August 28, 2000.

35   **Women make the vast majority of consumer purchases in this country—eighty-three percent:** Susan Estrich, *Sex and Power* (New York: Riverhead Books, 2000), p. 24.

35   **Women buy one fifth of all homes:** Edwards, "Flying Solo."

35   **Women represent more than half of full-time college enrollments:** "Who Needs Men? Addressing the Prospect of a Matrilinear Millennium," a forum with Barbara Ehrenreich and Lionel Tiger, *Harper's*, June 1999, pp. 33–46.

35   **An overwhelming majority of women—estimates range from eighty to eighty-nine percent:** See Steiner-Adair and Purcell, "Approaches to Mainstreaming Eating Disorders Prevention," p. 298; see also Deborah Pike, "Mental Makeover," *Vogue*, May 1995, p. 219; and "Searching for the Perfect Body," *People*, August 25, 2000.

36   **Women are three times as likely as men to feel negatively about their bodies:** "Mission Impossible: Deluged by Images from TV, Movies, and Magazines, Teenage Girls to Battle with an Increasingly Unrealistic Standard of Beauty—and Pay a Price," *People*, June 3, 1996.

36   Eighty percent of women have been on a diet: Ibid.

36   Half of all women are actively dieting at any given time: Ibid.

36   Half report feeling dissatisfied with their bodies all the time: Ibid.

36   Congress is still ninety percent male, as are ninety-eight percent of America's top corporate officers: Estrich, *Sex and Power*, p. 8.

36   Ninety-five percent of all venture capital today flows into men's bank accounts: Ibid., p. 12.

36   The two hundred highest-paid CEOS in America are all men: Ibid., p. 8.

36   Only three women head Fortune 500 companies: Ibid.

36   Women are still featured in only fifteen percent of page-one stories, and when we do make front-page news, it is usually only as victims or perpetrators of crime: Naomi Wolf, "The Future Is Ours to Lose," *The New York Times Magazine*, May 16, 1999, p. 134.

36   Women continue to make eighty-four cents for every dollar a man makes: "Ask a Working Woman," AFL-CIO Working Women Survey, 2000.

36   Women who take time off from work to have children make seventeen percent less than those who don't even six years after they return: Estrich, *Sex and Power*, p. 104.

36   Men with children earn the most money while women with children earn the least: Ibid., p. 93.

43   In order to stay connected, Gilligan theorizes: See Carol Gilligan, "Women's Psychological Development: Implications for Psychotherapy," in Carol Gilligan, Annie G. Rogers, and Deborah L. Tolman, ed., *Women, Girls and Psychotherapy: Reframing Resistance* (New York: Harrington Park Press, 1991), pp. 12–13. Also see Mary Pipher, *Reviving Ophelia: Saving the Selves of Adolescent Girls* (New York: Ballantine, 1994); Dana Crowley Jack, *Silencing the Self: Women and Depression* (Cambridge, Mass.: Harvard University Press, 1991).

44   "Girls stop being and stop seeing": Pipher, *Reviving Ophelia*, p. 22.

45   "The tyranny of freedom": See Erica Goode, "In Weird Math of Choices, 6 Choices Can Beat 600," *The New York Times*, January 9, 2001, p. A1.

Chapter 2: The
Mother Connection

63   In *The Feminine Mystique*, first published in 1963, Betty Friedan began to articulate what women of my mother's generation were feeling,
the "problem with no name": Betty Friedan, *The Feminine Mystique*
(New York: W. W. Norton, new edition, 2001).

65   "It is too often assumed that a mother . . . ": Jessica Benjamin, *The
Bonds of Love: Psychoanalysis, Feminism, and the Problem of Domination*
(New York: Pantheon, 1988), p. 24.

73   "The stressed-out, sometimes burned-out front line of the women's
movement. . . ": Ellen Goodman, "Feminism Hits Home for the Women
on MIT's Faculty," *The Boston Globe*, April 11, 1999, p. D7.

75   "Suddenly, in coming of age and entering the world . . . ": Kim
Chernin, *The Hungry Self: Women, Eating, and Identity* (New York:
Harper Perennial, 1985), p. 91.

79   "Pay-as-you-go plan": Louise J. Kaplan, *Female Perversions: The Tempta-
tions of Emma Bovary* (Northvale, N.J.: Jason Aronson, 1991), p. 230.

79   "All the time she has been. . . ": Ibid.

81   In her collection of essays . . . : Vivian Gornick, *The End of the Novel of
Love* (Boston: Beacon Press, 1997), p. 73.

Chapter 3: I Hate My
Stomach, I Hate My Thighs

86   "Anonymous disciplinary power": Sandra Lee Bartky, "Foucault, Femi-
ninity and the Modernization of Patriarchal Power," in *Writing on the
Body: Female Embodiment and Feminist Theory*, K. Conboy, N. Medina, and
S. Stanbury, eds. (New York: Columbia University Press, 1997), p. 148.

87   "Panoptical male connoisseur": Ibid., p. 140.

90   "This not only makes real intimacy impossible. . . ": Jean Kilbourne,
*Deadly Persuasion: Why Women and Girls Must Fight The Addictive Power
of Advertising* (New York: The Free Press, 1999),pp. 261–262.

92   Describing the historic ubiquity of misogyny. . . : David D. Gilmore,
Misogyny: The Male Malady (Philadelphia: University of Pennsylvania
Press, 2001), pp. 1–9.

93   "This multitiered ambivalence creates an uncomfortable and endless tension. . . ": Ibid., pp. 14–15.

96   American companies spend more than $200 billion each year hacking women's bodies into bits and pieces: Kilbourne, *Deadly Persuasion*, p. 33.

99   The female adolescent "moment of revision": Gilligan, "Women's Psychological Development," p. 26.

100 Notion of inscription, an idea frequently evoked to explain the shaping of a woman's self-image: See collected essays in *Writing on the Body*; also see: Susan Bordo, *Unbearable Weight: Feminism, Western Culture, and the Body* (Berkeley: University of California Press, 1995) and Susan Suleiman, ed., *The Female Body in Western Culture* (Cambridge, Mass.: Harvard University Press, 1986).

100 Statistics on plastic surgery: Anne Barnard, "When Plastic Surgeons Should Just Say 'No," *The Boston Globe*, September 12, 2000, p. E1.

100 Image of calligraphy: Elizabeth Grosz, *Volatile Bodies: Toward a Corporeal Feminism* (Bloomington: Indiana University Press, 1994), p. 191.

104 "There remains a common coding of the female body as a body which leaks. . . ": Ibid., p. 204.

110 Oddball tips: Patricia Marx and Susan Sistrom, *The Skinny: What Every Skinny Woman Knows About Dieting (And Won't Tell You!)* (New York: Dell, 1999), p. 196.

114 *Fat!So?*, by Marilyn Wann, an early pioneer in what's variously known as the "weightism" or "size activism" movement: Marilyn Wann, *Fat!So?: Because You Don't Have to Apologize for Your Size* (Berkeley, Calif.: Ten Speed Press, 1999).

Chapter 4: From Bra
Burning to Binge Shopping

126 The "missing discourse of desire" among and in regard to adolescent girls: See M. Fine, "Sexuality, Schooling and Adolescent Females: The Missing Discourse of Desire," *Harvard Educational Review*, vol. 58, no. 1, pp. 29–53. Also see Deborah L. Tolman, "Doing Desire: Adolescent Girls' Struggles for/with Sexuality," in *Gender and Society*, vol. 8, no. 3, September 1994, pp. 324–342; and Deborah L. Tolman, "Adolescent Girls, Women and Sexuality: Discerning Dilemmas of Desire," in *Women, Girls and Psychotherapy*.

126 **Foucault and discourse about sexuality:** Michel Foucault, *The History of Sexuality, Vol. I: An Introduction* (New York: Pantheon, 1978), p. 69.

129 **A girl's sexual impulses and hungers become "the feelings that no one names":** Deborah L. Tolman, "Adolescent Girls, Women and Sexuality: Discerning Dilemmas of Desire," in *Women, Girls and Psychotherapy*, p. 57.

130 **"Many girls may in fact solve the dilemma of their own sexual desire. . . ":** Ibid., p. 65.

132 **Feminist sex researchers have argued about the persistence of this thinking throughout the twentieth century:** See J. H. Gagnon, "Scripts and the Coordination of Sexual Conduct," *Nebraska Symposium on Motivation*, no. 21, 1973, pp. 27–60; M. Jackson, "Sexology and the Universalization of Male Sexuality (from Ellis to Kinsey and Masters and Johnson)," in L. Coveney, M. Jackson, S. Jeffreys, L. Kaye, and P. Mahony, eds., *The Sexuality Papers* (London: Hutchinson Press, 1984); Gina Ogden, *Women Who Love Sex* (New York: Pocket Books, 1994), pp. 9–13; Lenore Tiefer, *Sex Is Not A Natural Act and Other Essays* (Boulder, Colo.: Westview Press, 1995), pp. 97–102.

132 **"Normalcy can be easily summarized. . . "** : Tiefer, *Sex Is Not A Natural Act and Other Essays*, p. 102.

134 **Girls appear to be physically maturing at earlier ages today:** Barbara Kantrowitz and Pat Wingert, "The Truth About Tweens," *Newsweek*, October 18, 1999, p. 62. Also see Richard Saltus, "Growing Up Too Soon? Ready or Not, Sexual Maturity Comes Earlier Than Ever for Today's Girls," *The Boston Globe*, October 10, 2000, p. E1; and Paul B. Kaplowitz, Sharon E. Oberfield, and the Drug and Therapeutics and Executive Committees of the Lawsun Kilkins Pediatric Endocrine Society, "Reexamination of the Age Limit for Defining When Puberty Is Precocious in Girls in the US: Implications for Evaluation and Treatment," *Pediatrics*, vol. 104, no. 4, October 1999, pp. 936–941.

134 **Nearly half of all teenagers lose their virginity by age sixteen:** Lynn Ponton, M.D., *The Sex Lives of Teenagers: Revealing the Secret World of Adolescent Boys and Girls* (New York: Dutton, 2000), p. 257.

134 **"As a society, we discarded the Victorian moral umbrella around girls. . . ":** Joan Jacobs Brumberg, *The Body Project: An Intimate History of American Girls* (New York: Random House, 1997), p. 200.

135 **Figures on teenage sex-education—Most kids today (about 89 percent) will get some kind of sex education between grades seven and twelve:**

See "Sex Education in America: A Series of National Surveys of Students, Parents, Teachers, and Principals," Henry J. Kaiser Family Foundation, September, 2000. Figures on abstinence-only curricula: see Leora Tanenbaum, *Slut: Growing Up Female With a Bad Reputation* (New York: Harper Perennial, 2000), p. 216.

136 **In its 1999 report on sexual dysfunction:** Laumann, Paik, and Rosen, "Sexual Dysfunction in the United States: Prevalence and Predictors," p. 537.

140 **Americans spend three to four times as many hours shopping as Western Europeans:** Juliet Schor, *The Overspent American: Upscaling, Downshifting, and the New Consumer* (New York: Basic Books, 1998), p. 107.

140 **Americans consume more than $5 trillion worth of goods and services a year:** John Cassidy, "No Satisfaction: The Trials of the Shopping Nation," *The New Yorker*, January 25, 1999, p. 88.

140 **Americans rack up a staggering amount of credit card debt:** Robert H. Frank, *Luxury Fever: Why Money Fails to Satisfy in an Era of Excess* (New York: The Free Press, 1999), p. 46.

141 **Four billion square feet of the total land area have been converted into shopping centers:** Schor, *The Overspent American*, p. 107.

141 **In 1995, financial institutions sent out more than two and a half billion preapproved credit card applications:** Frank, *Luxury Fever*, p. 46.

142 **Gap between haves and have-nots; emergence of extremely high earners within more and more occupations; growing insecurity in the middle class:** see Robert Frank's discussion of "winner-take-all" markets in ibid., p. 44; also see Juliet Schor's discussion of social changes leading to shifts in the nature of comparative consumption in the 1970s and 1980s, *The Overspent American*, pp. 9–24.

144 **A Time/CNN poll found that only thirty-three percent of women called themselves feminists, only sixteen percent of college-age women:** Naomi Wolf, "The Future Is Ours to Lose," *The New York Times Magazine*, May 16, 1999.

144 **Membership in the League of Women Voters began its precipitous decline in the eighties:** Susan Estrich, *Sex and Power* (New York: Riverhead Books, 2000), p. 228.

145 **The number of women running for state legislatures began to level off, then decline:** Ibid.

146 **Karl Marx described the ways in which commodities become substitutes for "real human and natural faculties":** Karl Marx, *Economic and Philosophical Manuscripts*, Third Manuscript, "Need, Production, and Division of Labor," Gregor Benton translation, 1974.

149 **Advertisers spend $1.1 billion a year marketing alcohol:** Janet Evans and Richard F. Kelly, Bureau of Consumer Protection, Division of Advertising Practices, "Self Regulation in the Alcohol Industry: A Review of Industry Efforts to Avoid Promoting Alcohol to Underage Consumers," Federal Trade Commission report, Appendix B, September 1999.

150 **Magazine circulation figures:** Laura Q. Hughes, "Print Rolling out Heavy Artillery," *Advertising Age*, July 30, 2001, p. S2.

151 **Women today still spend on average about twenty-five hours a week doing unpaid household labor:** "A Man's Place: A Panel of Experts Looks at Women's Economic Power," *The New York Times Magazine*, May 16, 1999, p. 48.

151 **More than half of all women and nearly two thirds of women with children expect to be responsible for caring for an elderly parent or relative in the future:** *Women's Voices 2000*, Center for Policy Alternatives /Lifetime TV poll, September 29, 2000.

151 **About one quarter of working women have no employee-sponsored health coverage at all; one third have almost no control or flexibility over their work hours, and no paid leave to care for a child or an ill family member:** AFL-CIO Working Women Survey, 2000.

155 **"I was in an orphanage. . . ":** Joyce Wadler, "Turning a Corner: A Model at Size 12," *The New York Times*, August 12, 2001, Sunday Styles, p. 1.

Chapter 5: Body As Voice

165 **"Desire has indestructible permanence":** Judith Butler, "Critical Terms for Literary Study," *Desire*, Frank Lentricchia and Thomas McLaughlin, eds. (Chicago: University of Chicago Press, 1995), pp. 369–386.

166- **Post-Freudian conceptions of infantile life and mother-infant relation-**
167 **ships:** For an excellent summary of this shift in thinking, see Jessica Benjamin, *The Bonds of Love: Psychoanalysis, Feminism, and the Problem of Domination* (New York: Pantheon Books, 1988), Chapter 1, "The First Bond," pp. 11–50.

167 **"Each of us spent some time as an overwhelmed, enraged. . ."**: Polly Young-Eisendrath, *Women and Desire: Beyond Wanting to Be Wanted* (New York: Harmony Books, 1999), p. 20.

168 **Lacan on the difference between infantile need and demand:** Elizabeth Grosz, *Jacques Lacan: A Feminist Introduction* (London: Routledge Press, 1990), pp. 61–62.

177 **The contemporary sight of the weeping woman:** Christopher Lydon interview with Germaine Greer, WBUR's "The Connection," June 11, 1999; for more detailed discussion of the topic, see Germaine Greer, *The Whole Woman* (New York: Knopf, 1999), pp. 181–190.

Chapter 6: Swimming Toward Hope

180 **. . . her long, finally successful effort to make peace with her appetite, which she subsequently detailed in a memoir called *Holy Hunger*:** Margaret Bullitt-Jonas, *Holy Hunger: A Memoir of Desire* (New York: Knopf, 1998).

182 **Weigh Down Workshops boasts 30,000 chapters nationwide:** Rebecca Mead, "Slim for Him: God Is Watching What You're Eating," *The New Yorker*, January 15, 2000, p. 48.

182 **First Place is taught at an estimated 12,000 churches:** Diego Rihadeneria, "Recipe for Weight Loss: Pass the Prayer, Please," *The Boston Sunday Globe*, March 14, 1999, p. 1.

Epilogue

196 **Documentary about anorexia:** "Dying to Be Thin," written, directed, and produced for *Nova* by Larkin McPhee; initial air date, December 12, 2000.

197 **Boys continue to have higher estimations of their academic abilities than girls do:** John O'Neil, "He Thinks He Can, He Thinks He Can," *The New York Times*, April 6, 1999, p. D7.

197 **Nearly half of girls in grades one through three reported wanting to be thinner:** M. E. Collins, "Body Figure Perceptions and Preferences among Preadolescent Children," *International Journal of Eating Disorders*, vol. 10, no. 2, 1991, pp. 199–208.

197 **Thirty-nine percent of girls in grades five through eight said they were on a diet:** Kantrowitz and Wingert, "The Truth About Tweens," p. 62.

197 **Thirty-one percent of ten-year-old girls say they're afraid of being fat:**
     Steiner-Adair and Purcell, "Approaches to Mainstreaming Eating Disor-
     ders Prevention," p. 297.

198 **More than fifty percent of adolescent girls think they're overweight:**
     Ibid.

198 **The earlier a girl begins to have intercourse, the less likely she is to use
     birth control:** Joan Jacobs Brumberg, *The Body Project: An Intimate His-
     tory of American Girls* (New York: Random House, 1997), p. 204.

198 **Girls under the age of fifteen in this country are at least five times
     more likely to give birth than girls of the same age in any other indus-
     trialized nation:** Ibid., p. 201.

198 **Nearly two out of every five girls will be physically or sexually as-
     saulted in their lifetimes:** Commonwealth Fund Survey of Women's
     Health, Associated Press report, *The Boston Globe*, May 6, 1999, p. A25.

198 **"A half-changed world":** Peggy Orenstein, *Flux: Women on Sex, Work,
     Love, Kids, and Life in a Half-Changed World* (New York: Doubleday,
     2000).

198 **An "open moment":** Naomi Wolf, "The Future Is Ours to Lose," *The
     New York Times Magazine*, May 16, 1999.

BIBLIOGRAPHY

Brumberg, Joan Jacobs. *The Body Project: An Intimate History of American Girls*. New York: Random House, 1997.

Bullitt-Jonas, Margaret. *Holy Hunger: A Memoir of Desire*. New York: Knopf, 1998.

Chernin, Kim. *The Hungry Self: Women, Eating, and Identity*. New York: Harper Perennial, 1994.

Coward, Rosalind. *Female Desires: How They Are Sought, Bought and Packaged*. New York: Grove Weidenfeld, 1985.

Gilligan, Carol. *In a Different Voice*. Cambridge, Mass.: Harvard University Press, 1994.

Gornick, Vivian. *The End of the Novel of Love*. Boston: Beacon Press, 1997 ("exulted . . . forgotten to play Chopin," pp. 73–74).

Grosz, Elizabeth. *Volatile Bodies: Toward a Corporeal Feminism*. Bloomington: Indiana University Press, 1994.

Marx, Patricia and Sistrom, Susan. *The Skinny: What Every Skinny Woman Knows About Dieting (and Won't Tell You!)*. New York: Dell, 1999.

Orenstein, Peggy. *Schoolgirls: Young Women, Self-Esteem, and the Confidence Gap*. New York: Anchor Books, 1995.

Tiefer, Leonore. *Sex Is Not a Natural Act and Other Essays*. Boulder, Colo.: Westview Press, 1995.

Young-Eisendrath, Polly. *Gender and Desire: Uncursing Pandora*. College Station: Texas A & M University Press, 1997.

_____. *Women and Desire: Beyond Wanting to Be Wanted*. New York: Harmony Books, 1999.